All the Campus Lawyers

All the Campus Lawyers

LITIGATION, REGULATION, *and the* NEW ERA OF HIGHER EDUCATION

Louis H. Guard · Joyce P. Jacobsen

HARVARD UNIVERSITY PRESS

Cambridge, Massachusetts

London, England

2024

Publication of this book has been supported through the generous provisions of
the Maurice and Lula Bradley Smith Memorial Fund.

Library of Congress Cataloging-in-Publication Data
Names: Guard, Louis H., 1985– author. | Jacobsen, Joyce P., author.
Title: All the campus lawyers : litigation, regulation, and the new era of
higher education / Louis H. Guard and Joyce P. Jacobsen.
Description: Cambridge, Massachusetts : Harvard University Press, 2024. |
Includes bibliographical references and index.
Identifiers: LCCN 2023036584 | ISBN 9780674270497 (cloth)
Subjects: LCSH: Universities and colleges—Law and legislation—United
States. | Education, Higher—Law and legislation—United States. |
Universities and colleges—Admission—Law and legislation—United
States. | College students—Legal status, laws, etc.—United States.
Classification: LCC KF4225 .G83 2024 | DDC 344.73/074—dc23/
eng/20230929
LC record available at https://lccn.loc.gov/2023036584

Lou:

To Thomas J. Guard,

a believer in the power of education and the law

Joyce:

To Bill

Contents

Introduction

For college administrators, the day often begins with checking email. If they are lucky enough on any particular morning not to become engulfed by an urgent matter at their own institution, then there is a good chance they might begin by scanning a few of the daily compendiums offering a rundown of recent happenings at other institutions.[1] Inevitably, many of those stories relate to legal matters at other campuses. Whether it is a tenure denial lawsuit, a college running afoul of new federal regulations, new legislation being proposed in a state that would restrict what can be done on campuses, or an athletic compliance quagmire, not a day passes without some campus legal matter being highlighted and scrutinized in the higher education press. But beyond the alluring legal controversies that rise into the limelight of press and public scrutiny, legal issues also permeate the quieter facets of modern academic life, from detailed intellectual property or sponsored research problems to complex tax questions and real estate deals. On today's campus, the long arm of the law is inescapable. Policies, procedures, trainings, and forms reign supreme. When and how did higher education become so dominated by the law and by lawyers?

The core purposes of higher education—both for its students and society at large—have been extensively articulated, and the mission statements of many universities reflect these purposes well. Oxford University, founded in the eleventh century and thus the oldest university in the English-speaking world, holds as its core function "the advancement of learning by teaching and research and its dissemination by every means."[2] On this side of the Atlantic, Harvard University was founded in 1636 and today carries the mission "to educate the citizens and citizen-leaders for our society."[3] The many universities founded subsequently, including nonsectarian and land-grant institutions, echo these themes. The University of California, Berkeley, proclaims that its mission is "to serve society as a center of higher learning, providing long-term societal benefits through transmitting advanced knowledge, discovering new knowledge, and functioning as an active working repository of organized knowledge."[4] Cornell University's mission is "to discover, preserve and disseminate knowledge, to educate the next generation of global citizens, and to promote a culture of broad inquiry throughout and beyond the Cornell community."[5] The mission of Johns Hopkins University is "to educate its students and cultivate their capacity for lifelong learning, to foster independent and original research, and to bring the benefits of discovery to the world."[6] The liberal arts colleges, while focused mainly on teaching rather than research, echo the same themes. Amherst College, for example, proclaims that its mission is to educate students "so that they may seek, value, and advance knowledge, engage the world around them, and lead principled lives of consequence."[7]

At their core, these mission statements coalesce around themes of the search for and discovery of knowledge and the transmittal of such knowledge to students and the broader world for the ultimate betterment of humankind. But in the act of carrying out this mission, colleges and universities hope to become, and can become, even more. Bart Giamatti, former president of Yale University, describes a college or university in one of his musings on the "Academic Mission" as an "ethical center by which culture is transmitted and in which independent thinking is done."[8] In his view, colleges and universities are not merely seekers of knowledge for knowledge's sake, nor are they simple transmitters of knowledge. If one accepts Giamatti's view, the charge for colleges and universities becomes even more profound: they are also ethical guardians and primary vehicles for transmitting culture, whatever that may be. One of the summative points of Giamatti's essay is that his greatest fear for colleges and universities is that "those who are responsible for the legal processes and those who are responsible for the daily life of the mind will see themselves as somehow engaged in different things."[9]

But have colleges and universities realized Giamatti's dream—or Giamatti's nightmare? Have the legal strictures and constraints on colleges and universities overly constrained the actors—both faculty and administrators—charged with carrying out such a lofty mission and, in turn, compromised their institutions' fundamental mission? Is the law helpful or a hindrance to colleges and universities and their core purposes? Is the culture that colleges and universities are transmitting to our nation's future generations becoming one of legalized processes and bureaucracy, due in part to increasing legal and regulatory pressures? We think it is time to start both asking and answering these questions.

We wrote this book to try to make some sense of what has happened—and what is happening—at the nexus of the higher education sector and the law. Colleges and universities today are in a distinctly new era of regulatory oversight and litigation pressures, facing increased public scrutiny from regulators, legislators, and the public at large, and decreased deference from courts.[10] From the paired perspective of a college president/economics professor and a college general counsel/law professor, this book examines the rapid acceleration in the legal and regulatory landscape for colleges and universities, focusing in particular on developments over the last ten to fifteen years and the realized and potential impacts of these developments on the higher education sector, its fundamental mission, and its future.

While tracing recent legal developments and their interplay with the core purposes of higher education and the educational missions of institutions, this book also addresses the practical impact of this increased legal and regulatory burden on both the strategic leadership and operational management of institutions of higher education. The new legal environment for colleges and universities has sparked an increased demand for and reliance on legal services and counsel that shows no signs of receding. So this book also serves as a guide for college and university boards, presidents, counsel, and other leadership to understand how to engage legal counsel, whether internally or externally, in support of their institution's core mission. The book provides a vital and up-to-date assessment of the role of contemporary college counsel that is situated within the current context of breakneck legal developments and challenges facing colleges and universities. The implication of our work in this regard is that effective campus counsel and an integrated strategic approach to legal issues on campus are critical to preserving the fundamental essence and mission of colleges and universities moving forward.

We hope that this book helps readers make some sense of the most recent legal trends and headwinds facing colleges and universities. We hope that for those readers in positions of campus authority, this book will offer valuable insight and advice on how best to navigate these headwinds in the days, weeks, and years ahead. We hope that for those readers in positions of influence with regard to policy, this book will provide a true-to-form assessment of the impact of the current legal and regulatory environment on colleges and universities and their core mission. And for the purely interested reader, we hope that we give you interesting information regarding the fascinating range of legal and regulatory topics that affect the higher education sector—a sector that affects us all, whether directly or indirectly, and also make clearer what the legal and regulatory trends are that affect the sector's operations.

The "Lawyerization" of Higher Education

What does it mean to say that higher education has become "lawyerized?" Not so long ago, it could be fairly said that colleges and universities had relatively little interaction with "the law." Faculty, students, and even administrators carried out their studies and duties largely unencumbered by the legal strictures that were enveloping other sectors, whether commercial or nonprofit, or preprimary, primary, and secondary education. But as the twentieth century progressed, the gates of the academy opened to more than just successive generations of students. Finding their way to campus were federal, state, and local governments and associated agencies, accreditors, quasiregulatory agencies, influential professional associations, insurance companies, and plaintiffs.

The early stages of this shift and its narrative have been well studied and documented.[11] In the 1960s, the federal government officially put its handprint on higher education in the form of the Higher Education Act—and a professional association for higher education lawyers, the National Association of College and University Attorneys, was formed in Washington, DC. By the 1970s, a few well-heeled major universities were hiring in-house legal counsel to deal with the novel legal issues facing their institutions and the academic sector at large, but these institutions were the exception rather than the rule. Most other colleges and universities continued to think of the law as mostly not relevant to their internal processes, other than the occasional lawsuit that could be cordoned off from the institution's main workings.

In the latter part of the twentieth century, the number of institutions using in-house counsel continued to increase as legal and regulatory issues grew more complex. Empirical legal analyses have shown that private enforcement of federal statutes—many of which figure prominently in the world of higher education, including Title VII, Title IX, and the Americans with Disabilities Act (ADA)—in the form of lawsuits has increased steadily since the 1960s.[12] The data further show a strong upward trend in lawsuits beginning in the early 2000s and indicate that discrimination lawsuits specifically are the single largest category of litigation in federal courts.[13]

Campuses are not immune from feeling that heat. A simple search of both Westlaw and Lexis, the two main legal case databases, similarly reveals that the number of cases in these databases that involve a "college" or "university" as a party (generally, the defendant) has increased steadily over the last hundred or so years, reaching a peak around 2018–19. Figure I.1 demonstrates this pattern using data from both primary case law databases, Lexis and Westlaw, over the 1900–2021 period.

While litigation, or the avoidance of litigation, takes up much of the attention of the campus lawyer, it is also the case that many campus lawyers are involved either in simply understanding and assisting in the implementation of governmental regulations or are in

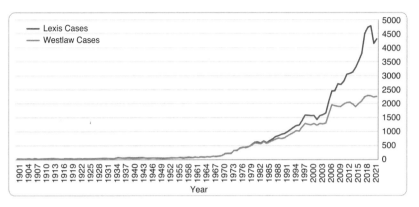

Figure I.1 Cases in Lexis and Westlaw with a University or College as Party, 1900–2021. Data sources: Lexis; Westlaw.

the process of understanding what is currently going on in the federal and state legislative sessions. Each year, additional regulations are proposed by administrative agencies and additional statutes passed by the legislatures in the federal or state governments; many local government regulations also affect campuses and require campus legal inputs. The incredible range of legislative proposals that can affect campuses that occur each year takes much legal and administrative campus time to consider and often to lobby for or against, even if not all of them are enacted into law. Whether it is protecting or prohibiting the carrying of weapons on campuses,[14] banning drag shows on college campuses,[15] restricting spending on campus diversity initiatives, banning legacy admissions, or taxing university endowments, the range of campus issues that legislators may decide to take an interest in is vast. Governors may also take more or less activist stances toward campuses; Scott Walker, governor of Wisconsin from 2011 to 2019 is often cited as having written the playbook on how to affect higher education; at one point he even attempted to change the mission statement of the University of Wisconsin System, "The Wisconsin Idea," from spreading knowledge to workforce preparation.[16] Meanwhile, the federal government appears to be in a continued upswing regarding proposed regulations directed at campuses, or regulatory overreach;[17] in mid-2023, the Biden administration released a large packet of new proposed regulations, including additional reporting requirements, additional tests for financial viability, and making university subcontractors subject to Department of Education regulations.[18]

Not surprisingly, all of this has led to an increase in the number of lawyers employed on campuses as well as the number of lawyers and support staff who spend all or most of their professional time working on academic legal and regulatory matters. Data compiled by the Chronicle of Higher Education between 2010 and 2019 show steady increases in the number of listings for the office of general counsel jobs during that period, with the number of job ads posted more than tripling between 2010 and 2018.[19]

It can fairly be said—and this book makes the case—that in this first part of the twenty-first century, the impact of the legal issues bearing down on institutions and their campuses has intensified to levels never before seen. In turn, the ways and extent to which institutions of higher education—IHEs, as we call them throughout this book—use legal counsel have expanded significantly. In our view, the "lawyerization" of higher education is simply a shorthand way of describing the increased regulatory and litigation pressures facing IHEs against the broader backdrop of the increasing operational complexity of IHEs and the increasing public scrutiny, politicization, and legislative interference with higher education and its campuses.[20]

It is a common refrain for those who practice higher education law to remark on the sheer breadth of their area of practice. From employment to tax, from tort and liability issues to technology transfer and intellectual property, the array of legal issues impacting a typical IHE is vast. Moreover, the unique nature of the corporate organisms that are IHEs requires an understanding of not only a broad array of substantive legal issues but also an innate understanding of the constituent parts of IHEs. This is both structural and theoretical. Counsel to IHEs must understand how each constituent part—student, faculty, staff, alumni, local community—feeds into the whole. In so doing, they must understand how quasilegal concepts such as shared governance, academic freedom, and academic deference bear on the issues at hand.

One of the goals of this book is to tell the story of legal developments over the past ten to fifteen years and their intersection with the core purposes of IHEs to provide a picture of where we are now and what these developments mean going forward. Such an inquiry is itself broad, and so when it is applied to an area of legal practice as oceanic as higher education, the challenge of our task intensifies. This is all to ask for our readers' patience. This book does not attempt to explain every technical detail of the law of higher education. We have attempted to write it in such a way as to articulate only the most relevant substantive legal details required to convey our core points. Thus, this book is not an exhaustive legal treatise: some technical details will be left out, and for the most part, this is intentional. We believe that the impact of the legal climate on the fundamental mission of higher education is significant, and its effects on higher education are wide ranging and in some cases downright alarming. As such, we believe it is a story that should be told in a way that is as accessible to as many people as possible.

This book is structured in two parts. Part I of the book focuses on what might be referred to as the "new" legal landscape, and it tells the story of the past fifteen or so years of rapid developments in legal issues facing IHEs. Part I is composed of seven chapters. The chapters are not grouped by substantive areas of law but rather by the broader realms of college and university life that have been impacted over this period. Chapter I addresses issues at the intersection of civil rights, discrimination, and the modern college campus, examining current and emerging issues in areas such as Title IX, the ADA, and various regulatory structures impacting issues of race and racism as well as gender, ethnicity, religion, nationality, and more by virtue of how protected classes of individuals have been defined by the law. Chapter 2 engages issues related to free speech and expression on campus. Chapter 3 is centered around student life and wellness and focuses primarily on the relationship of students to their campuses through the eyes of the courts. Chapter 4 looks at the legal issues facing the primary economic drivers on almost any campus: admissions and advancement, and related issues in community relations. Chapter 5 examines trending legal issues in matters of governance broadly speaking, from governing boards to the faculty. Chapter 6 examines new legal issues intertwined with what could be called the higher education "business model." In the final chapter of Part I, Chapter 7 looks at issues raised when crisis comes to campus, including the recent COVID-19 pandemic.

Having laid the groundwork for understanding the legal landscape for IHEs, Part 2 takes a more forward-looking and practice-based approach. The aim of Part 2 is to begin diving directly into solutions to the problems and tensions raised in Part I. Chapter 8 examines and advocates for the role of legal counsel not just as a necessity in reaching operational excellence, but also as a strategic partner. Chapter 9 reviews institutional considerations for campus counsel, and the nuts and bolts of how this role should operate to be most effective. Finally, Chapter 10 is our take on what to expect in the campus legal landscape over the next decade and how to prepare for those new challenges.

A Note on the Campus Context

It is cliché, but it bears repeating for our purposes, that campuses are profoundly singular places, unique not just in their functional role in society but also in their structure and composition. Across classrooms, dining halls, dormitories, labs, and playing fields, both commuting and residential students from all walks of life carry out the basic functions of life side by side in community—eating, drinking, recreation, entertainment—while also potentially embarking on the virtuous paths of knowledge exploration, knowledge development, and free inquiry. Traditionally aged students (as in the eighteen- to twenty-five-year-old age range) undertake this journey at a key juncture in their psychological and physical development, energizing the tenor and tone of campus life and raising the emotional volume, and with it, the institutional risk levels. For most students, for better or worse, attending college is a time unlike any other in a person's life. A long-serving dean at our institution was fond of reminding students that they had but "four falls and four springs"[21] as an admonition to fill their eight semesters by cultivating their intellect and interests to carry them forward through the rest of their life.

The workforce at IHEs is similarly unique in several ways. Many faculty members receive the privilege and protections of tenure, a contractual mechanism designed to promote academic freedom and protect free inquiry.[22] Hence a large percentage of the payroll at most IHEs cannot be terminated "at will," and do not serve "at the pleasure of the President." While, to quote Justice Lewis Powell, "at early colleges and universities the faculty were the school,"[23] the staff required to operate colleges and universities today is significantly more robust, specialized, and professionalized. A primary example is the campus lawyer, but many other examples abound, from admissions and fundraising professionals, accounting and finance professionals, human relations and technology experts, to still more specialized personnel such as health and wellness professionals, academic support personnel and advisors, diversity specialists, international student advisors, and student conduct and discipline professionals.

Against this backdrop, most IHEs are striving to diversify their student, faculty, and staff populations along numerous dimensions.[24] Many IHEs aspire to create a community that more closely mirrors the broader society, in service to academic, pedagogical, and social goals that have been articulated, documented, and litigated.[25] Given pedagogical and academic reasons to diversify IHE communities, and given their relatively focused efforts in recent decades to do so, higher education as a whole has increasingly become one of the more diverse sectors in the economy and nation when compared to other sectors, even as individual institutions may lag.[26] But there are also serious questions as to whether all members of the IHE community are really treated equally, both within and across campuses, or whether other forces, such as the effects of money, power, and privilege, lead to unequal treatment.

While IHEs are mindful of the patterns of their community, they also celebrate and cultivate individuality in a way that other sectors of the economy and society may not. This sense of individuality is inherent both in the pursuit of free academic inquiry and knowledge development undertaken by faculty and in the journey of knowledge acquisition and exploration undertaken by students. At least in principle, IHEs encourage students to pursue their individual academic and social interests and encourage faculty to freely inquire and create. While not perfect by any stretch of the imagination, the addressing of these goals means that the typical campus is likely to be more focused on fostering the unique interests of individuals, both employees and students, within the organization, even though these interests can sometimes come into conflict with other aspects of running an IHE and thus can lead to legal quandaries.

There has been extensive focus by many political commentators on the role that IHEs play in our democracy, and the synergistic relationships between IHEs and the growth and development of American democracy in particular.[27] As the argument generally goes, IHEs prepare students—future citizens—to more effectively contribute to our democracy by being more engaged citizens. Armed with the ability to think critically and communicate effectively, a more educated citizenry, in theory, creates better policy. Ronald Daniels, president of Johns Hopkins University, goes so far as to argue in his recent book that colleges and universities play a role and owe a duty to democracy akin to other key institutions such as the courts or media.[28] But there have also been concerns regarding whether modern IHEs actually fill this function, whether they have either turned into echo chambers for some political views but not others, or whether they have sidestepped fulfilling this participatory role completely. For most students, life on campus is also the first time that they are interacting as adults with legal protections tied to the promotion of equity and can fully participate in democracy. This book is an examination of what has happened at the intersection of legal developments—many intended to ensure equality and individual rights in a democracy—and the institutions that were supposedly designed to inform and strengthen future participants in that democracy. It will be increasingly clear to the reader as you make your way through the book that the same political and social divisions that affect our society also find their way into op-positional positions on nearly every issue on a college campus.

In all these ways and many more, campuses are both a distinctive petri dish impacted by a variety of legal and regulatory strictures and a reflection of the divisions and concerns in society as a whole. The implications of these synergies between the goals that IHEs aspire to and the myriad ways IHEs are challenged every day on their campuses are examined throughout our book. While we do not provide all the answers as to how IHEs may serve society more effectively in light of every legal or regulatory challenge, we provide an overall structure for understanding and responding to the many ways in which IHEs are both aided and impeded by the web of legal strictures under which they now operate.

· I ·

THE NEW CAMPUS
LEGAL LANDSCAPE

Chapter 1

Civil Rights and Equity on Campus

W e begin this book by examining major legal developments bearing on the broad topics of equity, inclusion, belonging, and social justice on campuses in the form of civil rights and related statutes and regulatory structures. Like so much of what we discuss in this book, the subject matter addressed in this chapter is one of the most fast-moving areas in the higher education legal and regulatory landscape. Moreover, the legal landscape of civil rights on campus has a significant impact on the core mission of institutions of higher education (IHEs). The civil rights laws that touch our campuses directly affect who IHEs serve and how they do it. Martin Luther King Jr. famously wrote that "the arc of the moral universe is long, but it bends toward justice."[1] In many ways, the modern campus is a laboratory for testing the mettle of this statement,[2] and the last ten to fifteen years at the intersection of higher education and civil rights law bear this out. This chapter begins our examination of the civil rights laws and structures that contour the interactions between IHEs and the students they serve. At the same time, this is also a study of how these inter-actions shape the institutions charged with educating students to be members of our participatory democracy, and affect the perceptions, hopes, fears, and expectations of those students for the future.

While many civil rights laws affect our campuses, we focus closely on Title IX, Title VII, and the Americans with Disabilities Act (ADA).[3] This chapter contains an evolutionary overview of these laws as they relate to higher education to provide insight into how our campuses have evolved in their relationship with the law and these regulatory structures. This study is our first step in understanding how campuses have become so "lawyerized" and lays a foundation for assessing the impact that legal evolution in this area has had on the core mission of IHEs.

Combating Discrimination on the Basis of Sex: Title IX and Its Implementation

Signed into law in 1972, Title IX is a federal statute that is perhaps the most obvious standout when one thinks of civil rights laws and their impact on higher education over the last ten to fifteen years. It holds that "no person in the United States shall, on the basis of sex, be excluded from participation in, be denied the benefits of, or be subjected to discrimination under any education program or activity receiving Federal financial assistance."[4] Stated more plainly, Title IX and its implementing regulations[5] "prohibit[s] discrimination on the basis of sex in education programs or activities."[6] Promulgated pursuant to Congress's spending power, the primary regulatory mechanism to enforce compliance with this and many other federal regulations is the threat of a loss of federal funds. A private right of action for monetary damages—a mechanism allowing individuals to bring lawsuits directly against offending institutions—has also been recognized and has driven much current litigation.[7] As one observer has noted, in the early decades of Title IX "neither the courts nor the Office for Civil Rights had much to say about sexual harassment."[8] But recent history has seen a dramatic evolution in Title IX as it pertains to both athletics and sexual harassment on campuses.

In July 2021, Catherine Lhamon sat in Room 430 of the Dirksen Senate Office Building in Washington, DC. "OCR does its job best when it efficiently, fairly, and thoroughly resolves investigations to protect student rights," she told the US Senate Committee on Health, Education, Labor, and Pensions (HELP).[9] Lhamon was testifying before the Senate HELP committee on the path to Senate confirmation as Assistant Secretary for Civil Rights at the Department of Education's (DOE) Office of Civil Rights (OCR). Eight years earlier, on another July day, Lhamon had breezed through the same committee without testimony before her eventual confirmation to the same position.[10] Her nomination and confirmation as Assistant Secretary for Civil Rights in 2013 and her renomination and reconfirmation to the same post in 2021 stand as exclamation points in the whipsawing recent evolution of Title IX's enforcement.

When Lhamon ascended to the lead of the OCR in 2013, she entered a legal landscape that had subtly begun changing two years earlier. In 2011, the OCR released its most substantive guidance document in more than a decade on the topic of sexual harassment under Title IX in the form of a Dear Colleague Letter (DCL).[11] The 2011 DCL reiterated the principle that "sexual harassment of students . . . is a form of sex discrimination prohibited by Title IX" and went on to clarify that "the requirements of Title IX pertaining to sexual harassment also cover sexual violence."[12] In the late 1990s, the

Supreme Court cases of *Gebser v. Lago Vista Independent School District* and *Davis v. Monroe County Board of Education* had settled several significant questions of law around Title IX and sexual harassment as related to private rights of action—or lawsuits—under Title IX that could be taken up against institutions.[13] But the 2011 DCL made abundantly clear to educational institutions beholden to the statute that sexual violence is a form of sexual harassment that violates Title IX, and that IHEs needed to reevaluate and retune their efforts in regard to preventing and responding to sexual harassment and violence on their campuses, or risk enforcement action from the federal government.

The spring of 2014 ushered in sweeping changes for IHEs and their Title IX obligations related to sexual violence. In late April of 2014, then-Vice President Joe Biden publicly called on IHEs to "step up" on the issue of sexual violence on campuses.[14] New (and suggested) resources were released via the Obama administration's dedicated website, Notalone.gov, including model policy language, checklists, and resources for conducting a campus climate survey.[15] The White House Task Force to Protect Students from Sexual Assault—created by Presidential Memorandum and signed by President Barack Obama in January of 2014—rendered its first report.[16] While not technically agency guidance, the report nonetheless opined at length on the value of campus climate surveys, sexual assault prevention, and what in its view constituted effective responses to the issue of sexual assaults on campus.[17] On April 29, 2014, the OCR launched a comprehensive guidance document titled "Questions and Answers on Title IX and Sexual Violence (Q&A)."[18] This was deemed by the DOE to be a "significant guidance document"[19] explicitly issued to provide IHEs "with information to assist them in meeting their obligations, and to provide members of the public with information about their rights, under the civil rights laws and implementing regulations" under the OCR's purview.[20] Some forty-five pages in length, the April 2014 Q&A provided a detailed outline of the OCR's specific expectations for all facets of sexual assault prevention and response. Almost simultaneously, on May 2, 2014, the DOE published its first publicly searchable list of IHEs under investigation for allegedly mishandling sexual assault complaints.[21] According to Lhamon, these lists were made public to "spur community dialogue" and "in an effort to bring more transparency to [the OCR's] enforcement work and to foster better public awareness of civil rights."[22]

One of the schools mired in the sweeping changes of spring 2014 was Tufts University.[23] In September 2010, a Tufts student filed a formal complaint with the OCR alleging that Tufts had failed to properly handle her report of sexual assault.[24] By April 17, 2014, the OCR had concluded its review of the matter and Tufts had signed a voluntary resolution agreement and effectively closed the matter. The resolution agreement contained language indicating that, by signing the agreement, Tufts was not admitting a failure to comply with Title IX. By April 29, the press reported that Tufts had withdrawn its signature from the agreement.[25] According to media reports, officials in the OCR's regional office informed Tufts by phone that officials at the OCR in Washington, DC, had required language in the OCR's final report indicating that not only did Tufts' previous actions violate Title IX but that its existing policies and practices continued to do so.[26] Tufts released a statement saying it "could not, in good faith, allow our community to believe that we were not in compliance with such an important law."[27] In the wake of student protests and outcry, Tufts announced on May 9 that it would be recommitting to the agreement.[28] The revocation of the Tufts signature was couched by the OCR as a "breach" of the agreement, and threats by the OCR to invoke its authority to revoke federal funding to Tufts, coupled with student activism, appear ultimately to have carried the day.[29]

During the remainder of 2014, and for some time after, considerable public attention was focused on the handling of sexual assault on campuses as robust accounts of specific cases began to dominate headlines both nationally and locally. Many of these articles were well-intentioned and rightly focused on highlighting the devastating impact of what continues to be a disturbingly pervasive issue across higher education and our culture more broadly. Other influential pieces from this period included coverage of cases at Florida State University,[30] the University of Montana,[31] and Amherst College.[32] A case at Columbia University garnered national attention when a sexual assault survivor initiated a performance art piece called "Mattress Performance (Carry That Weight)." The piece involved the Columbia University student carrying a fifty-pound dormitory mattress on her senior-year travels around the university campus, up to and including her graduation ceremony.[33] This coverage ensured that public attention stayed focused on the issue of how sexual assault was handled or mishandled on campuses. Some stories, however, relayed to readers only a singular perspective, having seemingly proceeded to press without rigorous fact-checking or substantive comment from other parties involved in the case. At least one very prominent article of this period was retracted in its entirety.[34]

Underlying the institutional response in Title IX cases following 2011 was not simply the substance of the laws (or "guidance") around Title IX but also the actual manner in which the OCR used its enforcement powers under Title IX. During the Obama administration, methods of enforcement were the subject of careful attention and much scrutiny. Many IHEs attempted in vain to navigate the rapidly changing legal landscape in light of the shifting external expectations.

As Terry Hartle, senior vice president for government and public affairs at the American Council on Education stated bluntly in a 2014 article: "Many universities that have found themselves in a conflict with OCR believe that this agency does not act in good faith and that it's little more than a bully with enforcement powers."[35]

Early critiques of the actual mandates in the 2011 and 2014 guidance and the 2014 White House Task Force Report were abundant as well. The Foundation for Individual Rights in Education (FIRE), referring to the Task Force Report, described it as "doubling down on a broken system."[36] Of specific concern were considerations of due process. Greg Lukianoff, FIRE's president, specifically called out the administration's endorsement of the use of a single-investigator model, citing concerns that it bundles the roles of investigator, judge, and jury into one person and thereby nullifies the ability of accused students to challenge the testimony of their accuser.[37]

While FIRE's response was to be expected given its stated mission, there were concerns from a broader array of voices, including many in academe, as each institution, under time pressure, developed and began implementing updated policies and procedures and handling new cases. In October of 2014, in response to the issuance of new university-wide policies around sexual assault and harassment, twenty-eight members of the Harvard Law School faculty signed an open letter voicing "strong objections" to the new policies.[38] They opposed the policies on due process grounds and "basic elements of fairness," calling out the amalgamation of functions such as investigator, appeal body, and fact finder, and pointing out that the policy "failed to ensure adequate representation for the accused, particularly for students unable to afford representation."[39] Perhaps most notably, the law professors pointed out that Harvard crafted a definition of sexual harassment that went "beyond" Title IX and Title VII statutory and regulatory law, signaling that the university should have considered more closely the actual legal weight of the 2011 and 2014 guidance document that undoubtedly influenced the policy. "Harvard apparently decided simply to defer to the demands of certain federal administrative officials," the professors wrote, "rather than exercise independent judgment about the kind of sexual harassment policy that would be consistent with law and with the needs of our students." This statement is particularly poignant, and perhaps only with the benefit of hindsight does it reveal the significant pressure even the most prominent universities in the world felt to interpret administrative guidance as the rule of law during this period in the face of unpredictable enforcement. The faculty at Harvard were not alone in decrying blind compliance with administrative mandates that went against basic principles of justice and due process. Members of Penn Law's faculty authored a similar letter in early 2015. "Ultimately," they wrote, "there is nothing inconsistent with a policy that both strongly condemns and punishes sexual misconduct and ensures a fair adjudicatory process."[40]

By the spring of 2020, the world of Title IX again underwent a major overhaul when the DOE under President Donald Trump issued updated implementing regulations for Title IX.[41] This was a significant development. While Title IX regulations did exist before 2020, they were skeletal and were rarely relied on by the department in enforcement actions. Codifying rules around Title IX compliance in the form of regulations as opposed to sheer administrative guidance answered at least some of the concerns raised by groups like the Harvard law professors. Before the 2020 regulations were issued, virtually all enforcement of sex discrimination complaints under Title IX related to sexual harassment occurred because of the significant guidance documents issued by the department during the Obama administration.

According to Education Secretary Betsy DeVos, the new regulations were intended to "rebalance the 'scales of justice.'"[42] Perhaps most notably, the new regulations implemented a requirement that IHEs allow cross-examination during a live hearing, thereby eliminating the so-called single-investigator model. Other changes included allowing IHEs the ability to choose a standard for the burden of proof, narrowing the scope of off-campus incidents that required action by an institution, and further defining parameters for when institutions would be deemed to have notice of an incident such that it required action on the part of the institution. The 2020 regulations also prohibited adjudicators in a Title IX hearing from considering statements in their final decision from individuals who did not subject themselves to cross-examination,[43] a rule that would later be struck down in the courts.[44]

As one might expect, the 2020 regulations were met with significant apprehension and disappointment by advocacy groups, members of the political left, and many who viewed themselves as supporters of sexual assault survivors.[45] But despite the controversy surrounding the 2020 regulations, some people had a sense that the regulations were not all bad. Jeannie Suk Gersen, one of the Harvard law professors who crafted the 2014 Harvard law faculty statement critiquing Harvard's Title IX policies, pointed out that while the regulations were not perfect, "they clarify the rights of both victims and the accused in a way that is likely to lead to improvements in basic fairness."[46] Among the aspects of the 2020 regulations that Gersen pointed out as arguably positive are the flexibility for institutions to choose a standard for the burden of proof and the reintroduction of so-called informal methods of resolution such as mediation and restorative justice approaches.[47] Another legal scholar wrote in the *Chronicle of Higher Education* that "regardless of their source, the new regulations are still a tremendous improvement over what existed before," citing specifically that the regulations "rectify the due-process wasteland that existed in the wake of the 2011 'Dear Colleague' letter."[48]

In the spring of 2021, the presidential administration of Joseph R. Biden issued interim guidance interpreting the 2020 regulations and announced a "comprehensive review" of the 2020 regulations.[49] By July 2022, new proposed regulations had been released by the DOE.[50] Among many significant changes, the proposed regulations reverted to expanded reporting requirements for certain classes of campus employees, expanded obligations of IHEs related to conduct occurring off-campus, an expanded definition of harassment, and an elimination (though still permitted) of the requirement to hold live hearings with cross-examination, effectively opening the door once again to a single-investigator model on campuses.[51] The proposed regulations also explicitly expanded Title IX protections to "pregnancy or related conditions" and clarified protections based on gender identity and sexual orientation as alluded to further below.[52]

One observer remarked that the proposed regulations continued the "political ping-pong" over Title IX.[53] This is an apt way to describe the reaction of campuses throughout the period from the 2011 DCL to the current day. Successive rounds of regulatory changes have kept campuses swirling. Indeed, while this book was going to press the Biden administration again extended its timeline for the release of a final set of regulations to late 2023.[54] Such changes require underlying systemic revisions to policies, programming, trainings, and supports, which have in turn led to a significant expansion of administrative roles. Campuses should be, and most are, focused on doing the right thing for their students. Nevertheless, amid sea changes like those seen in the last ten to fifteen years, it can be difficult for campuses to maintain credibility in their goal to support all students.

Additional Antidiscrimination Statutes and Their Intersection with Title IX

Like Title IX, Title VII of the Civil Rights Act of 1964 prohibits discrimination on the basis of sex, as well as for the protected classes of race, color, religion, sex, and national origin; specifically in the employment context.[55] One of the forms of sex discrimination in the workplace that Title VII prohibits—like Title IX—is sexual harassment. Given that both Title IX and Title VII are federal statutes and that both prohibit discrimination on the basis of "sex," the regulatory history and case law on issues and questions related to one statute at times informs or persuades the other,[56] so much so that the statutes inform each other's interpretation of the very word "sex." In *Bostock v. Clayton County*, the Supreme Court held that discrimination on the basis of "sex" under Title VII includes discrimination on the basis of gender identity as well as sexual orientation.[57] This logic has been extended to Title IX by the Executive Order of President Biden and by the 2022 Title IX regulations promulgated by the DOE.[58]

Sex discrimination under Title IX and sex discrimination under Title VII also share the terms "severe" and "pervasive" in the standard for establishing that sexual harassment has occurred or is occurring.[59] The Title IX implementing regulations require "unwelcome conduct" that is "severe, pervasive, and objectively offensive."[60] Title VII requires conduct to be severe "or" pervasive.[61] Regarding Title VII, the US Equal Employment Opportunity Commission (EEOC) further elaborates that "petty slights, annoyances, and isolated incidents (unless extremely serious) will not rise to the level of illegality."[62] While this standard may appear sensible on paper, it can prove challenging to apply.

Complicating matters, Title IX's reach on campuses is not limited to students but extends to employees as well. When faculty members interact with Title IX as a party to a case, things can get still more complicated and involve Title VII, tenure and contract issues, and other employment issues.[63] Particularly challenging are situations that involve both a student and a faculty member. What happens when evolving expectations under federal civil rights laws collide with the notion of academic freedom and the contractual protections of tenure? Are sexual harassment and protected exercises of academic freedom always mutually exclusive? In what ways do notions of academic freedom and its contractual protections serve as a bar to effectively dealing with issues of sexual harassment under Title IX or Title VII? There is no one-size-fits-all answer to these questions, but several recent cases illustrate these tensions and issues.

At the University of Rochester, a prominent professor of brain and cognitive sciences was accused of sexually harassing students and colleagues.[64] He was investigated by the university pursuant to Title IX and related policies for allegations of inappropriate and untoward comments as well as behaviors including allegedly having sexual relationships with graduate students involving coercion and abuses of power.[65] Following multiple investigations, the university concluded that his behavior did not rise to the level of sexual harassment or violations of university policy.[66] In September 2017, a group of eight individuals made up of colleagues and former colleagues of the professor filed a complaint with the EEOC against the university "for failing to act appropriately against a faculty member who has engaged in sexual harassment and has created a hostile environment for graduate students, and for retaliating against those of us who filed and pursued a complaint through university procedures."[67] By December 2017, the group had filed an action in federal court against the university alleging violations of Title VII, Title IX, and the New York Human Rights Law.[68] The lawsuit settled in the spring of 2020 to the tune of $9.4 million paid entirely by the university's insurance carrier and with no party "admitting liability or fault."[69] At the time of writing, the faculty member at issue was still a tenured member of the faculty within the brain and cognitive sciences department and had returned to teaching following a period of academic leave.[70]

Similarly, Jed Rubenfeld, a prolific scholar and prominent academic at Yale Law School was suspended for two academic years (2020–22) following an investigation into allegations of sexual harassment of students. According to media reports, the allegations against Rubenfeld included that he "inappropriately touched students, made harassing remarks, and attempted kissing" students.[71] Rubenfeld became the subject of scorn when, in 2014, he penned an opinion piece in the *New York Times* that argued in part that not all people under the influence of alcohol are incapable of giving consent and that IHEs had gone too far by adopting policies stating otherwise.[72] One colleague of Rubenfeld's referred to the piece as a "defensive" measure.[73]

The case of John Comaroff at Harvard is also illustrative. Comaroff faced multiple allegations of sexual harassment that resulted in a university investigation culminating in Comaroff being placed on paid administrative leave in August 2020 and then on unpaid leave in January 2022.[74] Three graduate student complainants in the matter subsequently filed a federal lawsuit in February 2022, and colleagues in the department of anthropology publicly called on him to resign.[75]

In all three of these cases, the universities involved were significantly impacted by the alleged behavior of an employee and weathered extensive media coverage and critique. In Comaroff's case, "hundreds" protested at Harvard, holding signs with statements like "we deserve real recourse" and taking aim at Harvard's Title IX coordinator who had openly commented on the integrity of Harvard's process.[76] These cases are rife with palpable frustration over the protections of tenure and its interplay with Title IX.

A complicating factor for IHEs as they navigate the public discourse regarding specific cases is that they are generally bound to confidentiality when it comes to discussing students due to the Family Educational Rights and Privacy Act (FERPA), a federal statute designed to provide basic confidentiality to what it defines as "education records."[77] Most IHEs, however, also decline to comment publicly in detail on student matters on the ethical grounds of wanting to respect the privacy of students. Entities that operate under such rigid constraints as those imposed by FERPA on what can be said and when and by whom it can be said are rare. Even rarer are entities like IHEs that operate with an ethical imperative of privacy and discretion toward those they serve as a matter of course, which generally extends to both tenured faculty and students and thus can come into additional conflict with the public discourse and desire to know the truth.

Two other federal statutes have played a formative role in campus responses to sexual assault and sexual harassment and interplay with institutional Title IX response: the Jeanne Clery Disclosure of Campus Security Policy and Campus Crime Statistics Act and the Violence Against Women Act (VAWA). Following the 1986 Lehigh University campus murder of Jeanne Clery, and her parents' fervent belief that the school did not do enough to safeguard and inform students regarding dangers on campus, the Clery Act was signed into law in 1990 and is designed to ensure the clear provision of statistical information to campus communities regarding crimes on campus.

The primary requirement of the Clery Act is that IHEs disseminate detailed statistics on campus crime, crime reporting policies, alcohol and drug use statistics, and information on sexual assault prevention.[78] VAWA is a more expansive statute administered by the Department of Justice (DOJ) and the Department of Health and Human Services that is aimed at the prevention of and response to domestic violence, sexual assault, dating violence, and stalking.[79] The 2020 amendments to the Title IX implementing regulations align certain defined terms shared by the three statutes, such as "sexual assault" and "dating violence."[80] Together, Title IX and its regulations and guidance, Clery, VAWA, FERPA, and in certain cases Title VII form the federal legal fabric of institutional responses to sexual harassment, which is then complicated further by relevant state statutes that can also dictate IHE responses to campus events.

A common question posed by trustees and other stakeholders to university presidents and legal counsel is how Title IX seemingly went from being invoked for preventing sex discrimination in the context of athletics to being more focused on sexual assault. To be sure, some of the evolution has to do with the parallels between Title VII and Title IX. The Supreme Court, having determined that sexual harassment can constitute sex discrimination under Title VII, eventually transposed this concept to cases brought under Title IX involving sexual harassment in the context of schools.[81] The evolution can also be traced to the early years of the Obama administration when, by using guidance documents and a very public enforcement campaign, the OCR directly linked what it had defined as "sexual violence" to "sexual harassment" under Title IX. Notwithstanding, Title IX has never ceased to be focused on athletics. Indeed, some of the first implementing regulations for Title IX centered on equality in athletics.[82]

In recent years, the focus in athletics has been on both the so-called three-part test for athletic program compliance and private lawsuits brought by students alleging Title IX violations for dropping certain athletic programs. For compliance purposes, the OCR uses a three-part test to determine whether an institution is "effectively accommodate[ing] the interests and abilities of members of both sexes" in accordance with Title IX.[83] An institution will be compliant under this test if it (1) offers athletic participation opportunities for male and female students in numbers that are "substantially proportionate" to the overall enrollment of male and female students, (2) can show a "history and continuing practice" of expanding programs in a way that is responsive to developing interests of students, or (3) can demonstrate "that the interests and abilities of the members of [the underrepresented sex] have been fully and effectively accommodated by the present program."[84] Exact proportionality under the first prong is not specifically required, and the test is relatively forgiving by offering three paths to compliance. Nonetheless, the test has spawned its fair share of controversy and litigation, with notable recent cases occurring at Stanford, Dartmouth, the University of Kentucky, the University of Connecticut, and others.

Recent cases have stemmed from institutions' deciding to downsize their athletics department programmatic offerings for budgetary reasons. At Stanford, five students from five of the eleven teams slated to be eliminated by the university sued the university alleging gender discrimination under Title IX because the proposed cuts would bring Stanford even further out of line with substantial proportionality.[85] Stanford reinstated the programs that had been moved back to club status, but the suit proceeded with the goal of promoting further compliance-based changes at Stanford.[86] The university and plaintiffs ultimately reached a settlement that required Stanford to undergo an extensive compliance review overseen in part by the university's Title IX office. The outcome at Dartmouth, which sought to eliminate various men's and women's programs, was substantially similar, with the college agreeing to reinstate teams and conduct multiple compliance reviews without a lawsuit ever being filed.[87] A federal district court in Connecticut issued a temporary restraining order against the University of Connecticut when members of the women's rowing team sued following the university's announcement that it would eliminate women's rowing as well as two men's teams.[88] Emphasizing the need for a "case-by-case" review specific to the circumstances of the institution, the court found that even with the reduction of men's participation opportunities, Connecticut could still not meet the substantial proportionality test at this stage of the litigation.[89]

As notions of gender identity and expression have continued to evolve, so, too, have the contours of Title IX. Like other aspects of Title IX, this process has been subject to fluctuation based on presidential administrations. In 2016, the OCR under the Obama administration issued guidance stating that the DOE and the DOJ would interpret Title IX as requiring schools to begin "treating the student consistent with the student's gender identity."[90] The guidance specifically included a reference to allowing transgender students equal access to locker rooms and athletic teams. The move was not without controversy, and in May 2020, the OCR under the Trump administration reversed course. In response to complaints received against the Connecticut Interscholastic Athletic Conference and the Glastonbury school board, the OCR found that these organizations' policies permitting students to participate on athletic teams based on the student's gender identity violated Title IX.[91] The Supreme Court's decision in *Bostock* that same year, referenced above, would plant seeds for settling the matter with the Court, holding that for purposes of Title VII, a person's gender identity or sexual orientation is inextricably related to a person's "sex" and that therefore discrimination on the basis of gender identity or sexual orientation constitutes sex discrimination under Title VII.[92] In response to this evolution, over twenty states have introduced legislation that would seek to limit participation in athletics based on gender identity.[93] Meanwhile, the National Collegiate Athletic Association came out with controversial guidelines early in 2022 regarding transgender athletes' ability to participate in their covered sports.[94] The Biden administration in 2023 has adopted a more nuanced approach, proposing regulatory changes that would prohibit outright bans against transgender athlete participation but that would afford schools a measure of flexibility in decisions regarding participation based on a variety of factors including aspects of the sport, the skill level of the team's athletes, and the competitive nature of the team.[95]

Title IX, Title VII, and Title VI of the 1964 Civil Rights Act, which prohibits discrimination on the basis of race, color, or national origin, place guide rails on the behavior of both public and private university actors in service to the broader goals of equality that underpin these statutes.[96] Private universities, because they almost all receive federal funding, are generally subject to these regulations, and although they could choose to forgo such funding, few find that to be an attractive alternative given the large amounts of financial aid, research funding, and other support the federal government provides to IHEs. Higher education is also subject to state-level civil rights provisions and protections around sexual assault and harassment and antidiscrimination laws and regulations, some of which may be stricter or require more reporting than do the federal laws and regulations.[97]

The Americans with Disabilities Act on Campus

The ADA, signed into law in 1990, is a key piece of civil rights legislation prohibiting discrimination on the basis of disability. Title I of the ADA bars discrimination on the basis of disability by public and private IHEs in employment practices, with enforcement carried out by the EEOC. Pursuant to Title II of the ADA, and in tandem with the antidiscrimination mandate of Section 504, discrimination on the basis of disability is barred in school and college programs, with the DOE holding enforcement authority over public IHEs and those private IHEs that are recipients of federal funds.[98] Title III of the ADA, which is enforced by the DOJ, prohibits discrimination against people with disabilities in places of "public accommodation,"[99] a term that encompasses most public and private IHEs. Thus, under the ADA, IHEs are required to make "reasonable modifications" for individuals with disabilities unless doing so would "fundamentally alter" the goods, services, facilities, programming, terms of employment, or other offerings. Litigation under the ADA has been on the rise, with one study finding that an "all-time high" of Title III lawsuits had been filed in the federal courts in 2021.[100]

In 2008, the ADA Amendments Act was signed into law by President George W. Bush.[101] This act eliminated ambiguities in the term "disability" that had been fought over in the courts and explicitly codified definitional aspects of the term "disability."[102] Regulations were promulgated in 2016 that clarified the applicability of the ADA Amendments Act to Titles II and III of the ADA.[103] Of obvious applicability to IHEs, the DOJ noted in a 2016 press release that the 2008 amendments to the ADA were spurred by litigation and definitional challenges related specifically to individuals with "attention deficit hyperactivity disorder, learning disabilities and other disabilities" being denied protections under the ADA.[104]

The mandate of the ADA, similar to Title IX and Title VII, is about promoting equity, in this case by ensuring access for people with disabilities. On campuses, the statute is far reaching, touching all constituencies on campus and various aspects of those individuals' interactions with each other and the institution. Moreover, one need not read too deeply to see the interpretive questions that abound in the language of the statute: what constitutes a "disability," what is "reasonable," what modifications can be said to "fundamentally" alter a job or program? But the questions grow still more complex when applied to the unique terrain of higher education. When does an academic accommodation fundamentally alter an academic program or course of study? When a school denies readmission to a student who left the institution over concerns related to self-harm or harm to others, is the institution discriminating on the basis of a mental health–related disability? How do institutions navigate accommodations related to student dormitories and living arrangements? How do technological changes and classroom innovations impact the accommodations process? How do accommodations intersect with the Title IX process or other processes that are aimed at either ensuring civil rights protections or providing disciplinary mechanisms? How have evolved understandings of cognitive disabilities had an impact on academic accommodations or on the right to receive an education more generally? These questions and more are just some at the heart of the intersection of IHEs and the ADA.

On many campuses, the primary interface for students and accommodations under the ADA is increasingly a dedicated office for disability services with one or more full-time staff members. At the postsecondary level, a student does not need to disclose that they have a disability.[105] However, if the student is requesting an accommodation from the institution, disclosure is necessary. If a student does request an accommodation, an institution may ask for reasonable medical documentation prepared by an appropriate professional. On request and having received any required documentation, campus professionals in a disability services office will then set about verifying, on an individual basis, whether a disability exists under the ADA; that is, whether there exists "a physical or mental impairment that substantially limits a major life activity."[106] On verifying a student's disability, the disability services office then engages in facilitating the provision of appropriate accommodations. Providing an accommodation is an interactive process, and actual accommodations vary in scope and type and are tailored to an individual's specific disability. For example, supportive screen-reading technology may be provided for a student with a visual impairment.

In recent years, a rise in the identification and understanding of various types of "invisible disabilities" has posed new challenges for disability services professionals. Diagnoses such as attention deficit hyperactivity disorder, posttraumatic stress disorder, anxiety disorders, and autism have presented novel issues in the context of both the traditional classroom setting and new and evolving curricular modalities. Reasonable accommodations can include steps such as allowing extra time on tests and providing note-takers, class recordings, or copies of PowerPoint slides. But faculty teaching a course are not, as a matter of law, privy to specific personal or medical details related to a particular student's accommodation. As such they may not agree with disability services professionals that certain accommodations are warranted, or they may be reluctant to concede such accommodations. Nevertheless, an institution is bound by the ADA to engage with the student in an interactive process of reasonable accommodations that ensures the student is not, on the basis of their disability, being deprived of the benefits of the educational program at that institution.

When properly applied, accommodations should be viewed as an effort to provide equal access to educational opportunities, not an attempt to lower academic standards or alter programs or curricula. Under the law, providing an accommodation never requires an IHE to "lower or waive essential requirements" of a course or degree program.[107] As an example, the DOE specifically cites that an accommodation may include providing additional time to complete a test. A reasonable accommodation would not include changing the "substantive content" of the test.[108] Where disability services coordinators have access to accommodation requests, supporting documentation, and professional expertise in honing accommodations, and when faculty have subject matter, pedagogical, and curricular expertise alongside putative notions of academic freedom in the classroom, there is the unavoidable potential for conflict. In the end, all parties should remember to put students first and remain cognizant of the underlying spirit of the ADA: to ensure that students are not denied the benefits of the institution's offering "by reason of" a disability.

Issues pertaining to student mental health–related disabilities, students who may self-harm, and the legality of involuntary withdrawals have also posed particular challenges for IHEs in the context of a rapidly evolving legal framework and an evolving understanding of the mental health challenges facing students.[109] For some time, the concept of "direct threat" reigned in campus decision-making about whether a student facing mental health challenges should be allowed to return to an institution.[110] This rule held that if an IHE determined that a student posed a risk of substantial harm to themselves or others, then the institution was justified in taking action that included removing the student. This rule later changed in 2011,[111] throwing campus disciplinary officials and lawyers into something of a tizzy. Expressing a sense of frustration three years after the change in 2014, one attorney wrote in a briefing paper for the National Association of College and University Attorneys (NACUA) that "there is still no formal guidance . . . regarding how IHEs, without applying a direct threat analysis, can properly care for students at risk of self-harm while maintaining compliance with disability laws."[112]

In the years that have followed the 2011 Title II regulatory changes, IHEs have piecemealed their way through situations involving students who posed a risk of harm to themselves. Institutions began looking to the OCR and DOJ findings against other institutions as instructive of how they should operate under circumstances where the institution was considering an involuntary withdrawal of the student or other type of separation. Noteworthy cases and resolution agreements included those at Princeton University, Fordham, Georgetown, SUNY, Spring Arbor, and Brown.[113] In 2018, in an effort to seek greater clarity for campuses, NACUA even hosted a special briefing with Candice Jackson, acting assistant secretary for the US Department of Education Office for Civil Rights in the Trump administration, in which she spoke to specific considerations for institutions to consider.[114] Several guiding principles emerge from Assistant Secretary Jackson's comments and prior resolution agreements including that IHEs should consider reasonable accommodations that would enable a student to remain enrolled at the institution, be sure to undertake an individualized assessment of the particular student at issue as part of a fair process that may consider input from qualified health providers and/or the student's provider, that institutions should prioritize voluntary action by the student, and that involuntary separations may be undertaken but only as a last resort. In general, these compose the basic guidelines for institutions weighing issues related to students who pose a risk of self-harm. Institutions struggle mightily to weigh procedural requirements and stated guidelines with the best interests of the student and sometimes, rightly or wrongly, the input of many other parties who may or may not truly have the students' best interests in mind.[115]

Students are not the only campus constituency to which the ADA applies; faculty and staff are also entitled to the protections offered by the statute by virtue of Title I. On the employee side, the human resources department, sometimes in conjunction with offices for academic and faculty affairs, is often the unit that coordinates efforts related to accommodations in the campus workplace. On disclosure of a disability and a request for accommodations by an employee, similarly to the academic setting, institutions are required to engage in an interactive process when determining accommodations but are not required to change "essential functions" of a job or position. This is because the individual must be "otherwise qualified" for the position under the ADA or able to perform the essential functions of the role with or without an accommodation.[116] The only exception to reasonable accommodations is where the accommodation might pose an "undue hardship" on the institution; that is, a "significant difficulty or expense" with a focus on the specific resources of the employer.[117] Determinations of when a requested accommodation poses an undue hardship or when a person's requested accommodation begins to change the essential functions of a job are not always easily made.[118]

Requests for accommodations, academically or otherwise, do not always align neatly with other legal, regulatory, or compliance constraints for IHEs. For example, the use of service animals is very specifically outlined by the ADA, which limits service animals to dogs or small horses that perform tasks directly related to a person's disability.[119] The Fair Housing Act however, which applies to campus dormitories, permits the use of a broader variety of emotional support or "assistance animals" that "alleviates one or more identified symptoms or effects of a person's disability."[120] Disability services coordinators and residential education officials must weigh both along with more local regulations related to all classes of animals and the needs of other students sharing residential space. The medicinal use of marijuana must also be considered. A student may possess a prescription card for the use of marijuana to treat a condition that constitutes a disability, but even in a state where marijuana use and possession have been decriminalized and fully legalized, it may be unwise for an institution to condone marijuana use as an academic accommodation if requested. This is because the Drug-Free Schools and Communities Act, enforcement of which is tied to federal funding, still categorizes marijuana as a "schedule one" drug.[121] Finally, providing accommodations during a disciplinary process may introduce thorny issues. Parties in a disciplinary or Title IX proceeding may require extra time to review key documents or may require accommodations for providing or processing testimony or other evidence in real time. At various points, the DOE has nodded to the issue of accommodations specifically in Title IX proceedings, but as with many things, there still exist significant areas of gray when institutions attempt to comply with both statutes on a case-by-case basis.[122]

Accommodations on campuses come in many forms and bridge the dimensions of the physical and the virtual. New campus construction must adhere to current accessibility standards but a variety of inaccessible preexisting buildings dot campuses across the country. While nearly all campuses aspire to full accessibility in their physical plan as a matter of principle, broad exceptions within the ADA do not require that preexisting structures be fully accessible unless such accessibility is "readily achievable," a fact-specific analysis that provides considerable room for interpretation.[123] Campuses must also ensure that their virtual presence (i.e., website) is accessible as well.[124] This includes accommodations such as appropriate color contrast and compatibility with screen-reading technology. In 2018, a single individual who uses screen-reading technology to navigate the internet sued fifty IHEs alleging that their websites were out of compliance with ADA standards for web accessibility.[125] The OCR has also ramped up enforcement of web accessibility in recent years, receiving complaints and opening investigations at hundreds of IHEs in 2018 alone.[126]

Conclusion: Civil Rights on Campus Are Here to Stay and Continuing to Expand

While several conclusions can be drawn from this chapter's material, a major takeaway is how the developments of the past ten to fifteen years have created a civil rights infrastructure with implications for IHEs that, while malleable across presidential administrations, will not recede any time soon for institutions. The amount of administrative bandwidth, costs, and energy that these matters occupy at institutions, regardless of their size, continues to increase. The rapidity of change in this area challenges the credibility of IHEs that are working in good faith and in the best interest of their students and broader communities to not simply "comply" with these legal evolutions but to also go above and beyond.

Another key takeaway of the chapter is that to the extent issues of equity are central to the educational mission and strategic success of IHEs in the future—as the authors think they are—an understanding of the legal waters into which institutions are being thrust, and effective counsel in navigating those waters, is essential for the long-term success of institutions and for educating and supporting students. Members of the campus community now go about their days asking many questions they never used to ask. While this presents challenges to IHEs as discussed herein, it is certainly a good thing overall, and IHEs must continually strive to be better. As administrators and educators, how we navigate issues of civil rights on our campuses is reflective of how our students experience them in practice and how they will enter the world as members of society at large.

Chapter 2

Free Speech and Expression on Campus

Embedded in the DNA of almost any institution of higher education (IHE) are principles of free speech and expression. Indeed, a higher education institution without some grounding in concepts of free speech and expression is, arguably, not properly considered a college or university. If an institution's fundamental mission is to create and discover knowledge and to disseminate knowledge to students and the broader public, an environment supportive of open inquiry must exist. Underpinning conditions of open inquiry are principles of free speech and expression. And yet, as central as these principles are, few concepts have been more challenging for IHEs to grapple with recently. While these concepts have always had some foothold in the First Amendment, they have taken on a decidedly more legalistic tilt in recent years as campus policies and practices have evolved alongside legal concepts impacting matters ranging from harassment to the use of technology and guest lecturers to trigger warnings. How does the layering of the legal framework regarding concepts of free speech and expression, as opposed to purely academic principles of free inquiry and open discourse, impact the core mission of the modern university? This chapter addresses this question by considering legal principles of free expression as applied to higher education in a way that sheds light on their impact on the sector and thus elucidates one of the most significant ways in which IHEs have become "lawyerized."

To explore the lawyerization of higher education from the perspective of free speech and expression, we first briefly discuss the basic framework of the First Amendment of the US Constitution and its formal legal interface with higher education. Then we explicate issues of speech and expression on IHE campuses through the lens of seven specific and highly evolving areas where the legal trends inform and impact—for better or worse—the core mission of IHEs today: academic freedom, codes of conduct and so-called speech codes, harassment, bias incident response, technology and speech, trigger warnings, and campus speakers. The depth and breadth of the scholarly work around the First Amendment, academic freedom, and other topics discussed in this chapter are too significant for twenty-odd pages to do them real justice. But we can provide an organizing structure to consider existing work and present issues in a concise and accessible format to understand better how discussions of free speech and expression on campuses are currently structured and constrained.

The First Amendment

The fount of our collective sense of free speech and expression in the American legal system and across American culture more generally is the First Amendment of the US Constitution. The First Amendment contains several protections, but most notably for our purposes, it contains the declaration that "Congress shall make no law . . . abridging the freedom of speech."[1] Critically, the First Amendment, like the other amendments that constitute the Bill of Rights, protects against infringements from government actors. The text after all instructs that "Congress shall make no law."

The text of the First Amendment says nothing specific about IHEs abridging speech, and courts have consistently interpreted the First Amendment as only applying to so-called state actors—entities found to be acting as or on behalf of the state.[2] In practice, this means that, as a purely legal matter, the First Amendment is the foundation for a cause of action only to public institutions, not private institutions. The First Amendment protects individuals against infringements by the state on their right to speak freely but does not generally protect them against such infringements by private actors, including private IHEs.[3]

So why do private IHEs still care about the First Amendment? There are myriad and varying reasons. Primarily, however, the fundamental principles behind the First Amendment are central to the principles of open inquiry that underlie the academic exercises involved in the search for knowledge. Just as articulating viewpoints on society or policy and subjecting them to debate in the "marketplace of ideas" can be healthy for democracy, so, too, do these principles aid in the search for knowledge and fundamental truth in the academic setting.[4] Similarly, the concept that an individual can publicly express a viewpoint without fear of reprisal from the government parallels the notion that scholars and students should be free to challenge a widely accepted academic concept or tout an unpopular scholarly viewpoint without fear of retribution from their employer or peers.

In short, private IHEs should care about the First Amendment, even if it cannot be invoked as a legal matter, because the linkages and analogies between First Amendment principles and principles of maintaining a scholarly climate of free and open inquiry are too close to ignore. Moreover, even if the First Amendment does not technically apply in all campus settings, people have simply come to think that it applies. Campuses are unique fora with porous boundaries, and the mores of the outside world do not wait at the wrought iron gates.[5]

Academic Freedom and the Law

The term "academic freedom" may be one of the most commonly, but loosely, used terms in the dialect of higher education. Like the First Amendment, academic freedom can be invoked as a sword or a shield. To an extent, and like the notion of free speech, it can be contorted to suit the purposes of the person or entity invoking its protections. It is central to the functioning of an IHE as one of the highest ideals of academia, and as such, like the First Amendment, it can by its mere invocation provoke hardened viewpoints and strong feelings.

Numerous scholars, lawyers, and courts have attempted to clarify and organize concepts of academic freedom and to settle notions of the concept within the law.[6] We cannot claim to do justice to such a task here, but for our purposes, we briefly explicate academic freedom's evolution, its relationship to the First Amendment, and the impact of this relationship on IHEs from a legal perspective.

It is useful to examine academic freedom from four different definitional angles that have been proposed by scholars, lawyers, and the courts. These are the so-called professional definition of academic freedom, the constitutional definition of academic freedom,[7] the institutional conception of academic freedom, and the individual conception of academic freedom.[8]

The professional definition of academic freedom emanates from the American Association of University Professors (AAUP), the formation of which in 1915 reflects an early twentieth-century shift toward defining a modern and professionalized conception of academia and the faculty's role within it. The AAUP's 1915 Declaration of Principles on Academic Freedom and Academic Tenure, which evolved into the AAUP's 1940 Statement of Principles on Academic Freedom and Tenure and has thus survived to the present day, is critical in this regard.[9] It is commonly thought that early twentieth-century pressures on faculty from governing boards, and then pressures on faculty exerted by the national government relating to concerns over communism from the 1930s and into the 1950s were the primary drivers of these policy statements.[10] In one example from the turn of the twentieth century, Stanford University failed to renew the contract of Professor Edward Ross.[11] Ross was controversial for his eugenicist beliefs, but he was also seen as critical of certain labor practices of the railroad industry, the source of Leland and Jane Stanford's wealth.[12] The failure to renew his contract apparently sent shockwaves through Stanford's faculty and resulted in the resignation of several professors, one of whom is said to have helped found the AAUP.[13] Hence today's professional definition of academic freedom appears to have evolved from a protective posture of the faculty induced by pressures and influences in part from inside the institution in the form of governing boards and in part from outside the institution in the form of government actors. The current AAUP statement proclaims that higher education is "conducted for the common good," that "the common good depends upon the free search for truth and its free exposition," and that academic freedom applies to "both teaching and research."[14] Academic freedom in research is "fundamental to the advancement of truth." And academic freedom in teaching is "fundamental" to the protection of both teacher and student. Notably, it is in the 1940 Statement that we are introduced to the concept of tenure and the notion that it "is a means to certain ends" in ensuring academic freedom.[15]

Constitutional renditions of academic freedom are composed of largely the same notes as the professional conception of academic freedom. But rather than emanating from the AAUP, the constitutional definition of academic freedom comes from a series of cases from the Supreme Court that some argue rather fortuitously tie together a theory of academic freedom.[16] These cases include primarily *Sweezy v. New Hampshire, Regents of the State of New York v. Keyishian,* and *Regents of the University of California v. Bakke.* Together, they have produced the language often associated with academic freedom as articulated by the Court. In *Keyishian,* Justice William Brennan stated that academic freedom is a matter of national concern and that academic freedom is a "special concern of the First Amendment, which does not tolerate laws that cast a pall of orthodoxy over the classroom."[17] Calling classrooms a "marketplace of ideas," he continued, asserting that "teachers and students must always remain free to inquire . . . to evaluate, to gain new maturity and understanding; otherwise our civilization will stagnate and die."[18] As in the professional definition, the constitutional conception supports concepts of open inquiry and expression, the free exchange of ideas, and the belief that these ideals should not be inhibited.

The constitutional strain of academic freedom formally introduces the dichotomy of institutional and individual academic freedom. *Sweezy* and *Keyishian* both involved instances where government actors sought to compel academics to divulge certain information or associations: in the case of Sweezy, the substance of a lecture he delivered; for Keyishian, his political affiliations by virtue of requiring a signed affirmation about his activities with the communist party. While the Court in these cases does refer generally to academic freedom rights of institutions, as a legal matter, both of these cases link academic freedom to the First Amendment rights of the individual faculty members involved. In *Bakke*, the seminal academic affirmative action case, Justice Lewis Powell relied on notions of academic freedom to articulate what has come to be called institutional academic freedom: the idea that an academic institution as a corporate body has an academic freedom interest rooted in the First Amendment "to make its own judgments as to education."[19] For Justice Powell, who invoked language from *Sweezy*, this includes an IHE's right "to determine for itself on academic grounds who may teach, what may be taught, how it shall be taught, and who may be admitted to study."[20] Interestingly, while the AAUP does appear to acknowledge forms of institutional academic freedom,[21] the AAUP's professional definition of academic freedom as articulated in the 1940 Statement has little to say about institutional academic freedom as opposed to the academic freedom of individual academics.

So what are the legal implications of these definitional turf wars? It helps to understand that, as an initial matter, tenure—the widely accepted bulwark against infringements on academic freedom—is a contract. The parameters of the protection that faculty receive in order to protect and ensure academic freedom are spelled out in faculty handbooks and bylaws. When defining the parameters of tenure at a specific institution, faculty handbooks often incorporate explicitly or by reference certain policy statements of the AAUP, such as the 1940 Statement. Where this is the case, and depending on other circumstances, the AAUP policies referred to or incorporated within the faculty handbook could be considered contractually binding on both the faculty member and the institution.[22]

There is, however, no explicit cause of action for a "violation" of academic freedom. In certain situations, mainly at public institutions, there exists the possibility that an individual faculty member could invoke constitutional theories of academic freedom that are cloaked in the legal doctrine of the First Amendment. But these arguments can be nebulous, are often highly fact-specific, and thus far have been statistically unlikely to succeed.[23] As one scholar points out, following the *Keyishian* case, the First Amendment rights of academics have essentially "merged" with the broader doctrine related to free speech and public employees.[24] As recently as 2006, the Supreme Court appeared explicitly to sidestep reconciling academic freedom with free speech doctrine as applied to public employees in *Garcetti v. Ceballos,* declining to opine on whether the analysis in that case would apply similarly to a speech case involving "scholarship or teaching."[25] This has been the subject of some confusion in the lower courts and splits at the circuit level.[26] The Supreme Court's musings on academic freedom, while stirring, have not provided a sound foothold for litigation where faculty seek solely to invoke their specific, individual rights to academic freedom. One empirical survey of First Amendment cases invoking academic freedom led the investigator to conclude that "faculty and courts define academic freedom quite differently," having found that faculty members lost 73 percent of the First Amendment–specific rulings he had reviewed.[27] Another scholar has observed that "the Court's glorification of academic freedom . . . has produced hyperbolic rhetoric but only scant, and often ambiguous, analytic content."[28]

The value and import of institutional academic freedom are also somewhat unformed in the courts. While there is certainly strong language supporting the concept—particularly in the line of cases including *Bakke* and *Grutter v. Bollinger*—the Supreme Court has never explicitly held "that academic institutions are entitled to either academic freedom or autonomy under the First Amendment."[29] Moreover, tensions between individual academic freedom and institutional academic freedom have not been firmly resolved as a doctrinal matter.[30] When the two do directly conflict, institutional interests tend to win out when institutions are acting in good faith and pursuant to contractual terms and other legal strictures.[31]

This section merely highlights a remarkably complex concept that is likely to continue to evolve[32] with controversies invoking academic freedom seemingly ever present.[33] In March 2021, around two hundred professors launched the Academic Freedom Alliance, a nonprofit "whose members are dedicated to protecting the rights of faculty members at IHEs to speak, instruct, and publish without fear of sanction or punishment."[34] The group promises "legal support to faculty members whose constitutionally, statutorily, contractually, or other legally protected rights to academic freedom have been violated or are under threat."[35] These statements capture and seem to acknowledge an important feature perpetuating academic freedom's elusiveness: that it is an academic aspiration that may, at times, be legally enforceable by contract, protections found in the Constitution, or through other statutes depending on the context. But belying this statement is the possibility that, in any particular case, academic freedom may not be legally enforceable at all. Whether academic freedom is of legal relevance will be a question of the specific claim or defense put forward and the facts at issue. Whether the claim or defense can succeed is then impacted by the jurisdiction and the precedent of case law in that jurisdiction. Either way, faculty and administrators navigating campus controversies across the terrain of free expression and academic freedom would do well to recall Chemerinsky and Gillman's description of the distinction between the two: as a legal matter, they are indistinct but concentric zones. "General precepts of free speech," they write, "apply without regard to the special teaching and research mission of college campuses" but may apply to the broader campus community nonetheless, while academic freedom principles "govern the expression of ideas within professional academic settings."[36]

Student Handbooks, Codes of Conduct, and Speech Codes

Student handbooks, codes of conduct, and expressions of community standards all seek to outline parameters of student conduct and behavior within a campus community. Thus, by their very nature, they involve issues related to speech and expression. Not unlike faculty by-laws and handbooks, student handbooks and codes of conduct can carry the weight of contract: the terms of the document delineate the relationship between the student and the institution where the student agrees to matriculate. From a disciplinary standpoint, adverse action against a student should only be taken in accordance with the terms of the applicable student policy.[37]

Many campus codes of conduct contain lofty—but worthy—stated expectations designed to create an ideal learning environment while fostering a climate of open inquiry. Stanford University's code of conduct, for example, states that the "university values integrity, diversity, respect, freedom of inquiry and expression, trust, honesty and fairness and strives to integrate these values into its education, research, health care and business practices."[38] The Student Handbook of Swarthmore College proclaims that the college "aspires to create an academic environment grounded in intellectual discovery and guided by rational discourse and civility" and that "Swarthmore promotes and fosters personal growth and learning; preserves both individual rights and the wellbeing and respect of others and the community."[39] The student code of conduct of Florida State University, which emphasizes a "responsible engagement of student freedoms," states that "the pursuit of responsible freedom is consistent with . . . efforts to promote civility at the University, as students balance their pursuit of excellence and exploration with consideration to the impact of behavior on themselves and others."[40] All of these statements identify that an environment of open inquiry is tied in some way to mutual "respect"; notions of "civility"; and the idea that by acknowledging the rights of others, we are preserving our own rights to a supportive learning environment.

Some observers couch portions of student handbooks or codes as "speech codes." The Foundation for Individual Rights in Education (now Expression) (FIRE), a nonprofit organization whose original stated mission was to defend and sustain the individual rights of students and faculty members at America's colleges and universities,[41] has created "speech code ratings" for IHEs that inform you of "FIRE's opinion of the degree to which free speech is curtailed at a particular institution."[42] FIRE is astutely aware that the First Amendment does not explicitly apply to private IHEs, saying as much on its website, but warns that those private institutions "that promise debate and freedom are morally bound—and may be contractually bound, depending on the circumstances."[43] FIRE maintains a database on its website providing ratings for "speech codes" at nearly five hundred IHEs. And, because higher education loves rankings, in 2020, FIRE teamed up with College Pulse and RealClearEducation to publish "the first-ever comprehensive student assessment of free speech on American college campuses" in the form of the College Free Speech Rankings, which they now update regularly.[44] FIRE is also not reluctant to engage in litigation, primarily by providing legal counsel or filing amicus briefs in cases it views as particularly noteworthy for purposes of First Amendment doctrine such as the 2021 case of a Shawnee State University professor who refused to use a student's preferred pronouns,[45] a faculty member who criticized institutional responses to COVID-19 and specific political figures on Twitter,[46] and "crude" social media posts made by a student that were investigated by the university.[47]

A legal reality for American higher education is that the First Amendment protects certain speech and expression that many people find repugnant or that may seem antithetical to the values or contours of an inclusive learning environment. As perhaps the most prominent example, hate speech is a form of protected speech under the First Amendment. Repeated attempts by IHEs to regulate hate speech through campus policies have been struck down by courts as unconstitutional, often on the grounds of vagueness or overbreadth.[48] In so doing, courts often refer to the principle that the First Amendment "prevents government from proscribing . . . expressive conduct because of disapproval of the ideas expressed"[49] on the theory that allowing government actors to regulate actual content, however repulsive the content, is a slippery slope. To paraphrase Justice Louis Brandeis, the best remedy for speech one disagrees with is more speech.[50] This approach is supported in many campus codes, including, perhaps most notably, the University of Chicago Statement on Freedom of Expression, which has been adopted in whole or in part by numerous other institutions:[51]

> the University's fundamental commitment is to the principle that debate or deliberation may not be suppressed because the ideas put forth are thought by some or even by most members of the University community to be offensive, unwise, immoral, or wrong-headed. It is for the individual members of the University community, not for the University as an institution, to make those judgments for

themselves, and to act on those judgments not by seeking to suppress speech, but by openly and vigorously contesting the ideas that they oppose.[52]

Hence campuses find themselves in a precarious middle ground where some of the most highly objectionable forms of expression are protected by the First Amendment and may wreak havoc in a community of scholars and students attempting to carry out their academic goals. Codes of conduct and student handbooks must do their best to articulate institutional values of respect and inclusion alongside academic freedom and the parameters of the First Amendment, and many do so admirably. Not all problematic speech or expression is "protected," but whether speech or expression is ultimately protected or unprotected, there is almost always considerable gray area and room for debate.

Harassment

Harassment is a form of speech or expression that is not protected by the First Amendment. But defining what constitutes "harassment"—and therefore what expression is not subject to the protection of the First Amendment—has proven more complicated. The task grows harder still on a campus, a place where a wide array of people from varying backgrounds are brought together to study, learn, and work in an environment that is, ideally, conditioned and primed for open inquiry.

Harassment can take many forms, and the laws prohibiting harassment are designed to protect a variety of "classes" of individuals from harassment's ills. Harassment in the employment context may violate Title VII, the Age Discrimination in Employment Act of 1967, (ADEA), and the Americans with Disabilities Act (ADA). Under these statutes, harassment experienced by an employee because of their race, color, religion, sex, sexual orientation, gender identity, pregnancy, national origin, age, disability, or genetic information is illegal.[53] As discussed in Chapter I, some of these are also protected classes under Title IX.[54] Title VI is another federal statute particularly germane to higher education in that it prohibits discrimination in the form of harassment on the basis of race, color, or national origin by institutions receiving federal funding, which is most IHEs.[55] The categories of people who may be subjected to harassment on campus in the eyes of the law are thus fairly well defined.

The general issue today on campuses is that the legal definition of harassment and popular interpretations of harassment can be at odds. A piece published by the American Bar Association articulates this issue well when its authors write that "as a society, we now use the term 'harassment' to mean being bothered, generically."[56] The Chronicle of Higher Education has given extensive coverage to this evolution in a piece on the expansive nature of harm to today's students, writing that "college students are redefining 'harm' as something that threatens not only their physical safety, but also their emotional safety."[57] Yet the Equal Employment Opportunity Commission (EEOC) specifically requires that harassing conduct be "severe or pervasive enough to create a work environment that a reasonable person would consider intimidating, hostile, or abusive," and applying a "reasonable person" standard rules out "petty slights, annoyances, and isolated incidents (unless extremely serious)."[58] Under Title IX, harassment must be "severe, pervasive, and objectively offensive" and must "effectively den[y] a person equal access to the school's education program."[59] In 2003, the Office of Civil Rights (OCR) issued a Dear Colleague Letter articulating that its regulatory actions are not "intended" to infringe on the free expression guaranteed by the First Amendment, though the OCR has said little to this effect since.[60] Under the above definitions, being offended or taken aback by a statement does not make a statement harassment in the eyes of the law. And under any definition, simply calling conduct "harassment," a "hostile environment," or "discriminatory" does not make it such.

One subject of much study in this regard has been the case of Laura Kipnis, a professor of film studies at Northwestern University who was purportedly investigated under Title IX in part because of her outspoken criticisms of Northwestern's Title IX policies that appeared in an article in the *Chronicle of Higher Education* and elsewhere.[61] Commentators have made much of Northwestern's willingness to invoke the legal conception of harassment explained above as the basis for investigation following the publication of an article expressing criticism of the effects of a campus Title IX policy.[62] As campus administrators, we know there is almost inevitably more on all sides of any given story than what is publicly reported. We also know that answering questions of whether certain conduct rises to the level of harassment necessarily involves embracing a facility and comfort level with operating in a "gray area." On its face, could a single article critiquing campus policies be conduct so severe, pervasive, and objectively offensive that it denies a person access to their education? This seems unlikely. But could there have been other facts known to Northwestern that made a review of the matter as potential harassment a reasonable approach at the time? Plausibly.

All of this is simply to say that while the law does seemingly offer some hard-and-fast guidance around harassment in the form of terms like "severe" and "pervasive," and the reasonable person standard, these terms do not assuage what is ultimately a series of judgment calls. This can be a hard reality for IHEs seeking to foster open inquiry and the free exchange of ideas. Institutionally, while putting the educational interests of our students first, we must avoid the tendency to use areas of unprotected speech such as harassment to drive a hole through open scholarly inquiry. We must embrace nuance and be comfortable with the fallibility of wading in a gray area, always keeping as our compass the educational best interests of our students.

Bias Incidents and Response Teams

According to one study, bias incident response teams (BIRTs) exist on over two hundred campuses, and their number may be growing.[63] Typically, a BIRT consists of representatives from several campus offices such as those across divisions of student affairs, equity and diversity, or campus safety that field complaints and concerns of all manners related to incidents of bias, hate, or discrimination.[64] BIRTs tend to focus on support for impacted students and proactive efforts aimed at reducing incidents of hate or bias. BIRTs generally do not have the authority to punish or discipline students or other community members, though they may refer matters to internal or external authorities that do have such authority.

BIRTs are not without controversy. Commentators have referred to them as "shadowy" assemblages, implied that they "muzzle" campus discourse,[65] and claimed that they "bring[] back the Soviet Union."[66] A central issue regarding BIRTs is the question of whether they "chill" speech on campus. This question occurs not only in the court of public opinion but also in the federal courts as a legal question. BIRTs have been challenged in lawsuits against public universities where plaintiffs argue that BIRTs and their related policies violate the First Amendment because they "stifle" and infringe on "protected speech through overbroad and vague prohibitions."[67] At least one court has rationalized that the BIRT at issue did not have a chilling effect because complying with the BIRT was entirely voluntary, and thus the BIRT did not have real disciplinary authority.[68] Other courts have disagreed, finding that because the BIRTs in those cases had the ability to refer incidents to campus disciplinary authorities or law enforcement who could then conduct a formal investigation, the BIRTs had a chilling effect.[69] The Sixth Circuit has also pointed out that BIRTs may have a chilling effect because a student who has been invited to meet with a BIRT might "understand the invitation to carry the threat: 'meet or we will refer your case.'"[70]

At first blush, BIRTs look like another example of the maxim "no good deed goes unpunished." In an attempt to create inclusive learning environments that holistically support students, IHEs have created BIRTs to address issues of bias—real and perceived—in a thoughtful and reflective way true to the educational mission and purpose of IHEs. And yet, despite these noble aims, these actions are not immune from litigation.

An aspect of the "lawyerization" of higher education in recent years is the proliferation of campus bodies, such as BIRTs and Title IX hearings, that engage in processes that are highly analogous to courts or administrative hearing bodies. Formality and process are positive features because they work to ensure fundamental fairness, speak to equity concerns, and lend legitimacy to an outcome, among other things. But in our zeal to create structures and processes, we need to take care not to lose sight of our educational goals and purposes by reducing their embodiment at the university to adversarial

processes steeped in the language of law and the courts, easily susceptible to further litigation.

Technology and Free Speech

Broadly speaking, "acceptable use" policies set the parameters for the
use of institutional technological resources such as networks, specific
pieces of equipment, software and applications, and tools such as
electronic mail. Acceptable use policies typically ban illegal activity
broadly; make statements requiring the "responsible" or "ethical" use
of resources; and often ban certain actions such as harassment, "bullying," or threats. The organization Speech First has brought challenges to technology use policies, often in cases where they are also
challenging BIRTs and campus codes of conduct.

At least one recent case suggests that institutions should look closely
at their acceptable use policies, particularly as they interplay with institutional codes of conduct and conduct that might be considered protected speech. In a case involving Virginia Tech, the district court
addressed the school's expansive computer use policy language that, in
the court's view, created prohibited conduct separate and apart from
that already used in the student code of conduct. While the student
code of conduct contained acceptable prohibitions and was linked to
the computer use policy, the court found that the computer use policy
went too far, and it granted a preliminary injunction halting application of the policy's language that barred use of computer systems for
the purposes of "intimidation" and "unwarranted annoyance."[71]

Policies have proliferated on today's campuses, covering nearly all
aspects of life at IHEs. They are also often interdependent and intertwined with each other. Policy setting is not an exact science, and in as
vast a sea of words as a compendium of campus policies, one is

destined to find language that is at times inharmonious. IHEs are not immune from scrutiny when these inconsistencies surface, and these can often lead to a contentious dispute or negative outcome in court.

Campus Speakers

Few topics have received as much attention in recent years as controversial campus speakers and the reactions they provoke on campuses. Several noteworthy events, ranging from the violent unrest at the University of California, Berkeley, in response to a scheduled talk by Milo Yiannopoulos to Charles Murray's speaking at Middlebury College, which generated a significant disruption on that campus, received extensive coverage and commentary and became emblematic of the myriad issues—legal and otherwise—at play in such a scenario.[72] More recent examples include the "shouting down" of speakers at the law schools of Yale and the University of California College of the Law, San Francisco.[73] Both theoretical and practical questions are rife in such situations. When, if ever, it is proper for an institution to disinvite a speaker or condemn a speaker's expression? Is it acceptable for student groups to functionally cancel speakers through violent or incendiary protest? What are the appropriate institutional responses when campus speakers create disruptions to the academic environment or civil unrest?

The framework that might apply in scenarios involving controversial campus speakers is multilayered. There are considerations rooted in First Amendment law (some or all of which may not even technically apply as a matter of law on private campuses), academic freedom considerations, and broader considerations of community-wide norms and expectations. As a matter of constitutional law, it is generally accepted that reasonable "time, place, and manner restrictions" that are "content neutral" may be imposed to address various issues presented by public speech and expression.[74] That is, the restrictions or constraints put in place by an institution cannot vary from speaker to speaker because of the substance of what a person or group is saying. These restrictions might include designating certain spaces or areas for speech and expression or events, restricting the occupancy of a room for safety purposes, requiring additional campus safety support for large crowds, and setting parameters for the time and duration of events to normal campus working or extracurricular hours. The key is to ensure that such restrictions are clear policy and universally applied and that they do not vary based on the views being expressed by the particular speaker or group. It is also settled that as a legal matter, the First Amendment cannot be used as a justification or defense for the destruction of property or to significantly disrupt campus operations.[75]

The lines between legal principles of free speech, perceptions of academic freedom, and community expectations and norms when it comes to invited campus speakers are subject to considerable blurring. The case of Dorian Abbott is an illustrative example. Abbott is a professor of geophysics at the University of Chicago who, unrelated to his scientific scholarship, is also an outspoken critic of diversity initiatives on campuses.[76] In the fall of 2021, he was slated to deliver the distinguished John Carlson lecture at MIT on the topic of climate and the potential for extraterrestrial life, but the lecture was canceled by MIT. According to Abbott, he was told that the Carlson lecture—a lecture that is apparently both a formative career accomplishment and also aimed at public outreach and high school students—had been canceled "in order to avoid controversy."[77] Abbott was subsequently invited by MIT to deliver a different talk without a public or recruitment component to "present his scientific work on MIT's campus to students and faculty."[78] Abbott claimed that the lecture was canceled because of a "small group of ideologues" who mounted a "twitter campaign" and succeeded in bullying the department chair into canceling the lecture.[79] The chair of the department hosting the Carlson lecture stated "We felt that with the current distractions we would not be in a position to hold an effective outreach event."[80]

As a private institution, MIT certainly has the ability to call off lectures hosted on its campus for any number of reasons. Abbott had no clear First Amendment entitlement to deliver the Carlson lecture at the stated time and place. But the overlapping academic freedom concerns in this instance are more nuanced. Is a talk delivered to current students and faculty the same as a named lecture open to a public audience? Is open dialogue in pursuit of knowledge and truth hindered by changing the character of the lecture given? MIT could not provide clear answers. MIT's president remarked in a campus-wide email that "there is no doubt that this matter has caused many people inside and outside our community to question the institute's commitment to free expression," and that "some report feeling that certain topics are now off limits at MIT."[81] Nevertheless, MIT's president went on to state that "freedom of expression is a fundamental value of the institute" and committed to a faculty forum to "engage in serious, open discussion together."[82] Abbott ultimately accepted the alternative lecture option offered by MIT and, with the support of members of the Academic Freedom Alliance, was also invited to deliver a public lecture at Princeton University on the same day he had been scheduled to appear at MIT for the Carlson lecture.

The fallout in scenarios like Abbott's invitation and disinvitation could have been dramatically different in a not-very-distant time and regulatory regime. In the spring of 2019, President Donald Trump signed an Executive Order aimed at strengthening "free speech" protections at institutions receiving federal research and education grants.[83] The president's actions were intended to "encourage institutions to appropriately account for [free speech and inquiry] in their administration of student life and to avoid creating environments that stifle competing perspectives."[84] The Executive Order stated that institutions should be held accountable for their own speech policies and directed the Department of Education and other agencies to use their regulatory power to craft regulations that ensure that institutions could be called to account for not living up to their stated values as articulated by their policies. The Department of Education (DOE) did promulgate final regulations, potentially paving the way for False Claims Act liability for private institutions not adhering to their stated free speech policies and tying vague notions of compliance with the First Amendment to receipt of certain federal grants.[85] However, the subsequent Biden administration has taken up a review of the regulations with an eye toward significant revision and rescinding certain aspects of the regulations.[86] Notably, and pragmatically, the DOE under the Biden administration has cited that "Federal and State courts are best equipped to resolve" First Amendment matters in this context.[87]

Instances like the proposed cancellation of the Carlson lecture also have had a notable impact on alumni of IHEs. In the fall of 2021, alumni from five prominent IHEs—Cornell, Davidson, Princeton, Virginia, and Washington and Lee—announced the creation of the Alumni Free Speech Alliance, an organization that touts its commitment to ensuring freedom of speech and academic freedom from beyond the physical campus.[88] The group essentially posits that as alums, they are in a unique and more insulated position to "push back" against free speech infringements than those tethered to a campus as faculty, staff, trustees, or administrators. In fact, a distinctive concern for campus administrators is whether alumni may reduce financial contributions to their schools if they are disaffected by campus doings. Thus the threat of financial harm coming not from litigation (which most campuses have insurance to mitigate) but from lost donations may have a more deleterious effect on the openness of campus climate.

Conclusion: Free Speech and Expression Continue to Engender Controversy on Campuses

While we have illustrated the issues in this chapter using incidents that were relatively current when we wrote this book, no doubt new incidents have occurred subsequently that might also be cited as examples of free speech issues on campus. While we could have used even older examples of challenges to free speech and expression on campus, both the rapidity of the spread of knowledge about these kerfuffles thanks to modern media technology, as well as the role of technology in causing the issues, differentiates the more recent issues from older examples. The rapid spread of both information and misinformation about events on campuses, combined with at times a very detailed public airing of documentation regarding such events and other times a veil of secrecy, can make the true story in either case that much harder to analyze objectively.

What is clear is that numerous outside parties consider whatever happens on campuses to be fair game for public analysis, condemnation, and interference. Matters such as BIRT proceedings, speech codes, lecture cancellations, and censoring of professor or student utterings are not considered to be purely internal matters, to be decided in internal legalistic proceedings or by administrative fiat. They are both tried in the court of public opinion and, in some cases, an actual court. As such, it is hard to imagine that IHEs act in such matters without first considering the external consequences of their actions, and thus it is also hard to imagine that they take the exact same actions that they would have taken had the public eye not been so firmly fixated on them in these situations. We cannot turn back time to the era when actions on campuses were largely ignored and not litigated. But we can consider whether IHEs are able to stay true to their missions when they are being so tightly scrutinized, or whether such scrutiny keeps them "honest" in their dealings with their employees, their students, and the public.

Chapter 3

Students, Student Life, and Institutional Liability

Students are the central concern of institutions of higher education (IHEs). It is no surprise, then, that students' interactions and relationships with their institutions are also the source from which the bulk of institutional legal and liability considerations derive. At the intersection of the institution's students and the law, one can see even more clearly how the law both exerts pressures on and yields to pressures from institutional values relating to students, the student experience, and higher education's core purposes. In this chapter, we examine legal issues deriving from various touchpoints of the student experience, focusing on institutional liability considerations. By this, we mean primarily the concept of private lawsuits by students against institutions. In other words, we take a closer look at what is going on when students or their parents say: "I am going to sue you" or "I am calling my lawyer."

This chapter explicates the evolving view of the courts toward higher education specifically through the lens of the student experience. This chapter does not attempt to chronicle the long and robust history of the legal relationship between institution and student. Rather, this chapter illustrates the many ways in which legal concerns have come to permeate nearly every aspect of student life in more recent years and explores what that permeation means to IHEs in their missions. In doing so, this chapter looks at the centrality of these legal considerations in guiding institutional policy and practice as it relates directly to key aspects of student life. In particular, this chapter examines the increased willingness of courts to impose a duty on IHEs as it relates to students, interrogating important questions related to the role of institutions as stand-ins for parents, the impact of the recent trend of courts to find a duty on the part of IHEs, and the multifaceted impact of this trend on institutions and their operations.

Before delving into specific topic areas, the chapter begins with an overview of a few key legal concepts related to tort or contract law that are often at play in this context. Having laid out this technical background, we then examine five areas in which IHEs have seen increased propensity for liability via private lawsuits, with reference also to relevant legislative and regulatory pressures: (1) Greek life (as in matters relating to fraternities and sororities); (2) intercollegiate athletics; (3) institutional liability in the context of study-abroad programs; (4) issues related to students with mental health challenges and suicidality, including the evolving case law related to the duty of IHEs to prevent self-harm; and (5) private actions against IHEs related to issues of sexual assault.

Students Suing the Institution: Legal Technicalities and Theories

When a student seeks to sue an IHE for a wrong allegedly committed against that student, there may be myriad ways to do so, but typically, the legal theory underpinning such action will be based either in a type of intentional tort, negligence claim, contract claim, or on a statutorily derived private right of action. Often, a lawsuit will contain some combination of all of these claims.[1]

An intentional tort is a tort with a specifically defined series of elements. Battery, for example, is an intentional tort and consists generally of the "causation of harmful or offensive contact with another's person without that person's consent."[2] To recover damages for an intentional tort, a plaintiff must prove each specifically defined element of the tort. Another commonly invoked intentional tort in the higher education setting is the tort of intentional infliction of emotional distress. While there are significant jurisdictional variations, this tort generally requires "outrageous" conduct committed by a defendant that is committed "for the purpose of causing the victim emotional distress so severe that it could be expected to adversely affect mental health."[3]

Negligence as a basis for suit can be more adaptable than intentional torts in that successful claims are highly dependent on the circumstances surrounding an incident and the conduct of the parties in light of those specific circumstances. Negligence as a theory of liability requires that a "duty" of care be found to exist running from the defendant to the plaintiff, and to succeed, a plaintiff must prove that the defendant's breach of this duty of care was the cause of damages to the plaintiff. A duty, a breach, causation, and the existence of damages are the elements of a negligence claim.[4]

The "duty" element of negligence is where matters become particularly interesting for higher education, as discussed in detail below in the context of specific cases, and as one might expect given the oft-evolving relationships and expectations between institutions and their students. A duty of care is merely the standard of care expected from an individual in a particular situation. Whether a duty is found to exist by a court is based on whether a certain harm is "reasonably foreseeable" in light of the circumstances surrounding the incident as well as public policy considerations.[5] So whether a student can sue an IHE for negligence depends on the existence of a duty of care owed on the part of the IHE to the student. And whether such a duty exists requires an examination of what was reasonably foreseeable under the circumstances with an eye toward public policy implications. In all of the areas of student life that we discuss herein—Greek life, athletics, study abroad, student mental health, and sexual assault—the law as it relates specifically to the duty of care owed by IHEs has been evolving and is by no means neatly settled.

Contract claims are another frequent source of liability for IHEs. In the student context, these primarily derive from instances when institutions allegedly deviate from stated policies. Courts with some regularity allow for breach of contract claims when institutions deviate from stated policies on the theory that students pay tuition and enroll in a particular IHE with the understanding that certain applicable policies will be enforced on their terms.[6] Student codes of conduct and disciplinary procedures are rife with opportunities for institutions to open themselves up to liability based in contract. For example, if a student is expelled or otherwise disciplined without use of the stated process for doing so, this may create the factual grounds for a breach of contract suit.[7]

Private rights of action provide yet another source of potential liability for institutions and a means for potential plaintiffs to recover against IHEs for specific wrongs. Private rights of action refer to explicit statutory authorizations, or implicit authorizations read-in by courts, for plaintiffs to seek redress of certain harms in court either for equitable relief such as an injunction or for monetary damages.

Title IX and the Americans with Disabilities Act are two prominent statutes providing prospective plaintiffs with a private right of action.[8]

A statute that does not provide for a private right of action but that is highly relevant in the context of the issues discussed in this chapter is the Family Educational Rights and Privacy Act, known as FERPA.[9] In the broadest terms, FERPA is a federal law intended to ensure the privacy of student education records. The term "education records" is defined expansively by FERPA as "records, files, documents, and other materials which—(i) contain information directly related to a student; and (ii) are maintained by an educational agency or institution."[10] FERPA applies to students of all ages, but its protections conspicuously shift from the parent to the student when the student enrolls in a college or university. FERPA requires that institutions have written permission from the student to release the education records protected by FERPA to anyone, including the student's parents. Detailed exceptions to this rule abound, but the primary examples are situations in which the information in question may not fit the definition of an education record to begin with, where a bona fide health and safety emergency exists, where disclosure is made to comply with certain specified judicial orders or subpoenas, or disclosure where the information could be deemed "directory information" and the party seeking such information has a legitimate interest.[11] Categories of so-called directory information include basic facts like a student's name, address, dates of attendance, and enrollment status, among others.[12] Students may restrict an institution's right to release directory information by not consenting to such information's categorization as directory information,[13] although sometimes students may overlook this right. FERPA applies to all institutions that receive federal funding through the Department of Education and is enforced by the

Family Policy Compliance Office of the Department of Education.[14] As stated at the outset, FERPA does not contain a private right of action. In other words, the statute does not explicitly grant plaintiffs the ability to sue under its provisions. However, the statute figures heavily in affecting institutional responses during litigation, including in managing public relations messaging during litigation and otherwise.

Scholars and practicing higher education lawyers alike have noted the trending propensity of courts to find that a legal duty exists on the part of IHEs in a wide array of types of private tort lawsuits.[15] The implication of this trend has aptly been described by one leading scholar on the topic as engendering what those of us familiar with campus life and operations might recognize as the "burgeoning responsibility to protect students with respect to foreseeable dangers in a campus environment."[16] This trend of courts finding a duty on the part of an institution to exist—or potentially exist—is apparent in all of the areas examined in this chapter.

As with most matters, the current state of the law related to duties imposed on IHEs by tort law is couched within and influenced by a broader historical context. In the simplest terms, this evolution of the duty of care required of IHEs can be described as having developed across three distinct eras: (1) a period dominated by the concept of in loco parentis; (2) a period of more and more theoretically complex standoffishness by courts dubbed by some as the "bystander era;"[17] and (3) the current period, which, as we see in this chapter, grapples with the legacy of both prior eras and which we call the "caretaker era."

As articulated recently by the Supreme Court in the context of a decision related to secondary schools, the "doctrine of *in loco parentis* treats school administrators as standing in the place of students' parents under circumstances where the children's actual parents cannot protect, guide, and discipline them."[18] As applied to early IHEs, the in loco parentis concept served to insulate them from early theories of tort and contract liability, among others. In the era of in loco parentis, a child could not sue their parents, and it followed that an institution that stood "in the place" of the parents also could not be sued.[19] For example, E. Hartley Pratt was a student at Wheaton College in the 1860s when he joined a "secret society" known as the Good Templars.[20] Membership in such societies was against Wheaton's rules, so the college suspended him pending the revocation of his affiliation with the group. Pratt's father sued on his behalf for his reinstatement to the college. In ruling for Wheaton, the Supreme Court of Illinois likened the authority of Wheaton College to that of a father, proclaiming that "a discretionary power has been given, . . . [and] we have no more authority to interfere than we have to control the domestic discipline of a father in his family."[21] Pratt's case is a clear articulation of in loco parentis and the principle that the institution's discretion in matters of student life is controlling and subject to absolute deference.

In the midtwentieth century, the judicial view of IHEs began to shift. Institutions were still largely protected from liability but not on the theory of in loco parentis as an absolute bar to suit. Rather, and in large part due to the civil rights movement, courts began to recognize the autonomy of students and the independence of students from their institutions.[22] Courts began holding that institutions did not have a duty to students in various contexts, largely because students were autonomous adults free to make their own choices and decisions. In this era, "the courts found that universities were 'bystanders' to non-educational student life, and that universities therefore owed no legal duties to prevent injuries students inflicted upon each other."[23]

In *Bradshaw v. Rawlings,* a 1979 case often cited as emblematic of the "bystander" era,[24] a student at Delaware Valley College was paralyzed in a car accident that occurred after attending a sophomore class picnic where alcohol was served.[25] A faculty member who was the sophomore class advisor helped plan the picnic and cosigned a check used to purchase "six or seven half-kegs of beer" that were consumed by about seventy-five students who had attended the picnic.[26] Fliers advertising the picnic were reproduced at the campus printing facility, were posted across campus, and featured renderings of beer mugs.[27] The Third Circuit Court of Appeals found that the plaintiff failed to establish that Delaware Valley College had a "duty of custodial care."[28] Citing the "freedom of the individual will," the court articulated that "the competing interests of the student and of the institution of higher learning are much different today than they were in the past . . . the change has occurred because society considers the modern college student an adult, not a child of tender years."[29] One would be hard-pressed to imagine an outcome like this in the current caretaker era.[30]

Greek Life

Perhaps no other area of the student experience is more emblematic of the tensions between institutional authority and student autonomy than Greek life. Since the advent of Greek letter organizations on campuses in the nineteenth century, tensions have abounded between institutional leadership and these organizations related to scope of authority, autonomy, and the general relationship of the Greek organization to the institution. These relationships figure prominently in legal analyses when assessing institutional liability. Meanwhile, the relationships between institutions and their Greek letter organizations have grown more complicated over time as Greek organization alumni have grown in numbers and become enmeshed with institutions as donors, trustees, faculty, and staff.

What degree of control can and should institutions assert over Greek organizations today—most of which are distinct legal entities from the academic institution—and what are the liability considerations and implications? Much of the debate today as it relates to Greek life and liability considerations tends to center around questions of how much intervention by an institution is too much.[31] For example, by doing things such as creating an approval process for parties held by Greek organizations, by having campus safety officers attend or check in on certain social functions, or by simply owning the dwelling used by a Greek organization, are institutions opening themselves up to a lawsuit if something goes wrong? The answer in most cases is yes.

There has been a distinctive and well-documented shift in the approach of the courts adjudicating such cases, beginning largely in the 1990s and continuing through today, toward holding IHEs accountable.[32] IHEs are more likely to be found by a court to have, or to have created, a duty of care, even if ultimately in a given situation they are not found to have breached that duty or are not the only party at fault.[33] The courts, and society at large, are aware of the large gray area that exists in the student-institution relationship. In other words, that relationship is not as simple as conceiving of students in every situation as independent adults subject only to the joys and follies of their own free will, or rigidly construing institutions as parent-like enterprises that are at once totally immune from suit and responsible for their student's every move.[34]

This evolution in the Greek life context can be seen in the willingness of some courts to allow negligence actions against institutions related to Greek life incidents to proceed beyond initial motions to dismiss, and in the settlement of some matters before they even result in the filing of a lawsuit. In one tragic case, *Tsialas v. Cornell University,* a New York State court denied defendant Cornell's motion to dismiss and allowed causes of action for negligence and premises liability to proceed where hazing at a fraternity rush party allegedly resulted in a student's death in the fall of 2019.[35] The plaintiffs argued that Cornell had a "duty to provide a safe environment for its students to live, socialize and attend school" and that this duty was breached for a variety of reasons including allegedly "failing to implement meaningful antihazing measures," failing to enforce its own policies regarding fraternity rushing, failing to discipline certain fraternity officers and members, failing to install security cameras in fraternity buildings, and failing to require hiring of independent monitors or campus safety spot checks, among other allegations.[36] This case ultimately settled for an undisclosed amount as well as the creation of a scholarship in the deceased student's memory and the implementation of various programming efforts.[37] It stands as a recent example of the willingness of courts to allow matters like this to proceed.

The case of Timothy Piazza at Penn State is another heart-rending recent example in this area. It is also a case in which the institution settled before the Piazza family even resorted to filing a lawsuit.[38] Piazza died of complications related to an extreme fraternity drinking ritual that resulted in him falling down stairs and suffering multiple traumatic brain injuries, a fractured skull, and other internal hemorrhaging in February 2017.[39] Evidence of the incident unfurling was captured on surveillance cameras that had been installed in the house. The fraternity also apparently had employed an independent security firm to assist in the oversight of social events. This security firm, along with over twenty former members of the fraternity, was sued by the family of Timothy Piazza in 2019.[40] In many ways, the death of Timothy Piazza was a seminal moment. Criminal charges were filed against certain members of the fraternity and jail time doled out.[41] A grand jury is reported to have found that fraternity members were "indifferent" to Piazza's alcohol poising and physical condition and "engaged in a vigorous effort to conceal evidence of hazing and underage drinking."[42] In October 2018, the Timothy J. Piazza Antihazing Law was signed into law by the governor of Pennsylvania and was widely lauded by the president of Penn State.[43] But unfortunately, incidents such as these persist, with student deaths and severe injuries continuing to be reported and new lawsuits continuing to be filed.[44]

The new realities of negligence and premises liability as applied to Greek life, specifically the expanded willingness of courts to find a duty on the part of the institution, has had wide-ranging implications for institutions. For one, it has resulted in not only campus counsel but also insurers and risk managers, promoting more hands-on and proactive approaches to management of Greek life on campuses.[45] These proactive approaches require time, expertise, and resources. The National Association of Student Personnel Administrators (NASPA), the professional association for student affairs professionals, dedicates programming and trainings to Greek life issues, including developing a "knowledge community" committed to connecting and educating professionals who work with fraternities and sororities.[46] In at least one recent instance, NASPA coordinated programming with Penn State's new Timothy J. Piazza Center for Fraternity and Sorority Research and Reform, a "multidisciplinary" center evolving from Penn State's settlement of the Piazza matter that is "dedicated to uplifting fraternity and sorority life."[47] Another notable trend involves Greek organizations completely disaffiliating with institutions, but the extent to which this will absolve institutions of liability in particular situations is still fact-dependent and likely to vary significantly, to say nothing of the impact such moves could have on the educational experience of students.[48]

Athletics

Collegiate athletics can be a critical part of the student experience for those participating as athletes and students supporting athletics from the stands. Athletics can forge aspects of institutional identity and have a tremendous impact—for better or worse—on campus culture, life, and morale. Athletics have also become a burgeoning powder keg of liability issues for institutions of all sizes and their leagues and regulating bodies. Lawsuits related to issues ranging from sexual abuse to concussion-related injuries and antitrust claims have proliferated in the last ten to fifteen years. Compliance concerns related to collegiate athletics, the expanding role of intercollegiate athletic governance structures, and the overall managerial complexity of athletics and its legal implications have all also flourished in recent years and have been the subject of in-depth elaboration in their own right.[49] Consistent with this chapter, however, our main focus is on the relationships among athletes, their teams, coaches, and institutions through the eyes of courts of law and the specter of liability.

In the area of athletics and institutional liability, perhaps few matters are as notorious as the 2011 case of Penn State University assistant football coach Jerry Sandusky, who was arrested and charged with fifty-two counts of child sexual abuse facilitated through a charity for underprivileged and at-risk youth that he operated from an office at Penn State. This case and the explicit critiques of university employees' failure to report and take action regarding what was happening was a watershed moment that caused states to examine and revise laws related to mandatory reporting and working with minors.[50] In turn, it caused institutions to review and revise policies and protocols related to minors on campus and their interactions with athletic teams.[51] As of 2019, forty-nine states had legislation penalizing mandatory reporters who fail to report instances of child abuse.[52] In Florida, a statute imposes fines of up to $1 million specifically "on any institution of higher learning, including any [s]tate university and nonpublic college, who fails to report or prevents any person from reporting an instance of abuse."[53]

The Sandusky case has sadly not stood alone.[54] In 2017, Larry Nasser pleaded guilty to charges related to sexually assaulting student athletes at Michigan State University in his role as director of sports medicine and as a doctor for the US women's national gymnastics team.[55] Another scandal, involving a wrestling team physician, enveloped Ohio State University in 2018.[56] In 2021, a campus physician at the University of Michigan was found to have sexually abused numerous student athletes and other students, including a former NFL player, over a thirty-year period. The university agreed to a record $490 million settlement, and over a thousand claimants have come forward.[57]

Stricter reporting requirements and state laws for abuse of minors;[58] the bolstering of Title IX as a tool to fight sexual assault, as outlined in Chapter 1; and evolved best practices for working with minors and student athletes more generally have further defined the standards of care for IHE athletic programs over the last ten to fifteen years. While factual circumstances vary from case to case and the law may vary slightly from jurisdiction to jurisdiction, in light of the legal developments of the past ten to fifteen years, it is almost beyond dispute that IHEs owe a duty of care to minors participating in campus-based programming. Campuses must abide by state laws for working with minors and ensure that their policies and procedures for doing so are up to date. These cases also illuminate the likely duty of IHEs to protect student athletes against sexual predators in the coaching and professionalized staff ranks, where IHE employees have extensive access to and in-depth personal interactions with student athletes.

In addition to the interpersonal dynamics of athletics teams and programming and the environment for risk this creates, participation in athletics or recreational activities in and of itself can create liability for an institution. Even though those participating in athletic and recreational activities are widely viewed as assuming the risk of those activities, suits abound against institutions and even coaches for injuries suffered as participants, including for activities such as the use of campus rock climbing walls.[59] Of particular concern of late have been cases involving concussion-related injuries, with litigation including widespread class actions also implicating the National Collegiate Athletic Association (NCAA).[60] In 2019, the NCAA settled a large putative class action suit that resulted in many member institutions adopting a standardized concussion protocol for student athletes.[61] As of this writing, there are still approximately four hundred suits pending against IHEs related to concussion injuries suffered by students while participating in collegiate athletic activities.[62]

Private lawsuits stemming from campus athletics have not simply been limited to tort suits. Coaches, for one, are college employees, and by virtue of this designation, they retain the standard protections granted to employees under federal and state laws.[63] Coaches at the elite Division I level may also have their employment terms articulated in a formal contract, which may tailor and constrain the rights and responsibilities of both the coach and the institution and can be a source of litigation.[64] One recent example is the October 2021 termination of Washington State University head football coach Nick Rolovich and four of his assistant coaches for "just cause" under their employment contracts when they refused to get the COVID-19 vaccine when a vaccine mandate was imposed by Governor Jay Inslee on state employees.[65] Critically, Rolovich's contract reportedly allowed the coach to be terminated for "just cause"—and thus not entitled to a severance—where the coach "deliberately" failed to adhere to university policy.[66]

As the business of athletics on campuses has become more complex, so, too, have the legal relationships between institutions and athletes. An example of this is a September 2021 memorandum from the National Labor Relations Board's (NLRB) general counsel that suggests that the NLRB views Division I Football Bowl Subdivision student athletes as "employees" under the National Labor Relations Act, an interpretation that could have a significant impact on the ability of players to collectively organize and may have other implications rooted in employment law.[67] The same memorandum warns institutions against "misclassifying them as 'student-athletes,' and against leading students to believe that they are not entitled to the [NLRA's] protection."[68]

Another example of this pro-college-athlete approach is the Supreme Court's June 2021 decision in *Alston*. In *Alston*, the Court held that certain NCAA prohibitions on education-related benefits violated antitrust principles;[69] in other words, the NCAA is not immune from "the normal operation of the antitrust laws."[70] A major impact of this case has been on the ability of college athletes to profit from their name, image, and likeness via paid advertising—a practice that was previously prohibited. In response to *Alston*, the NCAA immediately suspended its past rules on the subject and implemented an interim name, image, and likeness policy that allows athletes to profit from their name, image, and likeness. These developments are significant because they portend a broader evolution in the relationship between institutions and student athletes, at least as it pertains to larger Division I institutions. As the relationship between college athletes and their institutions evolves, it is safe to assume that questions of institutional liability will, in the longer term, evolve as well.

Off-Campus and Study-Abroad Activities

Modern IHEs are not constrained to the footprint of their own physical campuses. Students regularly venture beyond the borders of the physical campus for internships, service learning, and opportunities to study in another country—at another institution, through a program operated by the student's primary institution, or through a third-party provider. When students are engaged in activities off campus that are in some way related to their work or play on campus, it raises interesting and far-ranging questions of institutional liability. To what extent can a school be held liable for an injury suffered at an off-campus service-learning project that occurs one block away from campus? To what extent can a school be held liable for the injury of one of their students that occurs domestically on another IHE's campus? Does it matter if the student's institution paid for their transportation to and from the other campus or if the student was there for a reason related to their studies or for purely personal social reasons? To what extent can a school be held liable for the illness or injury of a student studying four thousand miles away in another country on another continent? Does it matter if the study-abroad program is operated entirely by another institution or solely by the student's own institution?

Such questions are not susceptible to quick or uniform answers at this point in the evolution of the legal standards governing this area. The detailed facts of the issue at hand as well as the jurisdiction, governing law, and precedent will all play a role. Thus these questions regularly challenge the brains of campus counsel and related administrative staff in this age when a college education is rarely constrained to the physical campus and the standard for the institution's duty of care to students continues to evolve.

Recent developments pertaining specifically to campus study-abroad programs are worth noting, as they relate to potential institutional liability and the increasing likelihood that courts will find that an institution has a duty of care in any particular case. While the case involves a secondary school rather than a college, *Munn v. Hotchkiss School* sent shockwaves through higher education circles when the Connecticut Supreme Court upheld a jury verdict of $41.5 million against the private Connecticut boarding school when one of the school's students suffered devastating injuries as a result of a tick-borne illness she contracted while on a Hotchkiss-sponsored trip to the Chinese countryside.[71] In addition to upholding the verdict, the court also held that Connecticut state law supports a finding that a duty exists to "warn about or protect against" severe insect-borne illness when organizing a trip abroad.[72] In upholding such a substantial jury verdict and finding that the imposition of a duty was proper, the court found a number of facts persuasive. Among others, these included that the trip's itinerary did not mention a visit to the wooded area where the tick-borne illness was contracted; that an email to students and parents about the trip erroneously included a Centers for Disease Control and Prevention link to medical information about Central America, not China; that insect repellant was merely mentioned as a "miscellaneous" item on the proposed packing list for the trip; and that no one affiliated with Hotchkiss warned the students on the trip of the possibility for tick-borne illnesses in wooded areas of that particular region of China. The court in *Munn* found that imposing a duty on Hotchkiss was appropriate because the possibility of a tick-borne illness was a reasonably foreseeable risk.

Given that Hotchkiss is a secondary school, aspects of the court's legal analysis in *Munn* are certainly not applicable to IHEs, most notably, perhaps, the court's reliance on the "special relationship" between students and secondary schools, a modern-day variant of in loco parentis. But the analogy to an IHE running a study-abroad program is too strong to ignore. The case stands as an example of the intricacies of managing an off-campus study program and the potential implications, no matter how unlikely, for IHEs to get it wrong. Moreover, the evolving propensity of courts to find that duties of care exist on the part of institutions requires institutions operating study-abroad programs to perform ongoing, real-time evaluations of risks in areas all over the world, supported by the best information available. Methods for conducting risk analysis on travel destinations have evolved in recent years, most notably with the Department of State updating its travel warning system.[73] During the COVID-19 pandemic, these data were routinely cited when IHEs decided to suspend their study-abroad programs.

Suicidality and Mental Health Concerns

Student mental health and well-being is a significant concern on campuses today, exacerbated by the COVID-19 pandemic. A nationwide survey conducted by researchers at Boston University found that half of incoming students in the fall of 2020 experienced some form of depression or anxiety, with 83 percent of respondents saying their mental health negatively impacted their studies, and two-thirds of college students "struggling with loneliness and feeling isolated."[74] While institutions rightly continue to do all they can and direct resources to support students facing mental health challenges,[75] the legal framework imposed by courts around issues involving student mental health continues to evolve and thus challenge institutions in developing their level of care.

A leading case is that of Han Nguyen, a twenty-five-year-old graduate student who committed suicide in 2009 while pursuing a PhD at MIT's Sloan School of Management. Nguyen's father filed suit against MIT alleging wrongful death following Nguyen's suicide, but the motion judge granted MIT's motion for summary judgment, finding that MIT had no duty to prevent Nguyen from committing suicide.[76] On appeal, in 2018, the Supreme Judicial Court of Massachusetts affirmed the motion judge's decision but concluded that in circumstances not present in Nguyen's case, specifically, when an institution has actual knowledge of a suicide attempt by a student, "a special relationship and a corresponding duty to take reasonable measures to prevent suicide may be created between a university and its student."[77] The Nguyen court's decision is significant precisely because it leaves open the possibility that under such circumstances—where an institution has actual knowledge of a suicide attempt—a future court could in fact impose a duty on an institution to prevent a student from committing suicide. While the case is strictly binding only in Massachusetts, it contains significant analysis on the topic of special relationships between students and IHEs as well as student suicides, leading one to believe that its reasoning may be persuasive for other courts dealing with this issue outside of Massachusetts and may evolve through future court interpretation beyond the specific context of student suicide.[78] More recent pending cases involve the suicide of a University of Florida graduate student, Huixiang Chen, who had accused his advisor of abuse and academic misconduct;[79] the case of a student at Vanderbilt University, Brian Adams, involving allegations of misconduct on the part of the institution's therapist;[80] and *Tang v. Harvard University*. In *Tang*, a Harvard undergraduate with known mental health issues, including a prior suicide attempt during college, tragically committed suicide. The Massachusetts Superior Court, considering the precedent of *Nguyen* and its requirement that institutions take "reasonable measures" ultimately dismissed the case finding that the defendants had met any duties that might have arisen under the particular circumstances of Tang's case.[81]

As mental health issues have an effect not only on the student suffering from a particular mental health disorder but also on the people around that person, this creates other unique complications for institutions. In *Regents of the University of California v. Rosen*, Rosen, a student at UCLA, sued UCLA in 2010 for failing to take action to prevent violent conduct on the part of another student.[82] Thompson, who suffered from auditory hallucinations and paranoid schizophrenia, attacked Rosen with a kitchen knife during a chemistry lab session in retaliation for what Thompson had perceived as Rosen's teasing him.[83] Thompson had previous interactions with campus police as a result of interpersonal conflicts stemming from his disorder, had been being monitored by the campus response team, and had undergone psychological evaluations at a local hospital and treatment from a campus psychologist.[84] Citing "the unique features of the collegiate environment," the court held "that universities have a special relationship with their students and a duty to protect them from foreseeable violence during curricular activities."[85]

Rosen and *Nguyen* are emblematic of the issues facing today's IHEs related to supporting students with mental illness as well as their peers and the trending extent of IHE legal obligations. It is very clear that IHEs cannot be "bystanders," and that future cases will further define the obligations of IHEs in this area.[86]

Sexual Assault and Domestic Violence

Chapter 1 has already given extensive treatment to the evolution of the regulatory regime under which instances of sexual harassment and assault fall, but it is important also to mention the potential for, and proliferation of, private lawsuits against IHEs stemming from matters related to sexual assault or harassment.

The legal theories in private rights of action related to sexual assault and harassment often include Title IX theories emanating from Title IX's private right of action,[87] negligence theories,[88] and contract claims,[89] among others. A suit may be brought by both complainants to a Title IX process or respondents: in other words, by the victim-survivor or the alleged perpetrator of the incident. When respondents to a Title IX process sue institutions for violations of Title IX, it is called a "reverse" Title IX claim.[90]

The underlying bases for private claims for discrimination under Title IX vary. One possibility is a lawsuit against the school for failing to take appropriate action to deal with sexual harassment. This is known as a deliberate indifference claim and is one of the earliest theories recognized under Title IX.[91] There is currently a split among the circuit courts related to several elements of the deliberate indifference standard.[92] At least one writ of certiorari has been filed—the process for appeal to the Supreme Court—in a case from the Fourth Circuit related to a public school district's actions following a report of sexual harassment on a school trip.[93] The Court did not take this particular case, but if it had, the ability of plaintiffs to sue institutions under a Title IX deliberate indifference theory could have been significantly narrowed. In a potential blow to plaintiffs, the Supreme Court in 2022 held that damages for "emotional distress" are no longer available in cases brought for violations of statutes passed pursuant to Congress's spending powers.[94] Title IX is one such statute, so plaintiffs seeking to recover financially against institutions that they believe violated their rights under Title IX will now have to rely on other damages theories and structure their complaints accordingly.

Other theories of liability under Title IX arise more specifically out of campus disciplinary processes and include erroneous outcome claims and selective enforcement claims.[95] Erroneous outcome claims are based on the notion that a respondent in a campus disciplinary proceeding was innocent but was found incorrectly to have committed an offense.[96] Selective enforcement claims, however, argue that either the decision itself to initiate a proceeding or the penalty under the proceeding was "affected" by the student's gender.[97] Negligence and contract claims are often included in Title IX private rights of action, and their factual basis is often intertwined with the specifics of the sexual harassment and the process by which it was handled.[98] Courts have recognized a duty of institutions to prevent harm to students stemming from sexual assault under certain circumstances and depending on the degree of reasonable foreseeability of the particular harm in a particular case.[99]

Many disturbing trends can be seen in the fact patterns of Title IX, but one such trend includes cases involving students in romantic relationships. Such cases might be categorized as "domestic violence" or "dating violence" cases under Title IX and the Clery Act. The case of Lauren McCluskey at the University of Utah is a jarring example. McCluskey was tragically killed by her partner after contacting campus police over twenty times regarding the man's behavior toward her in addition to speaking to counselors and housing staff.[100] Mc-Cluskey's friends had apparently also told residential life staff that the man who eventually shot McCluskey had intended to bring a gun to campus.[101] The McCluskeys sued Utah in federal court under Title IX for $56 million.[102] The suit eventually settled for $13.5 million, and McCluskey's parents committed to directing this amount to the foundation set up in McCluskey's honor aimed at improving campus safety.[103] Utah's president, Ruth Watkins, released a statement following the settlement, saying that Utah "deeply regrets that it did not handle Lauren's case as it should have and that . . . its employees failed to fully understand and respond appropriately to Lauren's situation."[104] Sadly, as of August 2022, another case rocked the University of Utah community, related to the disappearance of first-year student Zhifan Dong, who was found dead in a nearby hotel.[105] Dong's boyfriend and fellow Utah student was charged with murder. Utah's current president, Taylor Randall, pledged to "err on the side of transparency," and the university released an extensive timeline and other details on the matter.[106] In February 2023, the university announced that it would settle a lawsuit with Dong's parents in the amount of $5 million.[107] Both cases are illustrative of the institutional breakdowns that can occur with instances of relationship violence and the challenges presented to institutions in dealing with such cases.

Conclusion: The Caretaker Role for Colleges Is Not Receding

The caretaker era for IHEs has a way to go before it is fully articulated by the legal system through a combination of case law and regulation. But clearly, there are numerous pitfalls that an IHE can encounter while attempting in good faith to provide services and opportunities to its students. This is a stressful situation for those administrators who are charged with running the programs, such as athletics, residential housing, and study abroad. The caretaker standard is a significantly higher one than that of the bystander era and also does not have the implicit assumption of the in loco parentis era that administrators actually know what is best for students. While individual staff and faculty are unlikely to suffer personal monetary damage, even if they are individually named as part of a lawsuit, the stress and reputational damage that could occur if they are engaged in a legal action is not to be underestimated. Therefore, the worrying perception that they could be subjected to participation in a lawsuit while in the course of carrying out their normal work duties is not helped by the fact that such lawsuits seem to be reported constantly by the press and seem to be increasing in number and even settlement amount.

Besides the substantive legal considerations underpinning the expanding willingness of courts to find a legal duty for an institution, there may be other reasons why lawsuits against IHEs for student-related matters appear to be expanding. One reason may be the general litigiousness of society and people's tendency to want to hold involved institutions responsible for perceived shortcomings that have led to harm to a student. Additionally, a common litigation strategy is to sue as many potential defendants as possible. Similarly, perhaps the institution will be named because IHEs are generally perceived as well resourced and able to aid in the plaintiff's recovery of damages.

The modern IHE, as with any entity, wants to reduce liability and possible payouts and wants to avoid getting sued in the first place. These rational motivations lead to more "lawyerization" on campus of the IHE's operating procedures. This manifests in ways such as adding more "boilerplate," developing quasilegal structures, and adopting litigious language or the vernacular of law when not appropriate. Ironically, to the extent that duties and standards of care are spelled out more explicitly, it may also then be easier for litigants to find the IHE has fallen short of its own stated standards, as human error and oversight will almost inevitably occur as the systems of oversight and control become more complex. And, to the extent that both the need for boilerplate and internal regulation itself and the need to fight external legal challenges cause higher costs of doing business, the rising cost of education is a real "damage" coming out of this increased caretaker approach to student matters, and other matters, on campus. Are we balancing these costs effectively at universities, or are we overspending on damage control and also losing sight of our mission in doing so, as well as making it less affordable to achieve our mission? We return to this topic in the chapters to come.

Chapter 4

Admissions, Advancement, and Community Relations

A commonality among institutions of higher education (IHEs) of nearly all sizes is their reliance on admissions, fundraising, and community relations. The success of admissions and fundraising efforts ties directly to the institutional bottom line. Community relations and external affairs projects can have a similar, if more nebulous, effect on the institution's financial success and stability through reputation, goodwill, and overall community morale. This chapter is an examination of the recent pressures and tensions at the intersection of the law and these key institutional economic supports and drivers.

Our discussion of admissions centers on the question of using the courts to challenge admissions decisions, but it also considers operational concerns relative to admissions such as false advertising or contract claims and trending topics such as antitrust concerns. Regarding institutional development, this chapter reviews issues related to controversial gifts and the new prevalence of naming and gift acceptance policies. We include a discussion of the impact of legislation such as the Native American Graves Protection and Repatriation Act (NAGPRA) on university collections and museums, and issues surrounding the repatriation of parts of anthropological collections. This chapter also addresses the evolving "lawyerization" of issues across the spectrum of community relations, including payments in lieu of taxes, issues regarding campus-owned real estate, and how "town-gown" dynamics can have an impact in the courtroom.

This chapter demonstrates how legal issues necessarily impact strategies for institutional success and sustainability, given the critical role of admissions and institutional development offices as institutional financial drivers and the strategic importance of community relations initiatives for IHEs. If working well, the three-legged stool of advancement, admissions, and community relations helps sustain the academic mission of IHEs. The issues raised herein are demonstrative of the increased need for legal counsel to be engaged across the institution's operations and also provide a platform for discussing campus counsel's role as a strategic thought partner to these key economic drivers. Consistent with our overarching theme, this chapter demonstrates the recent proliferation of legal issues in these key operational areas for IHEs. As such, it provides another perspective for reflecting on how these legal pressures and tensions, through these additional avenues, impact the core mission of IHEs.

Admissions

Getting into their college of choice is top of mind for millions of high school students and their parents each year. No citations are required to support a statement that choosing and applying to colleges is often a complicated process, involving questions of personal fit, cost, academic and extracurricular interests and abilities, career aspirations, geography, and family considerations, all set within the already stress-inducing context of students transitioning to adulthood and independence. Despite the cheerful backdrop of sunny campus tours, smiling tour guides, and the excitement of entering a new phase in life, a 2019 poll conducted by Suffolk University and *USA Today* revealed a bleak statistic behind the college admissions process: fewer than 20 percent of Americans think the college admissions process is "generally fair."[1] Just over two-thirds of those surveyed agreed that the admissions process "favors the rich and powerful."[2] There is an old maxim in the world of medical malpractice law that "happy patients don't sue."[3] If there is an analogy here for the world of IHE admissions, institutions would do well to gird for more legal action in admissions in the years to come.

The work of IHE admissions offices is operationally critical to the financial bottom line of IHEs, but to consider only this point substantially minimizes the mission-critical task undertaken by admissions offices. To believe in the power of education, by implication, requires one to believe that there is power inherent in the process of deciding who receives such an education and on what terms. In this light, the admissions process is the hand that shapes our college student bodies. By extension, the admissions office is a hand that shapes the future of our democratic societies. Ron Daniels alludes to this concept in his recent book *What Universities Owe Democracy*: "Universities are places of such influence that they will . . . shape the society around them" and therefore "must look hard at who they admit."[4] Admissions is therefore central to the fundamental mission of IHEs not simply for its role in ensuring a steady revenue stream but also in shaping the campus community and, by extension, our future polity. When the law exerts its tensions and pressures on the process of college admissions, we must therefore carefully take note. Evolving legal constraints and new challenges in admissions impact not only institutional bottom lines but also the very composition of our campuses, questions of access, and the face of our democracy.

At a very general level, the admissions office and the admissions decisions its officers make have been largely afforded deference by courts. Indeed, it was the affirmative action case of *Regents of the University of California v. Bakke* that gave rise to a concept of institutional academic freedom inclusive of the notion that institutions retain discretion to determine who is admitted to study in their classrooms.[5] However, state courts that regularly hear more commonplace admissions claims arising outside of the discrimination or constitutional context also trend toward deference to the decisions of IHEs.

Courts are likely to uphold decisions related to college admissions across a broad spectrum of issues when those decisions are not arbitrary, capricious, or patently unreasonable.[6] A 2015 case involving St. John's University School of Law provides an apt example. In *Powers v. St. John's University School of Law*, New York's highest court upheld St. John's University's decision to rescind a student's admission to its law school when it was discovered that the student had failed to disclose accurate details in his application materials about a past arrest for dealing drugs and specifics related to his charges.[7] Stating long-standing precedent in New York that "courts have a 'restricted role' in reviewing determinations of colleges and universities" and emphasizing that the decisions of colleges and universities "will not be disturbed unless a school acts arbitrarily and not in the exercise of its honest discretion," the New York Court of Appeals found that the university's decision to rescind admission was rational.[8] The decision rested primarily on the fact that throughout the process of reviewing the student's application in light of new information related to the student's drug charges, St. John's had consistently followed its written and unwritten policies and procedures related to the rescission of admission.[9] Among other factors considered by the court, it cited that the student had been on notice that rescission of admission was a possibility when he had applied and completed the application. Cases like *Powers* illustrate that generally, short of blatant irrationality, an institutional admissions decision receives deference.

Legal challenges to admissions decisions grow considerably more complicated when claims are related to allegations of discrimination or constitutional violations. The Fourteenth Amendment of the US Constitution and Title VI of the Civil Rights Act of 1964 solidify that institutions may not discriminate on the basis of race or certain other classes in their admissions processes. Claims are typically brought against private institutions under Title VI and, in the case of public institutions, the Fourteenth Amendment's equal protection clause. Title VI prohibits discrimination on the basis of race, color, or national origin "under any program or activity receiving federal financial assistance"[10] and as such applies to private institutions that receive federal funding. The Fourteenth Amendment provides that "no state shall . . . deny to any person within its jurisdiction the equal protection of the laws" and as such by its language applies primarily to state actors; for example, state-affiliated institutions.[11] The Supreme Court has presumed that the legal analysis for the Fourteenth Amendment and Title VI in the context of race-conscious admissions programs are essentially the same.[12]

The companion cases of *Students for Fair Admissions v. Harvard* and *Students for Fair Admissions v. UNC* (hereafter referred to collectively as *SFA*) that were decided in 2023 have effectively barred the explicit use of race as a deciding factor in college admissions.[13] Those cases are discussed further, and their impact is woven into the discussion below, but the nearly fifty years of jurisprudence leading up to the *SFA* decision are still worth consideration for our overall purposes and as the higher education sector considers the future implications of the decision on its campuses.

From a legal doctrinal standpoint, any process or program that uses racial categories in admissions is subject to "strict scrutiny" when challenged in court under Title VI or the Fourteenth Amendment.[14] Strict scrutiny demands that race-based "classifications are constitutional only if they are narrowly tailored to further compelling governmental interests."[15] Before *SFA*, the attainment of a diverse student body was "a constitutionally permissible goal"[16] for an IHE and a "compelling state interest that can justify the use of race in University admissions."[17] The Supreme Court had also seemingly settled that "the decision to pursue 'the educational benefits that flow from student body diversity' . . . is, in substantial measure, an academic judgment to which some, but not complete, judicial deference is proper."[18] The Court in *SFA*, however, turned this analysis on its head, emphasizing what it saw as additional elements of strict scrutiny without considering the deference traditionally afforded to colleges and universities in this context and striking down the Harvard and UNC plans, effectively ending the use of race in admissions decisions. In short, the Court in *SFA* read further requirements into the strict scrutiny standard: first, the notion that race-based programs must be tested for using race as a "stereotype or negative," and second, that they must have a fixed end point.[19] The Court found that Harvard and UNC fell short on both.

Concerning the determination of whether programs that considered race were "narrowly tailored," deference has never been owed to an IHE.[20] When the Court considered narrow tailoring, the institution bore "the burden of proving that a "nonracial approach" would not promote its interest in the educational benefits of diversity."[21] In this regard, admissions policies adopting racial quotas to achieve student body diversity and those adopting a separate review process for applicants in certain racial categories have been roundly rejected on the grounds of narrow tailoring.[22] As considered further below, up until the Court's *SFA* decision, much of the current litigation centered around whether admissions programs considering race were narrowly tailored.

The cases that set the legal doctrine in this area before and including *SFA* are worth some explication and consideration. They are significant not only in their own right for the principles they once enshrined related to affirmative action in admissions, but also because these affirmative action cases make up the main corpus of the Supreme Court's proclamations on the nature and role of higher education more broadly. In examining the legal challenges brought against affirmative action programs, the Supreme Court, and to an extent the lower courts, has been forced to examine aspects of the admissions process bearing on the fundamental nature and purpose of higher education and of the ability of institutions to freely carry out this purpose. While the Court began its exploration of affirmative action issues in the 1970s and discrimination issues related to education more generally much earlier,[23] consistent with the theme of this book, several significant developments have occurred and continue to evolve in this first quarter of the twenty-first century.

Immediately before the *SFA* case was decided in 2023 (discussed below), the law of the land with regard to actually operationalizing a consideration of race or other personal classifications in IHE admissions was the process known as "holistic review." The pronouncements in the 2013 case of *Fisher v. University of Texas at Austin* (*Fisher I*) and the 2016 case *Fisher v. University of Texas at Austin* (*Fisher II*), as well as the lower court decisions in the *SFA* case, expound at length on holistic review. Setting the stage for these cases, however, is a pair of cases from 2003 stemming from both the law school and the undergraduate college at the University of Michigan.

In *Gratz v. Bollinger* (2003), the Court invalidated an undergraduate admissions process at Michigan that automatically allocated applicants a set number of "points" in the internal admissions scoring system if the applicant identified as being in a certain underrepresented racial or ethnic group.[24] This process was not viewed by the Court as being sufficiently narrowly tailored because it had the effect of making race a "decisive" factor without requiring any real close consideration of individual applicants and their circumstances. Meanwhile, in the companion law school case, *Grutter v. Bollinger* (2003), the Court upheld Michigan Law School's admissions process, which entailed a "highly individualized, holistic review of each applicants file" and which gave "serious consideration to all the ways an applicant might contribute to a diverse educational environment."[25] Notably, the law school's policy did not operate in a "mechanical" fashion or award set amounts of points based on an applicant's race.[26]

The *Fisher* cases that followed *Grutter* and *Gratz* stem from the college application of Abigail Fisher, a white woman, to the University of Texas at Austin. Fisher sued the university after being denied admission, claiming that UT Austin's policy of considering race in admissions violated the equal protection clause of the Fourteenth Amendment. Key to Fisher's argument was a Texas state statute that guaranteed admission to a public college or university in Texas to students finishing in the top 10 percent of their public high school class.[27] Because public high schools in Texas contained broader populations of individuals considered to be members of racial and ethnic minority groups, and because the 10 percent plan did indeed initially increase levels of underrepresented populations at UT Austin, the plan was championed by Fisher as an acceptable "race-neutral" alternative to the full file review plan that UT Austin had been using to build out the remainder of its incoming class. UT Austin's full-file review admissions policy—the policy under which Fisher applied by virtue of her high school academic standing and was subsequently rejected—entailed a matrix of complex indices composed of various inputs, one of which was an applicant's race. The trial court couched this involvement of race under this policy as a "factor of a factor of a factor,"[28] and as the Supreme Court articulated, while not a "mechanical plus factor," race could under this policy certainly have an impact on a prospective student's chances of admission.[29]

The *Fisher I* Court opined that under the narrow tailoring prong of the strict scrutiny analysis, courts should not be deferential to institutions as they are—or, rather, before *SFA*, were—in the compelling interest prong of the strict scrutiny analysis. Stating that "the higher education dynamic does not change the narrow tailoring analysis of strict scrutiny applicable in other contexts," the Court emphasized that all "racial classifications imposed by government" must be subject to the same exacting narrow tailoring analysis.[30] In this vein, the Court also found that institutions bear the burden of demonstrating that "no workable race neutral alternatives would produce the educational benefits of diversity" being sought by the institution.[31] In light of these clarifications, the Court vacated the decision of the court of appeals that had blessed UT Austin's plan and remanded the case for further action pursuant to its opinion. In a wry dissent, Justice Ruth Bader Ginsburg critiqued the characterization of the 10 percent admissions plan as race-neutral, writing that "only an ostrich could regard the supposedly neutral alternatives as race unconscious" because they were explicitly "adopted with racially segregated neighborhoods and schools front and center stage."[32]

In 2016, Fisher was at the Supreme Court again, this time after the Fifth Circuit Court of Appeals had again affirmed summary judgment in favor of UT Austin after applying the Supreme Court's directives in *Fisher I* regarding deference and narrow tailoring. The Court in *Fisher II* addressed a number of Fisher's arguments as to why UT Austin's plan was not sufficiently narrowly tailored and, in the process, articulated some significant points regarding diversity at IHEs and the role of admissions offices in shaping communities. First, the Court affirmed that diversity is not "a goal that can or should be reduced to pure numbers" and again disavowed the use of quotas.[33] The Court also gave considerable credence to the extensive self-study that had been carried out by the university and both statistical and anecdotal evidence and that supported the position that the 10 percent plan or other plans were not workable alternatives. The Court cautioned that while it affirmed UT Austin's plan at that moment, it did not necessarily mean that the plan could or should go unchanged in the future in the face of changing demographics. "Public universities, like the States themselves," the Court said, "can serve as 'laboratories for experimentation,'" but the Court warned that UT Austin must continually "assess whether changing demographics have undermined the need for a race-conscious policy; and . . . identify the effects, both positive and negative, of the affirmative-action measures it deems necessary."

While *Fisher I* and *II* seemingly settled many issues related to the use of race in admissions, the courts have not been quiet subsequently. The organization Students for Fair Admissions has been an outspoken challenger of admissions policies, including those at the University of North Carolina and Harvard University, both of which the organization took all the way to the Supreme Court.[34] In late June of 2023, in a much-anticipated decision, the Court struck down admissions policies at Harvard and UNC that explicitly considered race as a factor in admissions.[35] In the view of Justice John Roberts and the majority, the admissions plans at Harvard and UNC could not meet the doctrinal test of strict scrutiny. "Both programs," wrote Justice Roberts for the Court, "lack sufficiently focused and measurable objectives warranting the use of race, unavoidably employ race in a negative manner, involve racial stereotyping, and lack meaningful end points."[36] The opinion, moreover, gives short shrift to any deference as an aspect of academic freedom that had previously been afforded to institutions in determining the makeup of their student body. The closing stanzas of Justice Roberts's opinion, however, are likely to be the source of focus of IHEs for the near term. While the opinion seems clearly to ban admissions policies and practices that consider an applicant's race—even as part of a full-file, holistic review—Justice Roberts concludes by writing that "nothing in this opinion should be construed as prohibiting universities from considering an applicant's discussion of how race affected his or her life, be it through discrimination, inspiration, or otherwise."[37]

Private parties like Abigail Fisher or Students for Fair Admissions are not the only ones who may raise—and have indeed raised—allegations of discrimination in IHE admissions processes. While perhaps an outlier and most certainly a function of the executive branch as it existed at that time, in 2020, the Department of Justice (DOJ) commenced its own lawsuit against Yale University. The suit alleged discrimination on the grounds of race and national origin, alleging specifically that "Yale's discrimination imposes undue and unlawful penalties on racially-disfavored applicants, including in particular most Asian and White applicants."[38] According to the DOJ, the lawsuit was the result of a multiyear investigation stemming from a complaint filed by Asian American groups against Yale.[39] The suit was seen as baseless by Yale and higher education experts, particularly in light of the Supreme Court's long-standing precedent affirming the limited use of race in admissions as a part of a holistic, full-file review.[40] By February of 2021, and with the advent of a new presidential administration, the DOJ dropped the suit against Yale, citing as a reason for dropping the suit the then-recent *SFA* ruling.[41]

Another prominent area where the work of admissions offices collides with the law, and has more so in recent years, relates to antitrust issues. Substantiated allegations of institutions colluding to "fix prices" by trading information about accepted students trace their way back to at least the early 1990s when the DOJ cracked down on the eight Ivy League institutions for allegedly colluding over financial aid awards.[42] Calling the Ivies a "collegiate cartel," Attorney General Dick Thornburgh maintained that "students and their families are entitled to the full benefits of price competition when they choose a college," and said that the Ivies' work together "denied [students] the right to compare prices and discounts among schools."[43]

History has a way of repeating itself in this regard. Almost thirty years later, in 2018, the DOJ initiated an investigation into the admissions practices of several institutions using early-decision admissions programs. The investigation was centered on probing the extent to which names or other details related to specific accepted students were being shared among schools in an effort to enforce the binding nature of early-decision admissions.[44] That same year, the DOJ also initiated an investigation into the practices of the National Association for College Admission Counseling (NACAC) to review whether the professional association's code of ethics violated federal antitrust tenets by restraining trade in the area of recruiting students.[45] The investigation was panned by counselors as being "political" and was reported as having noted higher education experts "befuddled."[46] By the next year, however, NACAC and the DOJ had settled the matter with a consent decree in the face of the DOJ's threat of suit.[47] The consent decree required that NACAC remove several provisions of its code of ethics that the DOJ viewed as being in restraint of trade, including, perhaps most notably, a ban on offering incentives to students applying for early decision, such as preferred housing or special scholarships, and a ban on recruiting or enticing students who had already accepted offers of admission or "declared their intent" to another school.[48]

While the changing winds within the executive branch and administrative agencies have resulted in a diminished interest in policing admissions offices with regard to antitrust issues, private parties have quickly filled the void. A lawsuit filed at the start of 2022 revisited some common themes related to collusion over the awarding of financial aid, albeit with a twist. In *Henry et al. v. Brown University et al.*, a handful of plaintiffs filed a class action alleging specifically that sixteen schools that are "need blind"—those that make admissions decisions without regard to an applicant's ability to pay—are guilty of colluding on financial aid formulas to the disadvantage of students and applicants.[49] The suit rests not on the economics of need-blind admissions but on a provision known as Section 568 of the Improving America's Schools Act of 1994. Section 568 provides an exemption from certain antitrust laws for institutions that operate their admissions programs on a need-blind basis.[50] Specifically, schools that are need blind may agree "to award financial aid only on the basis of demonstrated financial need" as well as to "use common principles of analysis for determining the need of [applicants] for financial aid," including a common financial aid application form, without running afoul of antitrust laws.[51] The lawsuit alleges that because several of the named defendants that benefit from the so-called 568 exemption do in fact find ways to consider an applicant's ability to pay in the admissions process, these institutions are not entitled to the protection of the exemption and are therefore violating antitrust principles.[52] Whether the lawsuit will be successful has yet to be seen (but as of April 2023, one school, the University of Chicago, has already agreed to settle),[53] but its filing and argumentation support the notion that continued or growing suspicion, cynicism, and mistrust of IHE admissions are fueling creative challenges to their practices in the courtroom.

The past several years have also been marked by a diverse range of other novel legal issues and compliance woes for IHE admissions offices. For example, Title IV of the Higher Education Act, which governs the terms and provisions of federal funds for purposes of financial support for attending IHEs, has long held that incentive compensation or commissions may not be paid to individuals, directly or indirectly, based on students that an individual is able successfully to enroll.[54] The incentive compensation ban, however, does not apply to foreign students enrolled while in a foreign country who are not otherwise eligible to receive federal financial assistance.[55] Many IHEs structured compensation arrangements for international recruitment in reliance on this exception. In 2021, a law known as the Thrive Act cast this model into doubt when it authorized removing federal GI Bill funding for institutions that engaged in incentive pay–based international recruiting.[56] Subsequent legislation was introduced to address the provisions of the Thrive Act aimed at incentive-based pay.[57] The topic of legacy admissions has also been a legislative target, with Congress considering a bill to ban the use of legacy status in admissions and tying enforcement to the receipt of Title IV federal financial aid funds.[58] As of early 2022, Connecticut and New York have also introduced legislation targeting the practice of legacy admissions, although the bills did not pass in either state.[59] This issue is likely to heat up, as numerous organizations promoting increased access to education have also come out publicly against legacy admissions, with twenty such organizations signing a letter addressed to America's IHEs and pointing out that research shows no clear link between legacy admissions and alumni giving.[60]

Another evolving issue for IHE admissions offices centers around the role of social media in the lives of prospective students and questions related to the First Amendment; free expression; and, to a lesser extent, due process. Survey evidence has indicated that despite the potential for litigation, particularly at public IHEs, staff at many higher education institutions review social media in some shape or form in the admissions process, and that may be having an influence on admissions decisions.[61] Meanwhile, most institutions do not have policies in place that delineate the role of social media in admissions decisions. Work published in the *Hofstra Law Review* revealed that among 119 public institutions surveyed in 2020 about policies related to social media's use or impact in the admissions process, 61.4 percent of institutions indicated that no such policies existed, while 38.6 percent of institutions failed to respond at all.[62] As the use of social media continues to increase and platforms become more nuanced, they are increasingly likely to have some role in admissions decisions. The full legal ramifications are likely to be borne out in the years to come.

Gaining admission to the most prestigious IHEs is no doubt competitive, and is competitive to the point of driving some families of applicants to resort to criminal activity. No accounting of legal affairs related to IHE admissions offices would be complete without a mention of Operation Varsity Blues, the massive federal investigation into a college consultant's operations that resulted in the arrest of dozens of individuals on a variety of conspiracy and fraud charges in 2019.[63]

The investigation was centered around a consultant, his business and accompanying nonprofit organization, the actions of applicants' parents, and certain sports coaches with whom the consultant had developed a working relationship. The investigation revealed that, among other tactics, the consultant had cultivated mechanisms and relationships for facilitating large payments from parents made in exchange for their applicant-child's receiving recruited athlete status in the application process, even if the student did not play that sport.[64] The consultant allegedly also devised schemes for creating fraudulent test scores.[65] In most cases, payments went directly to coaches' personal coffers. Out of the fifty-seven cases stemming so far from this matter, only one defendant, a parent of a Georgetown student, was found not guilty at trial.[66]

The Varsity Blues matter is noteworthy for several reasons. For one, the public vitriol that the matter ignited is perhaps emblematic of the undercurrent of mistrust and angst plaguing the college admissions process, at least at the most elite levels of higher education. It is also worth noting that while the investigation centered around college admissions, it focused entirely on the conduct of a college admissions consultant, his clients and their conduct, and the actions of a few rogue collegiate coaches, not the universities themselves. In fact, the prosecutors involved "stressed that universities were not on trial," albeit perhaps in an effort to weaken various defenses attempting to conflate charitable giving under these circumstances with fraud or other crimes.[67] An exception in these cases is the situation of John Vandemoer, the former head coach of Stanford Sailing. Vandemoer's appears to be the lone case in which the money involved inured completely to the institution and its programs. Vandemoer maintains that he never personally accepted a dollar, that all donations went directly to Stanford and were gratefully acknowledged by Stanford's advancement office, and that despite engaging in the "development game" just like all of his colleagues, he found himself in the crosshairs of a federal investigation.[68] As media outlets are quick to point out,[69] it is clear that the Varsity Blues investigation writ large and the trials that resulted shed light on an unflattering reality: that admissions preference is often given based on athletic talent and on financial capacity and willingness to make large contributions.[70]

Institutional Advancement

The Varsity Blues scandal has helped bring more attention to the area of fundraising and gift receipt in higher education. Despite the relatively straightforward charge of "raising money," the fundraising arm of the modern university often known as "institutional advancement" comes into contact with a wide breadth of legal issues. As anyone who has ever made a modest donation to their alma mater or other non-profit organization knows, making and receiving donations can be simple and can often be accomplished through the click of a button or two on an institutional web page. But other gifts can be enormously complicated for both the institution and the donor. Securities, tax, trusts and estates, data privacy, and real estate matters constitute just a sampling of the substantive legal areas where one finds legal issues emanating from an office of institutional advancement. While we have time and space to give these myriad issues only cursory treatment, it is again clear that the legal issues coming to bear on institutional advancement operations have picked up steam just like those in so many other institutional areas over the last ten to fifteen years. Moreover, while the issues in many of these substantive legal areas do tend to be more "black and white" and susceptible to yes or no answers, the thorny gray area and more "policy" focused questions are often only answered after considering not only legal constraints but also the institution's values and the public relations aspects of some gifts.

The increased nuance around soliciting and accepting institutional gifts has led most institutions to adopt robust gift acceptance policies. The policies generally govern the acceptance and crediting of gifts, and in so doing, address issues such as when to decline gifts that are not in keeping with an institution's mission and vision, gift accounting standards, particulars related to pledges and gift commitments, and the types of gift assets that are accepted.[71] The rising popularity of cryptocurrencies in particular has caused institutions to evaluate whether or not to accept cryptocurrency as an asset and to revise gift acceptance policies and procedures to facilitate acceptance of this new asset type accordingly.[72] Gift acceptance policies may also opine on when the advice of legal counsel should be sought by advancement staff. Instances requiring specialized legal counsel might include gifts of closely held stock that are subject to restrictions, gifts involving real estate and other specialized contracts or ownership structures, or gifts that may give rise to the perception of or may in fact create a conflict of interest. Accounting standards such as those endorsed by the Financial Accounting Standards Board are generally also adopted by institutions in their gift acceptance policies.

Despite the seemingly straightforward nature of gift acceptance policies, this area has not managed to evade controversy, particularly as it relates to accepting gifts from donors who may have procured their wealth in controversial ways or a manner viewed as antithetical to the values of an institution.[73] This has caused a number of institutions in recent years to revise gift acceptance policies to provide for more transparency, flexibility, and discretion in the acceptance of gifts. Brown University, for example, was an early adopter of a revised and expanded gift acceptance policy in the face of controversy related to an alumnus whose corporation sold tear gas.[74] The Brown policy, as of 2019, states that the university "strives to ensure . . . that the gifts enhance the reputation and standing of the University and do not compromise its mission."[75] Policies like this are important from a legal perspective in that they set forth expectations of the parties clearly. Before a donor makes a financial decision that may have tax or other financial ramifications for themselves, they are on notice of the institution's positions and processes related to various issues around accepting the gift.

A second area of great concern has been former gifts that have led to unfortunately named buildings, professorships, scholarships, or other assets on campuses. The Sackler family has come under intense scrutiny for their company, Purdue Pharma, which manufactured and marketed OxyContin. While they have successfully won immunity in the courts from personal liability for the myriad of opioid use suits that have been filed against them,[76] Harvard University and other institutions, including the Metropolitan Museum of Art in New York City, have come under fire for accepting large-figure donations from the Sacklers and naming museum buildings and wings after the family. While the Met changed the name of its Sackler wing, Harvard has yet to rename its Sackler Museum of Art, even though local activists have decried the university's associations with the family.[77] Institutions may wait until there is a court verdict of wrongdoing before taking public action. For example, numerous higher education institutions had given Bill Cosby an honorary degree before assault accusations became public, but many waited to rescind their degree until after Cosby was convicted of aggravated indecent assault in 2018, even though that conviction was vacated in 2021.

A number of buildings have recently been renamed in response to far-past figures of praise on campuses now being viewed unfavorably, whether because of being slaveowners, antisemitic or racist statements, subscribing to eugenics, or a host of other possible issues. These can include former presidents of the institution as well as formerly prominent professors or trustees. In September 2022, the University of Richmond decided to rename the T. C. Williams Law School the University of Richmond School of Law because T. C. Williams, a former trustee, was found to be a slaveholder, and the University's Naming Principles (adopted in March 2022) does not allow any entity at the university to be "named for a person who directly engaged in the trafficking and/or enslavement of others, or openly advocated for the enslavement of people."[78] One of Mr. Williams's descendants, attorney Robert C. Smith, was outraged by this change and demanded that the university return both the original gift that the family gave to the law school in 1890 and all subsequent family gifts, which, with interest, would amount to more than the current value of the university's endowment (over $3.3 billion).[79] While Smith has yet to file suit, in Vermont, former governor Jim Douglas filed suit against Middlebury College for changing its Mead Memorial Chapel name to Middlebury Chapel due to Mead's role in eugenics policies (Mead was a former governor of Vermont and an alumnus of Middlebury who paid for the chapel's construction in 1914).[80] And a lawsuit continues in California over the dropping of the name of Hastings from the University of California College of the Law, brought by descendants of Serranus Hastings (a former chief justice and attorney general of California who gave the founding donation for the college in 1878 and served as its dean and as a professor but was involved in genocidal actions against indigenous peoples of California).[81]

Past gifts involving articles of questionable provenance are a third area of concern. For example, many IHEs that were in existence before the twentieth century had substantial holdings of anthropological and scientific collections, many of which were donated by collectors, not all of which were well documented regarding origin. Numerous institutions, particularly those with university museums, are subject to the provisions of NAGPRA.[82] Under NAGPRA, institutions must make a significant effort to return items that were taken inappropriately by either donors to the university or university employees, including providing inventories to all federally recognized tribes of their holdings and following up on any queries they receive regarding objects. Institutions must also serve as careful caretakers of objects in their holdings, including providing sufficiently respectful housing for such objects and refraining from displaying them publicly, including providing any photographs of such objects without permission of the governing tribal authority. While NAGPRA has been law since 1990, institutions have come under increased scrutiny in the past decade for their shortcomings in following its guidance, with large collections such as at the University of California, Berkeley, subject to significant criticism for its slowness in implementing repatriation;[83] Harvard University has still not released its full inventory of human remains in its collections, but a report leaked in June of 2022 indicated that the collections hold at least nineteen likely enslaved individuals and some seven thousand Native American remains.[84] Similarly, the University of Pennsylvania has come under increasing criticism to do away with its cranial collection, which includes the skulls of numerous enslaved peoples.[85] Other schools, including Yale, have also been subject to claims under international law regarding the repatriation of objects from countries such as Egypt and Peru.[86]

While NAGPRA governs and prohibits the sale or inappropriate transfer of objects under its control, there are other objects donated to IHEs that could potentially be sold, such as donations of land, houses, and other physical assets. A contentious area herein is the sale of art objects. For example, when Valparaiso University announced plans to sell three valuable paintings by Georgia O'Keeffe, Childe Hassam, and Frederic Church from its museum's collections to finance the building of new dormitories, not only was there outrage on campus; a former director of the museum and a professor at the law school sued the university to stop the sale.[87] The Association of Art Museum Directors and a number of other art organizations have always advocated that artworks only be sold from museum collections to support further acquisitions, not for other uses, and most university-affiliated museums as well as other museums generally follow this policy. However, many donations to museums and universities do not come laden with the stipulation that they cannot be deaccessioned; it is simply assumed that they will not be. In the case of some donations, however, the document governing the donation may stipulate that the donation must be displayed or cannot be deaccessioned. In the case of the Valparaiso donation, the governing document does not stipulate that the donation can be deaccessioned; therefore, the question is whether it cannot be. Often, public outcry, as well as legal action, can give a museum and/or IHE pause on whether to go through with a planned sale. When Brandeis University considered selling works from its collection in 2009, there was a widespread outcry and a lawsuit over the university's handling of its art museum; the suit was settled in 2011, and Brandeis did not sell the art.[88]

Community Relations

Similar to the relations that IHEs hold with their students and their families and alumni and other donors, the relationships between IHEs and the communities in which they operate are critically important for a wide variety of reasons. The vibrancy of a local community can be a boon to prospective students, drawing students to attend and parents and families to visit. Alternatively, challenges faced by a local community can provide deep and meaningful opportunities for students, faculty, and staff to learn, serve, and engage with a broad array of social and policy questions. IHEs are often major employers in a community and significant holders of real estate, giving them strong influence as a result of the direct economic impact they have on their local community.

These wide-ranging synergies and relationships between IHEs and their host communities often give rise to a broad array of issues and challenges that lead to a similarly broad array of legal questions or strategies that require legal guidance. For example, the fact of an IHE's tax-exempt status under the Internal Revenue Code entitles an IHE to hold real estate property free from taxation. This can create adversarial economic hostilities between an institution that is a tax-exempt end user of municipal services that are funded by tax dollars such as police and fire protection or public infrastructure and the municipality that is providing those services. Agreements to provide funding to municipalities in the wake of the 501(c)(3) tax exemption, sometimes referred to as "payments in lieu of taxes" (PILOT), are often used by institutions and their municipalities to address these issues. In addition to protracted negotiations and wrangling over legal details, the agreements can quickly become controversial and contentious in their own right and even give rise to threats of litigation or actual litigation. There are several prominent recent examples, such as in Philadelphia,[89] and some schools, like Yale, have recently increased their PILOT payments significantly, where Yale's planned payments of $135 million from 2022 through 2027 is the largest of any IHE to the community in which it resides.[90] Issues related to student housing abutting residential neighborhoods and other forms of IHE real estate use and development can also put institutions and municipalities at odds.

At the same time that a municipality and institutions may have conflicting or adversarial interests such as in the case of negotiating a PILOT agreement, they may also find themselves having shared legal interests stemming from specific partnerships or shared work together. As in any set of industries, legal issues can also arise when municipalities and institutions work together proactively. In *Ginsburg v. City of Ithaca and Cornell University*, for example, a judge allowed negligence claims against the defendant university to proceed when a student fell to his death from a bridge that was wholly owned by the municipality. The court found that while the defendant university did not own the bridge, its intensive involvement in the design, construction, and maintenance of the bridge gave the university a sufficient level of control over the bridge for a jury to find that the university indeed owed the plaintiff a duty of care.[91] Such cases are not only emblematic of the increased likelihood that courts will impose or at least not easily ignore a duty on the part of IHEs, as discussed in Chapter 3; they also stand as an important reminder about observing formalities and the distinctive roles of institutional or municipal actors in synergistic endeavors and projects.

The members of the local community and their opinions and feelings about an IHE can also have an outsized impact on the legal interests of an institution outside of official municipal-institutional relationships. This was displayed in one of the most significant pieces of litigation implicating "town-gown" issues in recent years, *Gibson's Bakery v. Oberlin College*. The case stems from the alleged shoplifting of bottles of wine from the Gibson's Bakery shop by a black Oberlin student, resulting in the white shopkeeper chasing the alleged shoplifter and later pressing charges against the shoplifter and other students involved in the incident.[92] Protests enveloped the local community in response to the incident by many who saw the chasing of the shoplifter and pressing of charges as racially charged.[93] In response to the public backlash, Oberlin College went so far as to suspend its dining services purchases of baked goods from the bakery for a period of twenty-eight days in an effort, according to Oberlin, to deescalate the situation.[94] Gibson's sued Oberlin College for slander, libel, tortious interference with business relationships and contracts, and several other causes of action under Ohio law, alleging that members of Oberlin's administration had actively supported the protesters who were alleging that Gibson's was a racist establishment through various means, including circulating fliers calling Gibson's a "racist establishment with a long account of racial profiling and discrimination."[95] Following the trial, in a stunning result that was upheld on appeal,[96] the jury awarded Gibson's some $44 million of combined punitive and compensatory damages.[97] As a defamation case alone, the outcome is interesting and seemed, in hindsight, unlikely.[98] As Oberlin asserted throughout the case, it is essentially blackletter law that "colleges cannot be held liable for the independent actions of students," and "employers are not legally responsible for employees who express personal views on personal time."[99] Nevertheless, the jury composed of local residents clearly had a distinct view of the factual circumstances sufficient to allow for this overwhelming monetary award that, although eventually reduced to approximately $31 million, is still largely unprecedented.[100] In late 2022, Oberlin ended up paying $36.6 million, including interest, to the bakery.[101]

Conclusion: Colleges Are Not Islands unto Themselves

While IHEs have never operated in a vacuum, the level of public scrutiny and involvement in internal IHE procedures appears to have increased in recent years and has become more likely to involve formal legal action affecting IHEs. For example, there was a long-standing question regarding whether there was a Jewish student "quota" at Princeton, Harvard, and other Ivy League universities, but the question, unlike the current question regarding the existence of an Asian student "quota," was never formally litigated. Rather, it was assumed that private institutions could conduct their matters with relative impunity so long as they cared little about public opinion, or if public opinion was either explicitly or tacitly approving of their actions. Similarly, IHEs did not worry much about public scrutiny regarding the source and type of gifts they received, let alone about how they curated their financial and physical holdings. IHEs always operated in a local context but were not under specific stipulations regarding community contributions and were generally considered to be assets to their communities rather than problems to be managed.

These various areas of university dealings have now been subjected to more public scrutiny, legal challenges, and governmental regulation. These processes lead to additional internal rules and controls for these areas as well, increasing the range and purview for college counsel. While Part 2 of this book discusses how college counsel can react proactively to manage these concerns, for now, it is sufficient to state that these areas cannot be overlooked by counsel and senior administration and that they serve as additional examples of the lawyerization of the campus.

Chapter 5

Governance and Oversight

Any analysis of the legal issues facing institutions of higher education (IHEs) today would be incomplete without including a discussion on matters of governance. Given the uniqueness of how IHEs operate, it can be difficult to understand the impact of the myriad evolving legal issues facing them without understanding their internal governance structures, some parts of which are a matter of law, while other parts derive from custom. A number of recent legal developments have had a direct impact on governance as a legal matter, such as more stringent oversight of not-for-profits under state statutory law, which in turn affect IHE operations and by extension their ability to deliver on their core mission. And there are recent noteworthy examples of how legal issues can be exacerbated or made more complex by breakdowns or tensions in existing governance structures. Times of crisis, whether real or perceived, tend to make tensions evolving out of governance issues more acute.

This chapter first lays out a framework for thinking about IHE governance as a legal matter. Then we look at concrete examples where governance challenges can impact or exacerbate trending legal issues in higher education. Thirdly, interwoven with the first two objectives, we examine recent substantive legal developments bearing on governance matters, ranging from faculty governance to institutional governance writ large. We examine recent cases relating to ousting trustees and concerns involving the behavior of presidents and senior administrators, while also exploring changes in the understanding of fiduciary duties over recent years. We then explore governance issues that arise when institutions face fiscal constraints, including considering whether or not to cease operations. The chapter also addresses the impact of the concept and custom of shared governance, including an analysis of recent conflicts over the extent—or lack—of faculty control over institutional governance.

Legal Parameters of Institutional Governance

Governance is both substantively broad and somewhat nebulous in its definitional reach. It is most generally described as being the structures, both internal and external, that govern an entity's internal affairs.[1] For the most part, US IHEs are corporations and, as such, creatures of state statutory law. The state statutory law under which the legal entity is formed—typically a state's not-for-profit law—can be viewed as the highest level of authority pertaining to the internal conduct of an organization formed pursuant to such statute. Still, in higher education, differences and distinctions abound. Some institutions operate as for-profit institutions and thus would not be formed under a state's not-for-profit law. Some institutions are state institutions and have specific enabling legislation on the state law books.[2] A rare few others are purely private institutions but are so old as to trace their roots back to colonial times and a specific state- or Crown-granted charter or governing statute.[3] Land grant universities—schools that trace their roots to mid- to late nineteenth-century investments in education by state legislatures under the 1862 and 1890 Morrill Acts—may have hybridized statutory enabling structures that relate to distinctions between the public and private aspects of a particular university (Cornell University is one such example, where some of its schools are private and others public).[4] In any case, the enabling legislation—be it a state's broadly applicable not-for-profit law or an institution-specific statute—is the ultimate authority on matters of internal governance.

Institutions are "chartered" pursuant to their enabling legislation. An institution's charter, or articles of incorporation, is subordinate only to the state statute authorizing the charter and as such is the highest internal governing document. The charter may contain provisions related to such matters as the type of degrees the institution may confer or the size of the governing board. Subordinate to the charter are the institution's bylaws. Bylaws tend to be more granular and operational, specifying officers, terms for directors or trustees, voting mechanisms and procedures, meeting protocols, information on committees and committee structure, and clarification of the spheres of authority delegated by the board and mechanisms for how such authorities are delegated. Subordinate to the bylaws are other items of board-adopted policy, such as resolutions pertaining to the authority to sign contracts and policies governing conflicts of interest.

Questions regarding board governance have been the subject of significant study in their own right, and we do not attempt to undertake such a project here, but it is worth mentioning a few key principles of board governance that impact institutions more broadly. Members of governing boards, or trustees, are often referred to as being "fiduciaries" of an institution and are thus responsible for holding the organization and its well-being "in trust" for the future perpetuation of the organization's mission.[5] Boards can be significantly different in scope and composition. Harvard University's primary fiduciary board, the President and Fellows of Harvard College's corporation—the "oldest corporation in the Western Hemisphere"—is composed of a mere twelve individuals;[6] the board of trustees at our institution of Hobart and William Smith Colleges currently has thirty-seven members, including the president, two elected student trustees, and four trustees elected by the alumni association. But regardless of size or complexity, trustees of IHEs are required to carry out their duties in good faith and with certain "fiduciary duties" at front of mind that are often articulated in state statutory law,[7] including oft-cited fiduciary duties of care, loyalty, and obedience.[8] In general, these duties require trustees to exercise diligence in fully understanding issues facing the organization, to act in their capacity as trustees with the best interests of the organization in mind, to be free of conflicts of interest, and to ensure that the organization hews to its mission and governing documents and policies.[9] Recent changes to state statutory laws governing not-for-profit corporations, such as the 2014 revised New York Not-for-Profit Corporation Law (NPCL), have spoken directly to further refining the fiduciary obligations of a board. For example, the NPCL contains specific provisions related to contemplating transactions between the institution and certain "related parties" and contains procedures for vetting and curing certain real or perceived conflicts of interest.[10] Moreover, internal governing documents such as institutional charters and bylaws can further spell out the role of a governing board and distinguish it from the role for a president or other administrative officers.

How does this structure layer onto and intersect with faculty governance? In most cases, either the corporate charter or institutional bylaws will speak to the function of the faculty in matters of institutional governance. Within these documents, this is often done by simply delegating matters pertaining to academic and curricular life at the institution to the faculty for them to form their own rules and standards of conduct.[11] For example, an institution's charter or bylaws might have language to the effect of "the work in instruction [at the college/university] shall be committed to the faculty under the direction of the President," and "the faculty may organize and govern itself through Bylaws as it may establish."[12] Mechanistically, the former clause delegates to the faculty matters pertaining to the curriculum and instruction, while the latter clause authorizes faculty to create an organizational structure to govern themselves.

The document pursuant to which faculty usually "govern" themselves is a faculty handbook or set of faculty bylaws. These may establish a governing body such as a faculty senate as well as faculty committees, work groups, or other faculty bodies within the overall structure of faculty governance.[13] The handbook or bylaws generally set conditions under which a faculty member may be eligible to vote on matters that come before the faculty as a whole pursuant to any delegation of authority emanating from the institution's charter or bylaws.

The various documents described above compose the legal structure of governance at the vast majority of IHEs. These documents also generally enshrine an important concept and operational reality that is highly unique to higher education: shared governance.

What Is Shared Governance?

Shared governance is a quasilegal concept in a state of significant flux within the field of governance writ large. The legal mechanics as described above are straightforward. An institutional charter and bylaws speak to the overall fiduciary obligations of the governing board as well as to the operational and managerial roles delegated to the president and senior leadership. Likewise, the faculty bylaws typically speak to the primacy of the faculty in curricular and academic functions and build out a structure for substantive involvement and input in other areas. But layering onto this structure is a rich history in academia that has led to generally held standards and norms that come to bear on these otherwise straightforward legal structures. For this reason, shared governance as it currently operates is best understood by also gaining an understanding of the historical roots of higher education and its subsequent evolution. Shared governance today is a function both of academic freedom, as discussed in detail in Chapter 2, and of the increased operational complexity of higher education.[14]

While colonial and early eighteenth-century American higher education institutions were typically religiously affiliated and existed to train clergy, the mid-nineteenth century saw the focus of higher education in America expand from simply teaching church doctrine to the discovery and generation of wider bodies of knowledge in an environment of free inquiry.[15] Law professors Erwin Chemerinsky and Howard Gillman point out an implication of this shift: for early IHEs to "become centers of rigorous inquiry, decisions about what ideas could be taught or expressed had to be taken out of the hands of boards, administrators, politicians, and donors and given to an expertly trained, independent faculty."[16]

There are few Supreme Court cases that opine on matters of academic governance and custom, but those that do are noteworthy. The 1980 case of *N.L.R.B. v. Yeshiva University* stands out. In deciding the question of whether faculty were considered "supervisors" or "managerial employees" under the National Labor Relations Act, the Court was forced to grapple with the role of shared governance in the university's overall operations. The Court recounted the general principle that in the early days, IHEs were composed primarily of two groups: scholars and the students they taught. "At early universities, the faculty were the school," wrote Justice Lewis Powell,[17] but modern IHEs evolved from a time "in which guilds of scholars were responsible only to themselves."[18] Early colleges and universities had few layers of administrative bureaucracy. What little administration there was consisted mainly of a president, who might have taught as well.[19] The Court acknowledged that ultimate fiduciary authority rested with the board of trustees of Yeshiva University, but they affirmed the judgment of the Second Circuit that had found that the Yeshiva faculty were "in effect, substantially and pervasively operating the enterprise" through the system of shared governance in effect at that time.[20] In the view of the Supreme Court in 1980, faculty still had significant operational control over the academic core of university life, at least at Yeshiva.

But well before 1980, faculty were concerned about incursions on their authority and their ability to operate independently of administrative strictures. In 1915, the American Association of University Professors (AAUP) was formed "in direct response to a wave of threats against the freedom of the faculty to hold and express unpopular views."[21] The formation of the AAUP in 1915 is emblematic of the early twentieth-century shift to define a modern conception of academia and the place of the faculty within academia. The AAUP's *1915 Declaration of Principles on Academic Freedom and Academic Tenure* and its progeny, including, in particular, the *1940 Statement of Principles on Academic Freedom and Tenure,* are evidence of this shift. Together with subsequent statements, these documents articulate the principles that higher education is "conducted for the common good," that "the common good depends upon the free search for truth and its free exposition" in the classroom, and that for the faculty teaching in those classrooms "tenure is a means" to ensuring academic freedom.[22] The 1915 and 1940 statements are often referenced or incorporated by reference in faculty handbooks and bylaws at institutions across the United States, baking the values of these statements into institutional governance structures and potentially giving them the force of contract. We discuss the significance of this further below.

As the story of higher education's evolution is typically told, over the twentieth century, enrollment at IHEs broadened to a more inclusive cross section of the United States, particularly following World War II, thanks in large part to federal funding efforts like the GI Bill. Through the process of this expansion, the enterprise of higher education became more interwoven with the outside world and, in turn, more subject to government regulation. Resultingly, administrative structures on campuses became more developed.[23] Campuses came to host not only larger numbers of faculty and students but also large numbers of staff. The fiduciary obligations and duties of boards of trustees and senior officers also became more complicated. The increased complexity of college and university operations did not easily comport with the traditional duties of teaching and research for the faculty, and institutional decision-making at all levels could not lie solely in the hands of the faculty in such a burgeoning system. By the mid- to late-twentieth century, IHEs were no longer the idealized enclaves of students and faculty isolated from society for purposes of free inquiry and scholarship. They had become increasingly complex organizations with various constituent groups, each with its own needs, wants, areas of expertise, and inputs or outputs from the campus community.

What is the role of the faculty in governance following such an evolution? The AAUP has expounded at length on shared governance, including in its still-oft-cited 1966 "Statement on Government of Colleges and Universities." Drafted as a collaboration between and among the AAUP, the American Council on Education, and the Association of Governing Boards,[24] the statement requires what it calls a "joint effort" in the operations and management of institutions due to the "variety and complexity" both among and within institutions and the "inescapable interdependence" of the various constituencies that this complexity creates.[25] The 1966 statement acknowledges that there are many possible approaches to navigating institutional decision-making and highlights two key principles. First, the statement notes that "important areas of action involve at one time or another the initiating capacity and decision-making participation of all the institutional components."[26] And second, that "difference in the weight of each voice . . . should be determined by reference to the responsibility of each component for the particular matter at hand."[27] The AAUP elaborates on all of this in further detail, but the practical upshot is this: because of the array of stakeholders in an IHE, institutional decision-making typically requires broad input, and the final say on a given matter rests with the stakeholder with the most responsibility for the issue under consideration. This reifies the role of the faculty in shared governance but also acknowledges the limit on the faculty's decision-making power for the institution.

There are direct legal and practical implications on many campuses to this historical evolution of shared governance. Shared governance is not just an academic tradition or aspiration; rather, its evolution gave rise to and underpins the legal documents that outline the governance systems of IHEs today. It is also well recognized in academic accreditation processes[28] and various state certification processes that have their own unique impacts on institutional operations and missions.[29] Notably, though it collects (voluntary) dues for membership, the AAUP does not function as a union (although faculty at some universities are unionized through employee unions) because then it could not advocate for the faculty's direct role in institutional governance.[30] The AAUP aims to speak for the professoriate as a whole, not just its dues-paying membership, and in particular speaks up in defense of faculty tenure in almost all situations where it senses a danger to that institution.

Governance and Tenure

Tenure is of significance not only because of its purported role in facilitating academic freedom and open dialogue as discussed in Chapter 2 but also because of the hold it has on institutions via their governance structures and processes. In a world where "at-will" employment generally prevails, one is hard-pressed to find any other industry where large swaths of the workforce are bound to their employer with what is essentially the force of contract. The contractual nature of tenure—which generally insulates a faculty member from recourse, as we discuss below, for a number of actions—engenders on most campuses an influential collective chorus of faculty input on matters that can extend beyond the academic core and into institutional operations. This is especially true in instances where the institutional governing documents specifically enable opportunities for faculty input by dictating the composition and structure of campus governing bodies—whether policy-making or merely advisory. As a prominent example, some institutions' governing documents provide that a seat on the institution's governing board be occupied by a tenured member of the faculty.[31] Tenure is valuable not only as a protection of faculty's ability to speak freely and to research topics that may be unpopular without fear of reprisal through losing their employ but also in linking faculty members to the institution for long periods, thus increasing their stake in institutional governance and their ties, both emotional and practical, to their students and the institution. Tenured faculty members are generally the faculty members most involved in faculty governance at their institutions, often serving as the primary staffing for faculty committees and as representatives on staff committees and to the trustees.

As a purely legal matter, the terms of faculty handbooks or faculty bylaws are typically deemed by courts to constitute the contractual arrangement between an institution and the individual faculty member or members to which the handbook or bylaws apply.[32] Offer letters to new hires that reference and incorporate the faculty handbook or bylaws can reinforce this interpretation. The contractual heart of these documents tends to be the provisions related to the path toward earning tenure and promotion to ranks (generally associate professor and full professor) as well as the provisions related to sanctions and termination. Deviation from the terms regarding these matters could constitute a material breach of contract on the part of the institution and could have the potential for damages significant enough to justify legal action on the part of the aggrieved faculty member.

Few things confound boards, students, rank-and-file staff, or casual observers of higher education so much as the fact that many faculty members cannot be terminated "at-will." Rather, tenured faculty members may only be terminated "for cause." As a legal matter, termination for cause is specific to the conduct of the tenured individual and the terms of the specific faculty handbook or bylaws. Many faculty governing documents require an act or acts of "moral turpitude" or similar conduct on the part of a tenured individual to justify their termination.[33] The governing documents may also lay out procedures related to a finding of such conduct, such as a hearing by a faculty committee before the administration could sanction or terminate.[34] Faculty governing documents also often contain provisions related to grieving institutional decisions that might adversely affect faculty status or academic freedom.

The AAUP has produced a chronology of the case law on any challenges to tenure, whether for an individual or group, that is searchable by state and available on its website alongside its various policy pronouncements related to tenure and faculty governance.[35] The AAUP policy statements are specifically designed to protect the interests of tenured and tenure-track faculty and should be read with this fact in mind. The AAUP is neither government regulator nor accreditor, though it carries weight in faculty governance as the preeminent professional organization of the professoriate. Moreover, campus AAUP chapters can be influential and persuasive in their own right. But as a purely external and truly "quasi" governing body, what legal weight, if any, do the various policy pronouncements expounded by the AAUP carry?

As mentioned above, faculty handbooks or bylaws may incorporate, either explicitly or by reference, the policy pronouncements or positions of the AAUP. If this is the case, then AAUP policies as referred to or incorporated into the faculty handbook might be found by a court to be contractually binding on an institution. Nuances, of course, abound. Courts may find that only parts of an AAUP policy statement that are explicitly incorporated are contractually binding, while other parts that are not explicitly incorporated are not contractually binding.[36] The version of the AAUP policy at issue matters as well. One court found that where an earlier version of an AAUP policy statement was the one explicitly adopted by a faculty handbook, the subsequently issued version of the same AAUP statement was not found to be a binding part of the faculty handbook.[37] Some institutions specifically limit or modify the AAUP policies and statements that are incorporated into faculty governing documents. Even when not explicitly adopted, however, an AAUP policy could be referred to by a court in the face of ambiguous language in a faculty handbook in order to understand academic custom or practice in a way that might inform the ambiguities in the contract.[38] As such, even when an AAUP policy statement is not explicitly incorporated into a faculty handbook or other faculty contract, there remains a chance that it could influence the interpretation of the responsibilities between and among the parties.

While the AAUP does not have real enforcement powers in a legal sense, it does occasionally launch public investigations into the activities of specific institutions where the AAUP detects that the rights of faculty members may have been infringed on. For example, in the wake of a number of faculty downsizings that occurred in the wake of the COVID-19 pandemic, the AAUP undertook a slew of investigations that led to a comprehensive report issued by the AAUP in 2021.[39] That report referred to the actions of several institutions in downsizing their faculty as "opportunistic exploitations of catastrophic events."[40] Institutions are not generally obligated to comply with such investigations, though faculty governing documents could theoretically give rise to such a responsibility. This was not the case for

Medaille College (now closed), whose president responded flatly to the AAUP's recent investigation of that institution following faculty cuts that Medaille "has no affiliation or relationship with the AAUP, does not have a faculty chapter of the AAUP, and does not have any faculty listed as members on the AAUP's website. The AAUP does not govern, accredit, or have any authority over Medaille College."[41] The other investigated institutions generally had no comment on or pretty much ignored the AAUP report, underscoring the question of how much power the AAUP has in a time of reduced tenured positions and general cutbacks.

Indeed, declining enrollments and rising costs have forced many institutions at various times to examine their expenses related to personnel—even those personnel with tenure. This situation was exacerbated throughout the COVID-19 pandemic.[42] Outside of questions of "moral turpitude" that might constitute cause for tenure stripping of an individual faculty member in certain cases; generally speaking, there are only two other ways that tenured members of the faculty can be removed: when an institution declares a "bona fide financial exigency," described more specifically by the AAUP as "a severe financial crisis that fundamentally compromises the academic integrity of the institution as a whole and that cannot be alleviated by less drastic means,"[43] or when an institution embarks on a "bona fide formal discontinuance of a program or department of instruction."[44] While an institution's faculty governing documents are, in general, the sole contractual constraints for the elimination of tenured faculty, many adopt the verbiage of the AAUP's policy guidelines related to financial exigency and program discontinuance.[45] Both the financial exigency path to eliminating tenured positions as well as program discontinuance require significant layers of process and faculty input.[46] The AAUP guidelines also require that institutions not make new appointments if they are terminating faculty appointments and that institutions make efforts to relocate faculty to "another suitable position" within the institution; the guidelines also spell out required notice periods and severance amounts for faculty whose positions are eliminated.[47] For institutions contractually beholden to these constraints, they create a large disincentive for pursuing reductions in the faculty workforce, though some institutions appear to have successfully navigated these procedures in carrying out faculty downsizing.[48] A noteworthy example is the College of Saint Rose, whose removal of four tenured music professors following "years of lower enrollment and financial hardship" using stated policies and processes withstood challenge in court.[49]

The tenure system has been the focus both inside and outside academia of a rising chorus of critiques and calls for reform or even elimination.[50] In 2022, a South Carolina legislator filed a bill that would have barred public institutions from awarding tenure from 2023 onward.[51] A similar initiative was introduced in Missouri in 2017.[52] A proposal by Lieutenant Governor Dan Patrick of Texas grabbed headlines in early 2022 when he announced his desire to end tenure for all newly hired faculty members at Texas state institutions, calling an end to tenure a "legislative priority."[53] While this trend began prepandemic, it seems to have gained momentum through the pandemic, as the aforementioned enrollment challenges and rising operational costs forced many institutions to take a closer look at their personnel budgets.[54] Louisiana, Florida, Iowa, and North Dakota have also entertained serious legislative proposals to end tenure at state institutions, though North Dakota's senate recently rejected the proposal.[55] In Florida, Governor Ron DeSantis has succeeded in pushing through regulations creating a more rigorous posttenure review process.[56]

But noteworthy critiques of tenure are not just related to the lack of financial flexibility. Some critiques of tenure have come from academics themselves, often advancing arguments that tenure creates a system of haves and have-nots among the professoriate; a "two-tiered structure of academic labor."[57] By and large, however, tenure remains the goal of aspiring professors and the industry gold standard, particularly for top institutions, even though the majority of those teaching in IHEs do not have tenure, a trend that has been underway for some time and appears to have accelerated recently. However, it is rare that an IHE of any repute does not have at least some tenured faculty; at least one institution that had abolished tenure, Chatham University, recently reestablished tenure in the face of low faculty morale and recruitment challenges.[58]

Other critiques of tenure are directed more squarely at the notion of tenure as an obstacle to terminating faculty with the same discretion as applied to traditional at-will employees. Several cases discussed throughout this book are examples of those that confound administrators because the contractual protections of tenure require a level of inappropriate conduct for termination that is far more egregious than the level of conduct that would normally be required to justify the termination of an at-will employee for the same policy violation. This result can be unsettling to students, faculty and staff colleagues, and the public at large, although faculty will sometimes rally in support of a colleague—and sometimes subsequently drop their rallying when more facts come to light. A recent example is the 2022 case of John Comaroff, a prominent anthropologist at Harvard that we mentioned in Chapter I. The university investigated complaints about Comaroff and found that he had violated Harvard's sexual harassment and professional misconduct policies.[59] The investigation resulted in a sanction of unpaid leave and revocation of advising privileges.[60]

Nevertheless, a group of students in the anthropology program filed suit against Harvard,[61] fourteen faculty colleagues of Comaroff's called on him to resign,[62] and thirty-five faculty colleagues revoked their signatures from a letter they had previously signed raising questions about the merits of the sexual assault investigation undertaken against Comaroff.[63]

The fact patterns of several recent cases surely exacerbate the negative trend in societal attitudes toward tenure, drawing attention to the very fine and nebulous lines between academic freedom and conduct that is widely deemed unacceptable and illustrating that there is often no quick and easy solution to faculty discipline in light of tenure. At SUNY Fredonia, a professor was placed on leave and under investigation for commenting on a podcast that it was "not obvious" to him that it is "in fact, wrong" for an adult male to have sex with a "willing" twelve-year-old girl.[64] Law professor Amy Wax has been a figure of controversy at the University of Pennsylvania for "incendiary and racist remarks and writings" taking positions such as "our country will be better off with more whites and fewer nonwhites" and "I think the United States is better off with fewer Asians and less Asian immigration."[65] She now faces the possibility of sanctions by the University Faculty Senate at the request of Penn Law's dean.[66] Some nine months after the law school's dean asked the faculty to initiate disciplinary proceedings against Wax, the matter still appears to be at a standstill with no hearing date set.[67] In a seemingly rare occurrence, in 2022, Princeton professor Joshua Katz was terminated by the university for allegedly misleading the university and not being forthcoming in its prior investigation into a relationship that he had with an undergraduate student.[68]

Whatever one's views on the virtues of tenure, there is no question of its impact on institutional shared governance. The contractual insularity of tenure protects faculty members to freely voice their concerns on a variety of matters impacting the life and health of an institution. Coupled with the structural impact of faculty bylaws on matters of governance throughout institutions, tenure as a construct has a significant impact on shared governance at IHEs overall. However, tenure as an institution is also under increasing attack from outside the academy and by some forces within it, making it clear that the faculty are not able to shield themselves fully from the force of the political situation in the wider society.

Governance and Politics

Matters of institutional governance are inherently political. This is true in one sense because governance quandaries often involve an analysis of the varied levels of buy-in required from the numerous constituencies of an institution in order to move a policy or initiative forward. However, and primarily for public institutions, governance can quite literally be political, linked inextricably to the state's internal politics. The resulting politicization of governance for IHEs both contours novel legal issues for the affected IHEs and dictates to some extent how legal issues, particularly at the board level, may be dealt with.

Some public institutions are so intimately linked to the political system of a state that a single election can have a dramatic impact on governance matters at that particular institution. As a prominent example related to general counsel—the function often thought to be the primary governance advisor to an institution—following statewide elections in Virginia in 2022, the commonwealth's newly elected attorney general unceremoniously removed the sitting general counsels of the University of Virginia and George Mason University.[69]

Critics of this move were quick to speculate that it was being carried out to pave the way for the implementation of various policy interpretations that the new attorney general sought to enforce, most notably a ban on vaccine mandates at the commonwealth's public institutions.[70] Indeed, shortly after the termination of the two university counsels, the newly elected attorney general authored an advisory opinion that articulated that public colleges and universities in Virginia could not require the COVID-19 vaccine,[71] resulting in the rollback of the adoption of vaccine mandates at these institutions.[72]

Sometimes, politicians themselves can ascend to leadership positions at prominent state systems by virtue of the search and appointment processes and the prominent role of state legislatures. Such moves can cast doubt on the continued strength and role of the shared governance tradition, particularly regarding the role of an institution's faculty in selecting a leader and principles of transparency in the search process. A recent example is the 2022 appointment of Sonny Perdue to lead the University of Georgia system.[73] Perdue, a two-term former governor of Georgia and former US Secretary of Agriculture, was approved by the Georgia Board of Regents despite "widespread opposition" that included critiques of the search process, lack of faculty input, and Perdue's lack of experience in higher education.[74] The search even prompted a letter from the university's main accreditor, the Southern Association of Colleges and Schools Commission on Colleges, warning of "political interference in the chancellor search process," though the association's president later indicated that she was comfortable with the ultimate process.[75] In 2022, the Florida legislature passed, and the governor signed, a bill that exempts certain information in public institution presidential searches from the state's open-records laws and bans revealing presidential candidates' identities until twenty-one days before the candidate is chosen.[76] This was merely one move in what some have called a "crusade"[77] by Governor Ron DeSantis against the state's public institutions that also included a bill he signed implementing further posttenure reviews in the state[78] and machinations to streamline authority of governing boards based on political appointees.[79] Governor DeSantis has also taken aim at a specific school, the New College of Florida, to turn it into a more conservative institution. To this end, the college's president was fired and a new one installed, along with a new set of trustees; a number of tenure cases did not go forward, and the legislature approved additional funding for the college to turn it into the "Hillsdale College of the South."[80]

Similarly, state legislatures have taken more direct paths at limiting the governance role, and in some cases, the substantive academic oversight of the faculty at state-run institutions in a number of states. These intrusions have come in the form of legislative attempts at weakening tenure, as referenced above, and even in the form of legislative attempts to regulate the content of the subject matter taught by threatening attacks on tenure, a move that implicates First Amendment considerations as well as governance concerns related to the scope of faculty authority in curricular matters at colleges and universities. A series of moves in Wisconsin, starting with the budget proposals of then-governor Scott Walker, resulted in state law changes that removed tenure protections from state statutes and gave broad authority to the state's board of regents, many of whom are appointed by the state's governor.[81] The regents subsequently adopted new tenure policies with broader flexibility for program discontinuation and regular posttenure reviews for faculty members, along with a process for termination in cases of poor performance.[82] The proposed policies provide much more flexibility than the standard AAUP policy language related to financial exigency or program termination discussed above. Other legislative attacks on tenure have been even less subtle. The Iowa state legislature has considered legislation that would allow its state institutions to "terminate any employee for reasons other than 'just cause, program discontinuance, and financial exigency,'" and similar proposals have been advanced in Kansas and South Carolina.[83]

Individual tenure cases at public institutions with politically appointed boards can also be illustrative. A noteworthy situation arose in 2021 at the University of North Carolina regarding the tenure case of Nikole Hannah-Jones, an acclaimed journalist and lead contributor to the *New York Times Magazine*'s "1619 Project." While obviously not carried out by a legislative body per se, the University of North Carolina's board of trustees—a group made up significantly of legislative appointees—declined to move forward with approval of Hannah-Jones for tenure.[84] It is highly unusual for a board of trustees to step in and override a recommendation for tenure. While the board ultimately did accept the recommendation of the faculty and provost and vote, 9–4, to award tenure, the initial failure of the UNC board to accept its recommendation created a media firestorm raising questions about whether the initial decision not to award tenure was in fact motivated by the content of Hannah-Jones's scholarship regarding slavery in the United States.[85]

Legislative intrusions into faculty governance become even more acute when they implicate the curriculum and, in turn, academic freedom concerns more directly. In 2022, Texas Lieutenant Governor Dan Patrick grabbed headlines when he proclaimed that in Texas "the law will change to say teaching critical race theory is prima facie evidence of good cause for tenure revocation."[86] Patrick's proposal appears on its face to be a content-based restraint on speech of faculty that impinges on not only their academic freedom but also, if indirectly, on faculty governance by leveraging tenure and the threat of tenure revocation to regulate the content of faculty speech. His proposal was by no means the only one. South Dakota has passed legislation aimed at the teaching of critical race theory (CRT), as did Florida with the "Stop Woke Act."[87] An ambitious project at the UCLA School of Law called the "CRT Forward Tracking Project" "provides a comprehensive database of anti-CRT activity across all levels of government and varying types of official action."[88] As of June 2023, the CRT Forward Tracking Project had identified 699 "anti-CRT" efforts being undertaken at all levels of government nationwide, with about 20 percent of such efforts being focused on IHEs.[89] The impact of these efforts and their interplay with curriculums at institutions across the county is sure to play out on campuses, and perhaps in legal challenges, in the coming years.[90]

There is no question that legislative oversight and, by implication, interference with public college and university systems create thorny governance questions and other substantive legal questions and that these relationships and the issues they create will continue to evolve. A 2020 study by the *Chronicle of Higher Education* that included extensive interviews, reviews of public records, and an analysis of appointments to public college and university boards revealed "a system that is vulnerable to, if not explicitly designed for, an ideologically driven form of college governance rooted in political patronage and partisan fealty."[91] The additional campus issues arising between the *Chronicle*'s study and now seem only to bolster the *Chronicle*'s findings. This includes what seems to be an increasing push to the exits of public university presidents: a recent study found that the rate of involuntary departure (where presidents are either directly fired or forced to resign) has risen from 10 percent of all departures from National

Collegiate Athletic Association Division I public universities from 2000 to 2006, to 19 percent from 2007 to 2013, to 29 percent from 2014 to 2020.[92] Specifically, the *Chronicle* reported that, "based on media reports and other sources, micromanaging or hyperpartisan boards were responsible for 24 percent of involuntary turnover at such universities in red states from 2014 to 2020, a rate more than four times higher than in blue states."[93]

Indeed, a number of the changes currently being introduced by state legislators and governors across a number of states look like systematic assaults that are related by an underlying political agenda to roll back or further limit IHE actions that politicians view as tied to a liberal academic agenda. On top of actions aimed specifically at prohibiting the teaching of CRT, these include numerous bills meant to limit IHE initiatives regarding diversity, equity and inclusion (DEI), including prohibiting or reducing funding at public institutions for DEI offices, banning diversity training on campuses, prohibiting the use of diversity considerations in either admissions or employment, and banning the use of diversity statements (where a faculty or staff applicant typically details how they have in prior positions worked to increase DEI initiatives or worked to make their teaching more inclusive) in hiring processes.[94] In January 2023, a report from the conservative think tank the Manhattan Institute provided model legislation to enable these changes.[95] According to the *Chronicle of Higher Education*'s DEI legislative tracker page, as of June 2023, thirty-eight such bills had been introduced, twenty-two had been tabled or failed, six had been passed by the legislature, and six had been signed into law by a governor.[96] This is not to say that changes are limited to red-state agendas; blue states also exhibit patterning of attempts to constrain IHE's ability to make their own choices, such as bills introduced to ban the use of legacy preference in admissions.

Governance and Fundamental Changes

Many of the financial pressures that have become more acute in recent years have resulted in not merely institutional belt-tightening; they have also involved situations that are literally existential for many institutions. Since 2016, over seventy colleges and universities have closed or merged or have imminent plans to merge.[97] This figure excludes consolidations carried out within public institution systems and excludes for-profit institutional closures, which have been rampant.[98] Situations involving closures or mergers trigger myriad governance considerations and legal questions. When an institution is on the verge of closure, what is the role of the governing board? How do issues related to the fiduciary duties of trustees, officers, and administration running to the perpetuation of the institutional mission manifest in this context?

In March 2021, Mills College in Oakland announced that it would not be accepting new first-year students.[99] A mere two months later, it announced that it would be merging with Northeastern University.[100] According to Northeastern's president, the merger, set to take effect in the summer of 2022, aims to create "a comprehensive, bicoastal university that leverages the complementary strengths of Mills and Northeastern for the benefit of students and society."[101] Not all stakeholders agreed on the plan's merits. Later in the spring of 2021, the alumni association of Mills College as well as one current and one former trustee sued Mills for allegedly withholding detailed information that the trustees and association felt was necessary for them to carry out their fiduciary obligations as trustees.[102] The complaint, which sought the production of certain documents and an order restraining the college from acting for a period of sixty days, also alleged that the Mills board of trustees never authorized the closure and wind-down plan that had been announced in March.[103] The Alameda County Superior Court granted a restraining order,[104] and the defendants also filed a cross complaint against the alumni association and trustees alleging breaches of fiduciary duty, tortious interference with a contract, and other claims.[105] After the production of some of the sought-after documentation and on the reluctance of the judge to extend the restraining order, the Mills board voted in September of 2021 to consummate the merger with Northeastern.[106] Subsequently, the alumni association and Mills College agreed to a mutual dismissal of their lawsuits.[107]

The 2020 case of Mount Ida College that ascended all the way to the First Circuit Court of Appeals is also illustrative.[108] In 2018, giving just six weeks' notice to its campus community, Mount Ida College announced that it would be closing its doors. Two Mount Ida students and a prospective student brought a putative class action in federal district court against the college, its trustees, and certain administrators, alleging that "defendants knew that Mount Ida was on the brink of insolvency but concealed this information, instead assuring current and prospective students that Mount Ida was financially stable" and bringing claims for breach of fiduciary duty, negligent misrepresentation, and fraud, among others.[109] The First Circuit Court of Appeals affirmed the district court's dismissal of the claim. Most notably, the court summarily rejected the plaintiffs' arguments that Mount Ida College owed a fiduciary duty to its students. In doing so, the court reiterated a principle that likely applies broadly in this context; that is, that Massachusetts law imposes only a fiduciary duty on directors that is owed to Mount Ida, not to its students per se.

This duty, according to the court, requires only that directors act "'in good faith and in a manner [the director or officer] reasonably believes to be in the best interests of the corporation, and with such care as an ordinarily prudent person'. . . . The duty is not owed to students."[110]

Not all institutions that initially intend to close or merge meet the fate of Mount Ida or Mills, and governing boards can of course, in the exercise of their fiduciary obligations, reasonably decide on other paths. The tales of Sweet Briar College, Hampshire College, and Antioch College serve as examples of colleges that went to the brink (in Antioch's case, over the brink for some time) and then continued (or returned to) operation.[111] Still, trustees maintain their obligations to the mission of the organization they serve, not necessarily the existing "bricks and mortar" manifestation of that mission. That is to say, when the mission of an institution cannot continue to be carried out in the exact form or fashion that it has been for some time, trustees, in exercising their fiduciary duties, must be open to and review other options. The case of Mills College illustrates how difficult this process can become in the shared governance-laden, multiconstituency context of higher education. Further, while the Mount Ida case makes clear that there is no explicit fiduciary duty that runs to students, considerations such as the financial implications for students and the disruption of their educational paths are a very real concern for colleges and universities at the brink of closure and should be considered alongside plans for teach-out agreements and other arrangements for students.

Conclusion: Governance Challenges Are Myriad and Fluid

The delicate balance of who runs the university and to what ends is central to this book's narrative regarding how the lawyerization of the university has affected its functioning. There are three key sets of actors involved in shared governance, one being the administration, one the faculty, and one the trustees. In addition, state governments, the AAUP, popular opinion in general, and the legal system all factor into how universities can evolve with the times. Whether it is responding to fiscal challenges, responding to emergencies, or determining what will be taught in college classrooms, if it is not clear what the required consultations are, or if one or more sets of agents do not want to consult with other sets, then the stage is set for confrontation and potential litigation. Meanwhile, the power balance continues to shift between groups as faculty undergo challenges to tenure and universities receive higher levels of scrutiny from state regents and legislatures.

Legal counsel must assist in stewarding governance tensions as they arise, as institutions face a wide variety of systemic and existential challenges. Chapters 6 and 7 discuss how governance issues, including who gets to make the hard decisions that institutions may need to make to survive and prosper and how others respond to those decisions through filing lawsuits, can complicate the ability of institutions to move quickly in response to external forces. Hence legal considerations cut to the core of institutional sustainability in the governance context and have made running the modern university that much more challenging.

Chapter 6

The Higher Education Business Model

The systems of higher education admissions and financial aid have undergone a great deal of change in the past fifteen or so years. These changes have made it more difficult for institutions of higher education (IHEs) to maintain business as usual. IHEs currently face a high degree of public scrutiny and suspicion regarding their finances. In addition, several changes regarding what IHEs can and cannot do in terms of admissions policies have shifted the power balance, particularly for middle- and upper-class families, so that it is harder for IHEs to cross-subsidize students from poorer families by charging higher prices to students from wealthier families. We have already seen that elite IHEs have been scrutinized regarding their admissions policies, whether it be for affirmative action or legacy students. However, changes in the rules regarding admissions affect a much wider swath of IHEs that cannot afford the same level of institutional financial aid as the elite IHEs. Meanwhile, top public universities have competed away much of the gains from attracting out-of-state students,[1] while also alienating their constituencies, thus potentially endangering their funding levels going forward.

In addition, IHEs face a higher level of scrutiny both by their accreditors, who have undergone their own antitrust deregulation recently with the breakup of the regional accreditor monopoly system, and by federal, state, and local governments. While we have already discussed governance issues relating to how legislatures and executive branches within states are increasingly scrutinizing decisions—whether curricular, hiring, or other—within universities, the federal government has also increased the public level of scrutiny on IHEs through producing increased comparative data on college outcomes, down to the level of individual majors at specific IHEs. In the for-profit college sector, this heightened level of attention regarding outcomes—and outcomes relative to loan burdens—has led to widespread closures, following an earlier era of easy money for such institutions. For nonprofit IHEs as well, this increased scrutiny may lead to additional concerns by the general public that at least some forms of higher education are not worth the investment.

Much has been written on whether or not our college system is in financial crisis,[2] whether or not college is "worth it," and how to reform the system.[3] Rather than recount what others have already discussed at great length, we take on a smaller but strategic topic in this chapter. We focus on several recent developments in how the sector is regulated that we think will have significant effects going forward. We should state at the outset that in general, we support antitrust policies and practices as well as policies that increase the amount of information available to the general public about the inner workings of IHEs and the outcomes they produce. Such practices hold the promise of increasing consumer sovereignty in the higher education market and reducing costs and loan burdens going forward. But policies can also have unintended consequences, such as reducing the ability of IHEs to subsidize the educations of poorer students, and thus potentially reducing access to college for those students. There are also both private and public costs to complying with and enforcing such policies.

We first lay out the fundamental elements of the current college business model; in particular, how college costs look from the student side and how they look from the college side. We then consider several recent changes and trends in the market for higher education: the recent boom and then bust in for-profit schools and what caused them, changes due to the interpretation of antitrust laws in how accreditation occurs in the United States and how admissions offices operate, and the federal government's increased work in making college affordable and transparent. We then turn to the question of whether these and other changes will lead to a wave of consolidation in the higher education sector and how legal structures and regulations can actually make it difficult for IHEs to merge or close gracefully.

Is the Current Model Sustainable?

At first glance, the US higher education sector is one of the great success stories of modern development. The US system rocketed to the head of the line as the center of research for the world, with government subsidization and encouragement of research responsible for the country's rise relative to nineteenth-century powerhouses like Germany and the United Kingdom.[4] The US system also offered the promise of heightened access to higher education relative to other countries' systems, with its greater number and range of institutions, from business and technical institutes to a whole range of two- and four-year colleges and universities. The United States has high levels

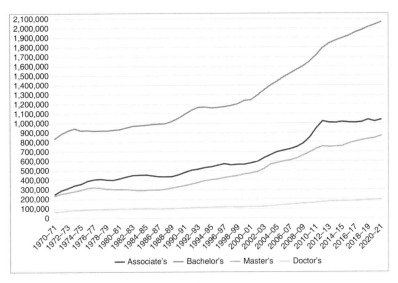

Figure 6.1 Number of degrees conferred by postsecondary institutions, 1970–71 through 2020–21. Data source: *Digest of Education Statistics 2022*, Table 318.40, https://nces.ed.gov/programs/digest/d22/tables/dt22_318.40.asp.

of high school completion (whether traditional, night school, or GED), with over 91 percent of the population ages twenty-five and over having completed high school or the equivalent, and also high rates of at least some college (63 percent) and bachelor's degree or higher (almost 38 percent).[5] Higher education is a significant export from the United States in terms of services, with many foreign students attending undergraduate and graduate programs in the United States, and many staying in the country to continue contributing to the economy. The annual number of bachelor's and graduate degrees granted, as shown in Figure 6.1, has risen continually, shown here from 1970–71 through 2020–21; associate degrees by contrast have stayed flat over the last decade.

In addition, the average financial return to a college education relative to attaining a lower level of education is still substantial. College-educated workers receive higher wages and have lower probabilities of unemployment (2.1 percent for college graduates vs. 3.5 percent for all workers in March 2023),[6] with, for example, a median wage in 2022 for twenty-two- to twenty-seven-year-olds of $52,000 with a bachelor's degree compared to $34,320 with a high school diploma.[7] These benefits accrue not only to the worker but to the state as well: one recent estimate is that an increase of 1 percent in the growth rate for each US state in its percentage of the population with a bachelor's degree or higher would have increased the overall gross domestic product (GDP) by over $130 billion.[8]

But these benefits are not equal across persons. Aside from individual variations in outcome, there are different returns to different major fields of study and to attending different schools. While raw data do not control for differences in ability across majors and schools to calculate actual value added by schools, they are nonetheless telling. Georgetown University's Center for Education and the Workforce has calculated returns on investment for over forty-five hundred schools, finding that for 30 percent of the institutions, more than half of their students earn less than a high school graduate ten years after enrollment.[9] This relates in large part to students not having graduated from the institution; meanwhile, other institutions, including such august schools as Cal Tech and MIT, pay off significantly, with returns of over $2.4 million in forty-year net present value at the high end.[10]

This indicates that, while many students find college to be a good investment and are also capable of financing their education through a combination of family and individual savings; earnings while in college; governmental, institutional, and nonprofit grants and scholarships; and loans—which they can then pay back in full; other students, particularly those who do not earn a degree, end up little better than a high school graduate in terms of increased earnings capacity and may have trouble meeting their college debt obligations.

The cost of attending college has risen over the long run in terms of the amount of purchasing power needed to pay for it. When Joyce was in college in the late 1970s and early 1980s, it was still possible to attend a state school and live at home, work significant hours during college while taking a significant course load, and graduate in four to five years with little or no debt. Similarly, Joyce received aid both in the form of a national merit scholarship and need-based financial aid from Harvard; her parents paid for much of the rest while she also worked two part-time jobs during the school year and full-time during the summers to cover her out-of-pocket expenses, including textbooks, music lessons, summer living expenses, and travel back and forth to school. She graduated with no student debt.

The late 1970s and early 1980s were in fact the lowest-cost years for college. Measured in constant (2022) dollars, the total for college tuition, fees, and room and board hit a local minimum (measured since 1963–64) of $10,097 in 1980–81, the year Joyce was a junior in college.[11] It has since risen every year through 2020–21, when it was $27,764, before declining to $26,903 in 2021–22.[12]

These rising real costs have led to increased total student debt. Total federal educational loans owed by individuals as of March 2022 was $1.62 trillion; by comparison, the annual US GDP at that time was $25 trillion.[13] This certainly sounds like a large number, and private educational loans increase the total educational debt yet more. As of 2020–21, 54 percent of bachelor's degree recipients graduated with some debt, an average of $29,100.[14] Additional debt is held by graduate school attendees and, most upsettingly, by those who fail to graduate. While student loan repayment was halted during the COVID-19 pandemic, restarting payments as of late 2023 will lead to additional pressures as well as additional calls for the government to forgive all or some of student debt, although President Joe Biden's wide-reaching loan forgiveness plan was deemed unlawful by the Supreme Court. However, total borrowing (federal and nonfederal, subsidized and unsubsidized, graduate and undergraduate) has been declining for eleven straight years, to $94.7 billion in 2021–22 after hitting a peak of $141.6 billion (in 2021 dollars) in 2010–11 (with steep increases in the preceding decade).[15]

Net prices for college, after rising for many years, have been dropping in the private sector and in parts of the public sector (where both published and net prices vary significantly by state and even by institution within states). This is mitigating the rise in the cost of college that had occurred in the longer stream. But this puts a strain on IHEs' finances as well. We shall see in the next section that the for-profit sector first rose and then fell in numbers and dollars based on significant changes in college financing and regulation. The for-profit sector is not representative of the rest of higher education, but what happened to it does signify the importance of regulatory changes for the well-being of higher education.

Boom and Bust in the For-Profit Sector

For-profit institutions have a long and illustrious history of participation in higher education in America. Many current nonprofits have their roots in formerly for-profit institutions, often business schools or other types of trade schools, and many trade schools, both for-profit and nonprofit, continue to operate, some general, and some very specialized (e.g., the Hobart Institute of Welding Technology, the Barber & Beauty Institute of New York). In addition, distance learning, including correspondence schools, has a long history in the United States. For aspiring students in rural areas, distance learning may be the only educational option, particularly for those whose work relegates them to areas without a brick-and-mortar educational institution nearby. These forms are not inherently suspect.

What is striking about recent decades is the growth of the for-profit sector, often in combination with increased distance-learning options, such as online learning. Online learning can exist in many forms (synchronous vs. asynchronous, controlled vs. open enrollment like massively open online courses, fully online vs. hybrid, etc.). While many large players in online learning include nonprofit institutions, both public and private, others have been for-profit, and they have received the larger share of negative publicity regarding student outcomes.

Figure 6.2, which shows the overall number of higher education and the number by control type (public, private nonprofit, and private for-profit) shows both the relative growth in the number of for-profit institutions and the recent drop in their number. While the numbers of public and private nonprofit institutions have stayed relatively constant over the past forty-five years, private for-profits rose from 214 in 1984–85 to 1,451 institutions in 2012–13 before dropping to 704 by 2020–21. Out of a total of 18.9 million students enrolled in higher education institutions in 2020, about one million were enrolled in for-profit institutions, a halving of that number relative to 2010, when total enrollment was 20.8 million.[16] While some prognosticators had thought that the number of nonprofit IHEs would decline significantly by now, that is not true, but it is the case that there has been significant recent shrinkage of both institutions and

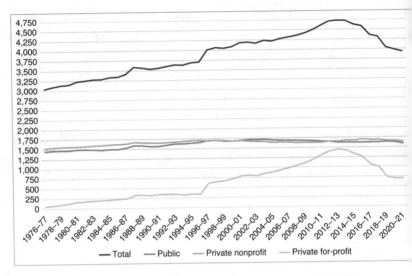

Figure 6.2 Number of higher education institutions, all and by
control of institution, 1976–77 through 2020–21. Data source:
Digest of Education Statistics 2021, Table 317.10, https://nces
.ed.gov/programs/digest/d21/tables/dt21_317.10.asp.

campuses in the for-profit sector, and this drop accounts for most of
the overall drop in the number of IHEs.

What caused first the expansion and then the contraction of this
sector? Interestingly, federal policy and regulation are responsible for
both. Students at for-profit institutions can receive federal (and nonfederal) loans and are eligible for Pell Grants and veterans' benefits
(and they and their families can receive tax credits for education at
for-profit institutions just as they can at nonprofit institutions). The
majority of the funding at many for-profits come from these sources,
as they do not receive public subsidies like public schools do, and do
not receive grants that only nonprofits can receive, nor do they generally have endowments. Without these significant sources of governmental funding, for-profits would be at a significant disadvantage

relative to nonprofits. The 90/10 rule requires for-profits to receive at least 10 percent of their funding from nonfederal sources, and it has now been tightened to exclude federal aid to veterans (which previously counted on the 10 percent side).[17] Many for-profit institutions hit up against this ceiling, and the vast majority of them receive 50 percent or more of their funding from the government.[18]

Many consumer complaints occurred following the expansion of this sector, in some cases leading to lawsuits, particularly between 2011 and 2014. Lawsuits were brought by both private individuals (students and investors) and states on grounds of misleading recruitment practices, misrepresentation of quality of services,[19] trumped-up placement statistics,[20] and hence securities fraud.[21] The courts have not always been sympathetic to these arguments, sometimes on the rough grounds of "consumer beware," but the onslaught has been sufficient to catch regulators' attention.

The case of Ashford University is instructive. Ashford University was an online for-profit institution owned by parent company Zovio (formerly Bridgepoint Education).[22] The state of California sued the company for making false statements to students about degree value and providing misleading information about cost, financial aid, market outcomes, pace of degree programs, and transfer credits.[23] In March 2022, the San Diego Superior Court ruled in favor of the state, ordering more than $22 million on penalties. Ashford had by then been acquired/absorbed by the University of Arizona Global Campus, with Zovio continuing to serve as the operating body; subsequently, in August 2022, the University of Arizona announced that it would take over management of its online programs from Zovio.[24]

These claims have also led recently to loan forgiveness for hundreds of thousands of students by the Department of Education (DOE).[25] When institutions are found to have made substantial misrepresentations, students become eligible for possible discharge of all or part of their debts. The DeVry University, ITT Technical Institute, Corinthian Colleges, and Westwood College situations, among others, have led to significant findings for these borrowers having been misled into taking out loans that are essentially consumer fraud.[26] This type of targeted loan forgiveness has been relatively noncontroversial compared to arguing that all student loans should be forgiven whether or not there is a finding of fraud.

The discipline that the legal system has placed on the for-profit higher education sector appears to be a very positive force: a positive aspect of the lawyerization of higher education. This is the legal sector and the government (federal and state) operating to protect consumers from fraudulent sellers.

Antitrust Comes to Admissions and Accreditation

Another area in which lawyerization comes across as a proconsumer approach is in antitrust law enforcement. An early example, as discussed in Chapter 4, was the breakup of the financial aid cartel that the top IHEs ran for many years. Now IHEs are forbidden to discuss financial aid matters directly and in general should refrain from discussing any kind of price-setting with each other, whether it be faculty and staff pay levels, tuition raise plans, or merit aid offers to students. For instance, in 2021, Duke University agreed to pay $19 million to settle an antitrust lawsuit wherein it was claimed that Duke and the University of North Carolina had an agreement not to steal faculty from each other and to set similar compensation levels.[27]

Recently, the National Association for College Admission Counseling (NACAC) came under scrutiny for its practices. NACAC had, at its founding in 1937, created a statement of principles of good practice and later, a code of ethics and professional practices. This statement included much self-policing, including the requirement that members be truthful when representing their schools to prospective students and make all due dates/deadlines clear. All members of the professional association were expected to comply with these statements.[28] However, in 2017, the US Department of Justice (DOJ) indicated that elements of the statement were anticompetitive and thus in violation of the Sherman Antitrust Act,[29] and the DOJ subsequently filed a complaint against NACAC in late 2019.

The association voluntarily changed its practices and published a new statement/code in 2020. The important changes were to drop three rules regarding transfer student recruiting, first-year student recruiting, and early decision incentives.[30] The effect of these three rules, the DOJ alleged, was to substantially reduce "competition among colleges for college applicants and potential transfer students and deprived these consumers of the benefits that result from colleges vigorously competing for students."[31] The transfer student recruiting rule kept IHEs from recruiting transfers unless the student initiated the inquiry or the college checked first to make sure that the college permitted transfer recruiting (e.g., community colleges encouraging students to transfer to a four-year college). The early decision incentives rule kept IHEs from offering preferential treatment to students applying for early decision. And the first-year undergraduate recruiting rule kept IHEs from improving their offers to students after May 1, the general decision deadline.[32]

IHEs were quick to change their behavior in the 2021 admissions season. For example, High Point University rolled out a slew of early decision benefits, ranging from preferential class scheduling and room selection to a personal parking spot.[33] Our school, Hobart and William Smith Colleges (HWS), sent out general inquiries to students who had previously applied to HWS but had not enrolled to see if they would be interested in transferring. We do not believe we were alone in these actions.

The net effects of these changes are many and continue to evolve. Students can continue to consider their options for changing schools and also extend financial aid negotiations up until enrollment (and beyond). IHEs may end up with greater summer melt (as in students agreeing to enroll in the fall and then changing their minds before arriving) than before as well as higher discount rates and more recruitment expenses as they continue to work to build the class far beyond the traditional recruitment season end. While somewhat more students may end up attending college because of these changes, the main effect is likely to shift students between institutions and reduce the net revenue associated with each student. In addition, schools that are less able to make competitive offers and spend the additional money on continued recruiting are likely to see enrollment drop. This should be advantageous financially to students, as many will be no worse off under these changes, and some, who are willing to bargain longer, lock in earlier, and/or transfer once or more during college, should come out significantly ahead. IHEs may also offer more favorable aid packages early on, both to early decision, early action, and regular action applicants, to secure students earlier and reduce melt.

In addition to the DOJ's targeting the college admissions system for change, the regional monopoly system of general accreditation was also ruled as inappropriate. Seven regional accrediting agencies controlled general accreditation (as opposed to specialized accreditation for particular programs or schools within universities, such as a chemistry major or a business school, which are generally managed nationwide). In 2019, the DOE ruled that regional accreditors could accredit schools outside of their region, to begin in 2020.[34] It took

another year for either accreditors or IHEs to make any moves to accredit outside of the traditional regions, as accreditors did not have to
agree to consider schools outside their region.[35] Still, once one does,
others generally follow, and at this point, the majority of the accreditors have announced willingness to consider schools from outside
their region for accreditation.

Accreditation issues were brought up well before these recent
changes. For one thing, the very fact that the awarding of Title IV
funds is based on an institution's being accredited causes a fundamental conflict of interest. The threat of losing funds is so great that
it is not clear that accreditors move in quickly enough to deal with
problem cases; the Mount Ida case discussed in Chapter 5 is a case in
point. Indeed, accreditors rarely pull accreditation, although they do
occasionally put institutions on probationary status.[36] In addition, accreditation, given that the vast majority of those who serve as peer
reviewers of institutions and who serve on the accrediting agency
boards are employed by the very IHEs that the accreditors evaluate, is
an insider's game.[37] It is hard to see what incentives accreditors have to
consider radically different forms of education and educational institutions or what incentives they have to instill cost controls or tuition
caps on IHEs.

Are accreditors likely to toughen up in this newly competitive environment? The Middle States Commission on Higher Education
(MSCHE), which accredits schools (so far) in New York, New Jersey,
and Pennsylvania, announced in September 2020 that it would require IHEs suing it regarding adverse findings to go through arbitra-
tion, and also that it would more often require IHEs to have teach-out
plans (where they arrange for their students to finish their degrees at
one or more other schools if they end up closing).[38] Neither of these
announced changes seem likely to attract more IHEs to them, unless

those IHEs can somehow convince prospective students that these stricter requirements make them more attractive options. Meanwhile, the State of Florida passed a law in 2022 requiring Florida institutions to change accreditors every time they come up for reaccreditation (generally, in the five- to ten-year range),[39] apparently in an attempt to instill fresh perspectives regularly, although even the DOE warned that changing accreditors this often was likely to be very challenging and costly for IHEs to manage.[40] Subsequently, the DOE issued notice to all IHEs that they had to first get approval from the DOE before switching or adding accreditors, essentially reregulating this area.[41] And, in the current counteraction, in June 2023, Governor Ron DeSantis sued the DOE, arguing that this notice is an unconstitutional interference with the state's ability to carry through with its own law.[42]

It is interesting to contemplate the various pros and cons of this shift in how accreditation is done.[43] Accreditors are nonprofit agencies, but they still may care about the possible power and prestige that may come with having more clients. Alternatively, will accreditors develop more expertise in particular areas (e.g., specialize more in sectors, such as small nonprofits vs. large state schools), thus possibly becoming more effective in their specialty areas? Will they also develop different but equally positive reputations and allow for a wider range of standards that better match the specific needs and interests of different institutions? The Higher Learning Commission, which accredits institutions in nineteen states in the middle of the country, announced in March of 2021 that while it would apply the same basic evaluative criteria to all schools regardless of size, type, and so on, it would start considering differential standards in view of the differences across schools.[44] Or, is this simply going to make accreditors more lax if they are trying to draw business from other states and keep their current clients? As one commentator predicts: "With various accreditors vying for the business of selling access to Title IV financial aid, shenanigans are sure to ensue."[45]

It is also possible that more regulation will occur where before accreditation was essentially a self-regulating sector (but still necessary for federal funds eligibility) that could be relied on to provide the thorough scrutiny of institutional data necessary to provide good product and maintain oversight, thus freeing the government of a degree of those obligations. If the government does not trust the accreditors to carry out this function effectively, then it may step in and do more of this regulation itself. Indeed, that seems to be happening as the federal government (and some state governments) adds additional reporting requirements and takes it upon itself to make the collected data available to the public. Indeed, both presidential candidates Donald Trump and Ron DeSantis have indicated that they are interested in reworking the accreditation system, which they describe as a cartel, including making sure that diversity, equity and inclusion (DEI) considerations are not taken into account in accreditation processes.[46] Meanwhile, in 2022, the Biden administration finally fully revoked recognition of one controversial accreditor, the Accrediting Council for Independent Colleges and Schools, which had been investigated for some years for being the accreditor for a number of questionable institutions that ultimately closed.[47]

Increasing Transparency regarding College Affordability and Outcomes

The amount of data now required to be collected annually from IHEs who participate in Title IV funding has increased over time. IHEs have provided annual data into the Integrated Postsecondary

Education Data System (IPEDS) since 1993. These data span a huge range of information, ranging from number of students and faculty to admissions statistics, degrees conferred, prices charged, and aid granted. They are used by researchers, ratings creators, and the government itself to track patterns over time and across IHEs.

The federal government uses IPEDS data in combination with other sources to track college financial well-being and student outcomes. Currently, the DOE maintains an online College Affordability and Transparency Center[48] with a number of features, including net price calculators for each college,[49] a college scorecard center that allows one to compare graduation rates, cost, graduates' earnings, and cumulative loan debt of borrowers across selected sets of schools,[50] and lists of IHEs that have had particularly high levels and/or increases in tuition and net price.[51]

As of 2023, the federal government has made moves to further increase the amount of data collected. Under the proposed College Transparency Act, schools would have to collect and report detailed data regarding enrollment, persistence, transfer, and completion for all of their programs and degrees; these data would be disaggregated by student demographics, including race and ethnicity, gender, and age.[52] This would be a significant expansion of governmental data collection including having students' personal data linked to college outcomes.

These data could be used to measure more exactly whether or not IHEs and other institutions are making gainful employment possible for their graduates. The government could then move to penalize institutions with low gainful employment rates or low earnings for their graduates (as in lower than that of high school graduates). While so far, much of the regulatory focus has been on whether for-profit institutions provide gainful employment, these same data and concepts can easily be used to evaluate nonprofit institutions' outcomes. Indeed, in 2023, the Biden administration indicated that it wants an increasing focus on gainful employment with possible sanctions and penalties for institutions that do not meet certain standards; in particular, the termination of access to federal student financial aid.[53]

Perhaps perversely, while IHEs may worry about cost containment, they are also lauded for the level of services they provide. Rating projects, such as *U.S. News & World Report's* widely read annual college rankings, generally measure levels of inputs and award points for higher levels of inputs, such as high faculty–student ratios, and the amount spent on academic support. And while IHEs are sometimes highlighted for their fancy new dormitories and student centers, gyms and recreation centers, lazy rivers, and other amenities, labor is their main input. Indeed, increases in the number of and pay for staff rather than faculty seem to be responsible for much of the increased cost of college.

Yale University has come under particularly pointed criticism for its apparent administrative bloat. A 2021 article in *Yale Daily News* reports that the number of managers and professionals working at Yale has risen much faster than the increase in the student body, rising from thirty-five hundred administrators and managers in 2003 to over five thousand by 2019 for an over 40 percent increase; meanwhile, the undergraduate student body increased from fifty-three hundred to fifty-nine hundred, an 11 percent increase.[54] Similar rises, though not generally as notable as this, have occurred at many other schools. From 1976 to 2018, while student enrollment increased by 78 percent and faculty increased by 92 percent, executive and administrative staff increased by 164 percent, other professionals by 452 percent, and nonprofessional staff by less than 1 percent.[55]

What do these staffs do? Some of the increase appears to be because students and their families expect more services from IHEs.[56]

Mental health centers, centers for teaching and learning, staffed recreation centers . . . the list goes on. This is not unreasonable, given that many of these services are not readily available outside of IHEs; much as has happened to our primary and secondary school systems, these services have moved inside of IHEs rather than being available to the general population through public provision.

Some of the increase appears to be because of increased regulation, including the record-keeping and reporting requirements that are placed on IHEs. IHEs must file not only the data needed to run the information systems discussed above but also a myriad of other documentation required to show their appropriate use of Title IV funds, research grants, and state opportunity program funds. They must file yearly Clery reports, Title IX reports, and tax documents. They must maintain documentation on their foreign students and all their employees, and undergo regular audits. All of these tasks require staff to do them. A 2015 study that considered the overall costs of federal compliance on the IHE sector calculated the cost of federal compliance at between 3 to 11 percent of total nonhospital operating expenditures and that the sector as a whole was spending $27 billion on compliance, which would be around 4 percent of sector revenue.[57] Compliance on research grants was estimated to be between 11 and 25 percent of grant revenue. Another study at Loyola Marymount University that attempted to measure all federal, state, local, and National Collegiate Athletic Association compliance costs arrived at 3.5 percent of revenues, with over 23 percent of staff spending at least some time on compliance matters.[58] Both of these studies, however, argue that their calculations likely underestimate the true costs of compliance, including potentially many staff positions that would not exist if it were not for compliance. Already, given the narrow margins that most IHEs work with, 3.5 percent can erase that margin of budget balancing in many cases.

Finally, some staff growth may be because of simple bureaucratic bloat. Bureaucracies can develop their own internal momentum, as administrators naturally wish to expand their span of control and do more of whatever they are in the process of doing. While many of these positions may come about through the natural desire to do a better job in providing services, whether they are mental health, student engagement, or academic support, they nonetheless can add to bloat and are not necessarily meaningful positions. The concept of "bullshit jobs," as popularized by David Graeber's 2018 so-named book, wherein many jobs appear meaningless even (or particularly) to those holding them, is not unknown to academia. Consistent with this theory's predictions, a recent study finds that "other professionals" have a much higher expressed dissatisfaction with their job than either executives or faculty.[59]

Aside from concerns about incentives for administrative expansion and expanded record-keeping burdens, numerous commentators have voiced concern about whether well-intentioned transparency and accountability measures lead to overemphasis of some outcomes over others. While no one wants earnings to be lower for college graduates than for high school graduates, it is reasonable to ask whether the focus on earnings as the measure of whether college is "worth it" is overly reductive. For example, researchers Wendy Fischman and Howard Gardner[60] argue that higher education "has become a largely transactional endeavor, focused entirely too much on jobs and bogged down in well-intentioned institutes, centers and programs that distract from its main purpose" of getting "the mind to work better."[61] To the extent that liberal arts education has focused more on the development of the whole human being to function well at work but also in one's personal and public-serving life, its supporters have argued that its benefits are likely undermeasured by earnings alone.[62] For example, Richard Detweiler claims that it can be shown empirically that liberal arts graduates are more likely to be ethical, to appreciate art and culture, and to lead fulfilling and happy lives.[63]

Is Consolidation the Answer?

Assuming that the various changes discussed above continue, IHEs face significant challenges. They must increasingly justify their educational options on the basis of their graduates' earnings while reducing their charges, competing more aggressively for a share of the shrinking next generation of college students, and complying with an increased level of regulation and accreditation requirements.

Of particular concern are the many US colleges that are under one thousand students, on the view that they are unlikely to achieve any economies of scale for cost control, that they tend to have little or no endowment, and that they are often located in rural areas experiencing population declines. The consulting firm Parthenon analyzed 2,275 colleges and universities in 2016, finding 932 (41 percent) of them to have a "strong niche," 538 (24 percent) to be "large and thriving," 735 (32 percent) to be "small and at risk," and 70 (3 percent) to be "large and languishing."[64] Similarly, a 2020 study, *The College Stress Test*, studied over 2,800 institutions and found that 10 percent face substantial market risk, 30 percent struggle, and the other 60 percent face little or no market risk.[65]

Given these challenges, it is not hard to find doomsayers regarding the future of the traditional higher education industry, or at least large segments of it. The late Clayton Christensen became well known for predicting in 2017 that over half of American colleges and universities would close over the next ten to fifteen years.[66] Earlier (November 2013), he and Michael Horn had decided together that "the bottom tier of every tier . . . will disappear or merge in the next 10 to 15 years."[67] Horn subsequently hedged the bet, writing in 2018 that "our predictions may be off, but they are directionally correct."[68]

While Christensen's prediction period has not yet ended, unless the pace picks up significantly, his forecast will not be realized. The pandemic, similarly, was forecast to cause some closures, based on stress test analysis,[69] but instead, federal and state funding appears to have improved many IHEs' finances, to the point that they ran surpluses during 2020–21 when enrollments were at their lowest. In 2022–23, when most IHEs had run out of pandemic-related funding but were still experiencing enrollment reductions, about twelve closures and mergers occurred. Indeed, many colleges that were assumed to have been lost causes seem to return from the ashes, including Hampshire College, Sweet Briar College, and Antioch College, which closed but subsequently reopened.[70] Additional small colleges, whose size would seem to make them unviable, continue to operate, such as Sterling College in Vermont, with all of 125 students.[71] While it is essentially unheard of for a college to close that had not been previously tagged as being in potential trouble, many colleges continue even though they meet a number of criteria that make them likely candidates for closure.[72]

A more attractive option to outright closure may be acquisition or merger, either between a weaker and a stronger partner, or between two relatively equal partners, where one may complement the other. For instance, the Berklee School of Music and the Boston Conservatory merged in 2016, with clear synergies and complementarities between those two institutions.[73] There has been significant consolidation in the for-profit sector, with stronger institutions taking over weaker ones, and some for-profits (like Ashford) being acquired by nonprofits that want to expand their online programs. However, nonprofits who tried to develop online courses have also devolved their programs in some cases, notably when MIT and Harvard's joint venture of edX was sold to 2U, a for-profit online program management company.[74]

Traditional nonprofit colleges have merged in some cases as well, often with one becoming a subset of another larger institution. For instance, Wheelock College became a part of Boston University in 2018, continuing to exist as the Wheelock College of Education and Human Development at Boston University.[75] A more litigious case was the 2021 merger between Wesley College in Delaware and Delaware State University, which also involved the case of a public school acquiring a private one.[76] This situation led to two lawsuits, one claiming it was a sham to avoid paying Wesley's debts,[77] and the other brought by fourteen faculty members claiming it was a move to get around tenure and allow for firings.[78] Regulators, including the U.S. Education Department, State Departments of Education, and accreditors, appear to be taking increasing interest in the details surrounding various mergers, making the environment more difficult for effecting a merger, and in at least one case in 2023—Paul Smith University and the nonprofit Fedcause—causing the merger to be called off entirely.[79]

Meanwhile, a number of state systems have considered reorganizing their systems to consolidate by having more central administrative authority (thus theoretically reducing the amount of administration at individual schools), by creating regional systems with a central authority, and/or by closing some campuses. Such moves have to pass state scrutiny and planning and then also be approved by the relevant accreditor. A consolidation of the entire twelve-institution Connecticut community college system into one college (CT State Community College)[80] and consolidation of part of the Minnesota community college system are examples of the first type of reorganization.[81] While faculty generally lamented the Connecticut consolidation, central administration lauded the ability to avoid having twelve separate systems.[82]

An example of the second type of reorganization is occurring in Pennsylvania, where authorities plan to merge six institutions into two,[83] with the first merger—of Northeast Pennsylvania Bloomsburg, Lock Haven, and Mansfield Universities into a combined institution to be called the Commonwealth University of Pennsylvania, has been approved.[84] A similar plan to merge three state universities in Vermont is proceeding, albeit with faculty resistance.[85]

Reflecting the other side of the coin, a 2019 plan to consolidate Alaska's three universities into one system with branch campuses failed.[86] And what seems almost impossible to do, at least in the current climate, is to close any campuses as part of a state system consolidation plan. In both Vermont and Pennsylvania, early plans to close campuses as part of their consolidation were scrapped,[87] and in Maine, the chancellor argued that savings from closing branch campuses were small.[88] While this may be true, particularly if commuting costs of students are taken into account, it is hard to believe that all current branch campuses can continue to operate in some states (including New York, which has perhaps the most elaborate public higher education system of any state, with sixty-four separate State University of New York campuses and twenty-five separate City University of New York [City] campuses as of 2023).

Meanwhile, there are a number of efforts underway in higher education to create consortia and networks that could lead to reduced costs of operation without also forcing mergers and losses of independence for individual schools. Many consortia have fairly limited goals, such as sharing information and possibly courses between schools, while others are working on sharing more services, such as IT, payroll, library, and business services. One long-standing project is the Claremont College Consortium (five undergraduate colleges and two graduate institutions);[89] others include the Green Mountain Higher Education Consortium (Champlain, Middlebury, and St. Michael's Colleges)[90] and the Five College Consortium (Amherst, Hampshire, Smith, Mount Holyoke Colleges and University of Massachusetts Amherst).[91] At HWS, we currently participate in several consortia with different levels of involvement (the New York 6, the Rochester Area Presidents Group, the Upstate New York College Collaboration). A number of other groups, including five colleges in New Mexico[92] and four in Indiana,[93] have recently announced that they are following this strategy as well.

There is much at stake in these endeavors to control costs while maintaining independence and keeping campuses open. It can be devastating at an individual and a community level when a college closes. Judson College in Marion, Alabama, 185 years old, closed in 2021 after dropping down to 145 enrolled students, then filed for bankruptcy protection, leaving debts unpaid and the small town without a centerpiece.[94] Similarly, the 2021 closing of Becker College in Worcester, Massachusetts, which traced its origin back to 1784, included the laying-off of over three hundred employees.[95] However, there are also many barriers to consolidation and merger, including legal challenges by employees and alumni (as discussed in Chapter 5 with respect to Mills College), the regulatory challenges of having accreditors and states approve the changes, and the fundamental challenge of finding a willing partner or set of partners and working out the legal structures necessary to carry out the plan.

Conclusion: College Is Still a Good Deal . . . for Some

This chapter has considered fundamental matters pertaining to the sustainability of higher education as it is currently financed, the implications of financing challenges for IHEs, and the contribution of the lawyerization of higher education to these challenges.

Fundamental changes in the way IHEs do their business, ranging from how they interact with accreditors to how they compete with each other for admissions, have led to increased consumer sovereignty. Meanwhile, the federal government has turned an ever-closer eye on what IHEs are doing, scrutinizing and publicizing how they produce their "product" of degrees, whether they are successful in graduating students and granting their degrees, and what those degrees earn their holders. This has also potentially increased the power that students and their families have in the marketplace for degrees, putting additional pressure on institutions that seem impecunious, incapable of graduating most students in a reasonable amount of time, or that produce degrees that do not raise their holders' earnings considerably. The discipline of lawsuits combined with increased regulation have reined in the for-profit sector considerably. The result of all these changes appears to be a dampening of the rise in the cost of college and a flattening-out of the amount of newly issued student loan debt. However, students who do not graduate or who get a less valuable degree can end up burdened with debt payments, leading to public support for at least some level of debt forgiveness.

The current size of the sector in terms of the number of individual independent institutions seems unsustainable, but numerous factors make it difficult for IHEs to find merger partners or close gracefully and for public higher education sectors to shrink. Nevertheless, the process is occurring, and the pace may well quicken further over the next decade. We see a harbinger of shrinking and consolidation in both the for-profit sector and the public sector as well as changes in the proportions of two-year versus four-year institutions. However, the process may be more graceful than doomsayers have predicted, with potentially few outright closures and more mergers occurring and integrated networks forming. Such actions can be handled gracefully if managed correctly, with the aid of legal counsel.

Amazingly, while the big wave of college creation is definitely in the past, new enterprises continue to be founded. Two new enterprises of some note are Minerva University, a small residential college that rotates its students between dorms in several international cities while conducting all classes online,[96] and the University of Austin, the creation of which was announced in late 2021 on the basis of free speech, which immediately became controversial when several announced board members almost immediately quit.[97] New institutions tend to aim to fit some potentially underserved or novel segment, much as it is hard to believe that there could be underserved areas given the number of existing institutions. It is this very resilience and quest for innovation that gives one hope about higher education and also makes higher education able to withstand significant existential challenges, as we will see in Chapter 7.

Chapter 7

Crisis Comes to Campus

So many of the issues that we have discussed so far in this book have been critical to the operation of institutions of higher education (IHEs). But often, issues are slow to brew and develop over weeks, if not months or years. Particular inflection points happen when new regulations are announced or bills are passed, but their effects on IHEs may still take time to develop and give campus administrators time to adjust to them, as well as provide advance notice generally of their implementation date. However, administrators must also be on constant alert for fast-breaking matters and be prepared to deal with emergencies on an almost daily basis. Many of these issues have legal ramifications and require careful attention from counsel, both while they are in progress and subsequently. In this chapter, we consider these dynamics, both when they affect an individual institution and when they affect more than one institution.

Individual institutions, particularly those with high enrollments and large campuses, are likely to experience fairly regular crisis situations, during the academic year in particular. These range from situations affecting one or more individuals associated with the university, such as suicides, accidental deaths, assaults, and threats or scares, to situations involving damage to university property, such as fires. While these may be viewed as "routine," their effects on campus cannot easily be predicted, and even well-prepared campuses may not be able to withstand the negative effects of these incidents without experiencing financial and reputational damage.

A localized set of institutions may also jointly experience crises related to weather or other disasters, such as damage from hurricanes, tornadoes, flooding, earthquakes, or wildfires. Hurricane Katrina created such a situation in 2005 for institutions in New Orleans. Some places, such as Puerto Rico when Hurricanes Irma and Maria struck in 2017, have had their entire educational systems disrupted by natural disasters, and others, like Syria and Ukraine in recent times, by human disasters such as civil war or invasion.

There are also crises that all institutions must prepare for, even though only some will experience them. These include cyberattacks and bomb threats, such as the Accellion file transfer application data breaches in 2020–21 and a series of bomb threats at more than fifty Historically Black Colleges and Universities (HBCUs) in 2022. The role of insurance in mitigating these issues, but also in adding to the burden of management, needs discussion in this framework.

And finally, systemic crises may affect institutions across the world in times of war, natural disaster, and epidemics. Thus we also investigate in this chapter the legal and regulatory impacts of the COVID-19 pandemic in 2020–23 on higher education, with a particular focus on those legal and regulatory issues related to the pandemic that are likely to have a lasting impact, including impacts on shared governance, institutional downsizing and force reductions, online learning, and the use of online technologies for hearings or investigations in areas such as Title IX.

Many of the concerns addressed in this chapter reflect themes from preceding chapters, including the pressure on colleges to merge, issues of student wellness, and matters of financial viability leading to lay-offs and program closures. One question is whether regulation and litigation make it harder for institutions to react quickly and effect-ively to crises and to subsequently recover. On the flip side, has gov-ernment intervention actually saved institutions that have faced crises that were not of their making? We examine these two possibilities in more detail below.

Management during Times of Crisis

As mentioned above, in any academic year, IHEs as a group experi-ence a large range of crisis situations. No wonder administrators gen-erally breathe a sigh of relief when the summer comes! While college administrators routinely prepare for emergencies, including reviewing their handbooks regarding what to do when they occur and even run-ning simulations of various types of emergencies, when something actually happens, it is rare that everything proceeds according to script.

A large issue during unfolding crises is information management. Administrators grapple with what information to share with the gen-eral community and when to share it. Maintaining confidentiality can become an issue in both directions, as in what should be maintained and what needs to be told to the community as well as the timeliness of communications. For example, if a student's death is reported on campus, administrators generally wait to release information until they get confirmation of the student's identity and the exact facts of the situation, and take into consideration the input and wishes of the family so as to avoid any reporting errors. A mistaken identity case in 2006 involved a fatal car crash in which several Taylor University students died, but one was sent into a coma. At the scene, the students' college IDs were mixed up, leading to the mistaken identification of one student as dead who was actually in the coma, and vice versa.[1] But in the meantime, the rumor mills on campus may already start flying through word of mouth and social media, including asking why the authorities have not yet sent notice.

While this is normally just an "inquiring minds want to know" situation, sometimes there may be a more pressing matter, for instance if a perpetrator is still at large on campus. While the Clery Act addresses timeliness of notification, it could potentially be a matter of minutes or hours in situations where there might be a live shooter. In the 2007 Virginia Tech mass shooting case, Virginia Tech was faulted for not moving quickly after the first two shootings occurred, as two hours transpired between those killings and the later ones. The first campus mass shooting occurred at the University of Texas at Austin in 1966, and since then, there have been eight more such shootings (mass shootings defined as four or more dead), including four since 2012.[2] More recently, in 2021, one student was killed and seven wounded at Grambling State University; another shooting occurred the week before;[3] in 2022, three students were killed and two wounded at the University of Virginia;[4] and in 2023, three students were killed and five wounded at Michigan State University.[5]

On the other side, any perceived or actual breaches of confidentiality or inappropriate sharing of personal information could also lead to subsequent legal action. This could include issues of mistaken identity. At Wesleyan University, a shooter came on campus in May

2009, just as the school was about to celebrate its spring concert day. The shooter, who had been stalking a particular student ever since attending summer school with her at NYU, shot her at the campus bookstore café where the student was working behind the counter. The shooter then disappeared from the scene, causing the shutdown of the campus during the search for the shooter. A supposed photo of the shooter, Stephen Morgan, was shared widely over the media as the search progressed—although the photo turned out to be that of a Cornell University sociology professor (now at Johns Hopkins) by the same name. Professor Morgan subsequently sued Wesleyan, claiming humiliation, mental anguish, emotional distress, and injury to his career;[6] the suit was settled, and the university apologized to Professor Morgan.[7]

Sometimes, as was discussed in Chapter 3, the legal issues can center around what the university knew in advance concerning employees or students. In 2010, Amy Bishop, a biology faculty member at the University of Alabama in Huntsville who had not received tenure, entered a department faculty meeting and opened fire, killing three of her colleagues and wounding three others.[8] Two of the deceased faculty members' families subsequently filed wrongful death lawsuits against the university and the provost in particular for negligence; the suit was dismissed on the grounds that the provost did not know beforehand that Bishop was mentally unstable.[9]

The most notorious campus mass shooting may be the 2007 Virginia Tech massacre where undergraduate Seung-Hui Cho killed five faculty members and twenty-seven students and wounded seventeen others (another six were injured by jumping out of windows to escape) before taking his life.[10] Afterward, the investigation discovered numerous issues with how the situation was handled beforehand and during, but Virginia Tech was ruled not liable on appeal from a wrongful death suit brought by two of the students' families.[11] Federal privacy laws meant that Virginia Tech did not know about Cho's prior mental health history before he enrolled, and the university would not release his school medical records to the investigation panel, although it eventually did so. Similar to the Bishop case, the ruling was that Virginia Tech did not have sufficient information beforehand or during the event to have been able to prevent the killings. Subsequent legislation in Virginia required its IHES to establish threat assessment teams, and after the mass shooting at the University of Virginia in 2022, additional legislation was passed requiring timely action by such teams in obtaining, evaluating, and turning over to law enforcement complete criminal and health records of individuals deemed to be a potential threat.[12]

The tradeoff between real or perceived rights to know certain information and real and perceived rights to privacy is salient across these cases. In general, it appears that universities receive the benefit of the doubt regarding their responses to crises when they act reasonably and in good faith. Moreover, while there is a variety of guidance addressing a plethora of crises, there is no federal requirement that universities prepare for crises in any specific way. As we will see in the next section, IHEs have also been beneficiaries of Federal Emergency Management Agency (FEMA) funds for the COVID-19 pandemic crisis and natural disasters as well.

Systemic Crises

While any individual campus can experience one or more crises in a given academic year, sometimes a set of schools fall victim to the same situation. While being in miserable company generally does not make it any easier for each school to deal with the situation, it does make it possible to see the variety of responses to the situation and to learn a wider set of lessons from it. Just as with individual crises, these systemic crises can lead to changes in how institutions set up best practices as they learn from other schools what they need to do to be prepared to withstand crises. Systemic crises may also have larger effects on college insurance rates and coverage. Given that many of them are natural disasters, IHEs may be less impacted by principles of tort law than in individual crisis situations where tort law may apply more directly in particular jurisdictions to the individual crises and their legal aftermath.

Natural disasters can run the gamut from minor storms causing power outages, property damage, and flooding to significant disruptions from major storms. It may be that climate change is increasing the likelihood of such incidents. For example, in September 2021, Hurricane Ida caused significant damage in the Gulf of Mexico region and along the Northeastern coast, forcing several universities to close due to excessive rain, flooding, and tornado warnings. Some IHEs closed briefly, while others, including Tulane University, stayed closed for up to a month.[13] Wildfires in Oregon in September 2020 caused some disruptions to activities (in part due to diminished outdoor air quality) at the University of Oregon in Eugene but did not close the campus.[14] IHEs also serve as local shelters for communities affected by natural disasters; for instance, in the fall of 2021, a tornado destroyed neighborhoods in Bowling Green, Kentucky, near Western Kentucky University, and the university provided internet access, power, resting space, and showers for free to affected local residents.[15] Accredited IHEs in areas declared as subject to a presidentially declared major disaster with a public assistance clause are eligible for FEMA funding. This funding can be used for repairs of damaged facilities and provision of temporary classroom facilities to replace the damaged ones so long as insurance payments were not also provided for the same reasons.[16]

Sixteen years before Hurricane Ida, Hurricane Katrina struck New Orleans full-on in August of 2005. It is still the costliest tropical cyclone on record, tied with 2017's Hurricane Harvey.[17] Katrina devastated large swaths of New Orleans and drastically affected the local IHEs. Students had to be evacuated or sheltered, and classes were disrupted for some time afterward. The University of New Orleans managed to resume classes after forty-two days but suffered enrollment declines.[18] Dillard University, whose campus suffered severe flood and fire damage, closed for the semester and had to house its returning students the following semester at local hotels and hold classes at other campuses and at hotels.[19] Many New Orleans students were temporarily housed as provisional students at other IHEs, and not all returned. Tulane University laid off thousands of employees and took advantage of the crisis to do a wholesale restructuring of its programs, including cutting twenty-seven of its forty-five doctoral programs and suspending eight of its teams.[20] Tulane also dissolved its coordinate system, creating a single undergraduate college, Newcomb–Tulane College, rather than continuing with both Tulane College (for men) and H. Sophie Newcomb Memorial College (for women). The academic restructuring and layoffs at Tulane and other area universities drew significant criticism and attention from the American Association of University Professors (AAUP),[21] and the dissolution of the coordinate system brought a suit from the heirs of the founder, Josephine Louise Newcomb, which was ultimately unsuccessful. This idea of using a crisis situation to effect structural change in an institution has not gone unnoticed, and Tulane's president at the time, Scott Cowen, subsequently wrote a book about transformational leadership that discussed this period as well as other salient actions from his Tulane career.[22]

A more recent and even more systemic (as in island-wide) disaster was Hurricane Maria's effect in September 2017 on a number of Caribbean islands, including Dominica and Puerto Rico.[23] The hurricane killed over three thousand people and knocked out Puerto Rico's electrical power grid and the vast majority of its cell and cable networks. One month later, most of the power had still not been restored. As with the Katrina disaster, many US IHEs offered to take in students displaced from universities in Puerto Rico, including the University of Puerto Rico system. Coming on the heels of student strikes in the spring of 2017, these dual blows were highly disruptive to the university system in Puerto Rico, and a year later, most campuses had not fully recovered, including research programs, which were extremely disrupted.[24]

But natural disasters are not the only types of systemic crises to affect IHEs. Other crises are clearly human-caused and can disrupt sets of schools at the same time, which may or may not be able to coordinate an appropriate response to these disruptions. One example is the series of bomb threats directed at HBCUs during the early part of 2022. Over fifty-nine threats, none of which involved an actual device, were experienced in this wave by over one-third of HBCUs, starting in January 2022 and including eighteen threats on February 1, as Black History Month began.[25] In each case, the affected campus took the threat seriously and generally closed or locked down its campus in response, disrupting classes and other campus activities. On March 16, 2022, at which point no arrests had been made, the White House announced, among other actions, that funding would be available from the Education Department's Project School Emergency Response to Violence program. This funding could be used for enhanced security and targeted mental health resources, among other uses.[26]

Cybersecurity attacks are another growing area of crises for IHEs and other institutions. In December 2020 and January 2021, supposedly secure servers operated by technology company Accellion were breached and thousands of files captured. The Accellion breach affected numerous companies, governments, and IHEs, including the University of California, the University of Colorado, the University of Miami, and Stanford University.[27] Some schools reportedly paid ransom to the Clop ransomware gang (named after the website on the dark web where the gang would post files to show that they had accessed them), which was partially shut down when members were arrested in June 2021 in Ukraine.[28] Accellion reached an $8 million settlement for the December 2020 breach.[29] Ransomware attacks continue to occur, even though not all affected institutions reveal them. The University of Utah was one of the first schools to reveal that it had paid a ransom (of over $450,000) when it lost files with student information to a cybergang in July 2020.[30] Not surprisingly, cyberinsurance premiums have gone up substantially over the last few years, implying that more IHEs are paying ransom even if they are not going public with those payments.

A bigger crisis is when entire computer systems are closed down rather than simply files compromised. A number of community colleges were cyberattacked in this way in 2021, possibly because they, being poorer systems, have weaker defenses, but they also have cyber insurance through the government to pay for ransom.[31] Howard University was cyberattacked in September 2021 and had to cancel classes for several days while it brought its systems back online.[32] Lincoln College claimed a cyberattack in 2021 was directly responsible for its final decision to close in 2022; the attack affected its admissions and fundraising systems and took several months to recover from, at which point projections for enrollment were too negative for the college to stay open.[33] Overall, cyberattacks against IHEs appear to have risen since 2019 and are now staying steady at this higher level,[34] with the average total cost of an IHE data breach estimated at $3.9 million.[35] On top of the direct costs of dealing with the cyberattack and any possible ransom paid, colleges can also end up being sued by those whose data has been compromised: Hope College, Knox College, and Mercer University were all hit with multiple lawsuits in 2022–23 for negligence regarding the safeguarding of personal data after they suffered computer system data breaches (and, in Mercer's case, for lack of timely notification of the breach).[36]

While we cover the COVID-19 pandemic and related litigation and regulation in the next section, it is worth noting that health crises predate the pandemic even as they have had generally more limited effects on IHEs. IHEs are natural breeding grounds for multiple communicable diseases, given the close residential quarters and social events occurring on campuses. While many IHEs require a range of vaccines before a student can enroll, they vary on this front, and not all of them require all possible vaccines. One disease of significant concern for the traditional college-aged population is meningitis (more formally known as serogroup B meningococcal disease). A number of IHEs have experienced significant outbreaks of this disease,[37] particularly before the vaccine was approved in 2015 but also subsequently, including seven cases at the University of Oregon in early 2015, where one student died.[38] Generally, universities hold emergency vaccine clinics if a case is reported and inform the general student body that there has been a case. At Ohio University, a student died of meningitis in 2010, and her family sued on the grounds of negligence, wrongful death, and breach of standard of care: the university was aware of other cases on campus right before she contracted it but did not inform the student body, and the university's health center did not diagnose her correctly.[39] Ohio University settled in 2015 for $1 million.

Disputes over making the meningitis vaccine a requirement for college students provide a precursor to the types of debates over vaccine requirements that were seen in the COVID-19 pandemic. Before the serogroup B vaccine was approved in 2015, there were other meningitis vaccines that provided more limited protection against bacterial meningitis. While vaccine requirement controversies were not as widespread in the early part of the century as they are now, there were already hints of pushback. After a Texas A&M student died from meningitis in 2011, his parents pushed to have all college students vaccinated, but others were opposed to this vaccine mandate;[40] nevertheless, the mandate passed, and now all students must show proof of a meningococcal vaccine to enroll in Texas state schools unless they qualify for an exemption.[41]

The COVID-19 Pandemic

Referring to the COVID-19 pandemic, J. P. Morgan's CEO Jamie Dimon said, "The word unprecedented is rarely used properly . . . this time, it's being used properly. It's unprecedented what's going on around the world."[42] While we see that there are precedents of crises on campuses, the pandemic is nonetheless notable for leaving no campus untouched worldwide and for the duration of the disruption. It is also notable for the range of regulation that was imposed on IHEs, how that regulation varied from locale to locale (particularly by state), and for the amount of related litigation.

While initial cases of COVID-19 were reported in Wuhan, China, in December 2019, US IHEs gave it little note in the first few weeks of 2020, going about their usual busy schedules, even as the first US case was noted on January 13. In February 2020, the first inklings of a significant issue started to appear, with reports of infections occurring on both coasts. Starting with its first case on March 1, New York City and later New York State became an initial epicenter, with high rates of hospitalization and deaths, including high rates of incidence in nursing homes and other elderly care facilities. New York declared a state of emergency on March 7, and on March 12, all SUNY campuses were ordered to close within the next week and to shift to online for the rest of the semester.[43] On March 20, a statewide stay-at-home order was declared, and all nonessential businesses and gatherings had to close down. The stay-at-home and school closure order was subsequently extended, with phase one of reopening not beginning until May 15, and schools ordered to stay closed for the remainder of the school year.

We experienced this sequence at our institution after the World Health Organization designated the COVID-19 outbreak as a pandemic on March 11, the Wednesday before the beginning of spring break week. We asked all students to take what they would need to continue coursework home with them for the break but told them they could leave the main part of their belongings on campus, as we still hoped at that point that we could reopen. But by the end of the break, the New York shutdown order had been enacted. We pivoted to remote learning immediately after spring break week, a pattern followed by most other institutions, as similar orders occurred in other states.

Subsequent to these very similar initial reactions, states and university systems enacted varying regulations. In New York, we had to file a comprehensive fall semester reopening plan over the summer that detailed how we would provide a safe environment for our students, including regular testing, sanitizing, dedensifying classrooms and dormitories, having a plan for quarantining sick and exposed students, and requiring face coverings. In other states, legislatures refused to allow masking in classes. Some state systems, notably the California State University System, decided to stay remote for instruction and to keep their campuses closed for most functions, although researchers were generally allowed to return to their offices and labs. Some private colleges similarly decided to remain remote, and some stayed remote for the whole 2020–21 school year, while others opened in the spring of 2021.

Campuses that were open experienced significant outbreaks but low hospitalization and death rates, as traditional college-aged persons tended not to get as ill as older persons, and campus faculty and staff generally took precautions. In some states, campuses were barred from requiring students to wear masks and less social distancing occurred; many large university campuses had particularly significant outbreaks, but almost all campuses had at least some cases.

Vaccines were developed on a rapid timeline and started to become available in late December 2020. Each state developed a rationing system for who could get vaccinated first, with most states favoring health care workers, first responders, residents in nursing homes and other care facilities, and older adults. In New York, college professors became eligible in late January 2021, as all teachers were considered essential workers. In a subsequent round, many of our student workers became eligible by virtue of their jobs on campus, and as of April 2021, all persons aged sixteen and above were eligible. We hurried to get our students to the vaccination facilities, arranging for their transport; and later held vaccination clinics on campus.

Once vaccines became more widely available, the debates began on campuses about whether or not to require that students and employees be vaccinated. In some states, public institutions were barred from requiring vaccination, while in other states, vaccinations were required. Private schools varied when it came to requiring vaccination, with many religious colleges deciding not to require them. IHEs also varied about whether or not to allow various forms of exemptions.

Many if not most of the decisions that college administrators had to make during the pandemic were controversial. Faculty faced many governance decisions, ranging from whether to allow for tenure case extensions to whether to have grades during the spring semester of 2020. Debates were particularly fierce over the late spring and summer of 2020 regarding whether or not to reopen, whether faculty would have the choice to teach online or be forced to teach in person (we gave them the choice), and how we could guarantee safety on campus for all involved. Decisions had to be made about how to modify the 2020–21 academic calendar (many schools started later and/or ended earlier, often by dropping any breaks); what the COVID-19 testing schedule would be for students; how students would be housed; how classrooms would be dedensified; and, perhaps most controversially, whether or not to require vaccination and, if so, how to disenroll students and fire employees who did not comply. Athletic leagues mainly shut down for the year, and the National Collegiate Athletic Association circulated rules for reopening once sports started back in limited form in the spring of 2021.

Not surprisingly, many campus decisions led to litigation, although perhaps less than was initially predicted. A National Association of College and University Attorneys note in May 2020 suggested many possible grounds for suits, including landowner liability, negligence, and gratuitous undertaking, as well as concerns over violations of privacy, inability to provide reasonable accommodations, and breach of contract.[44] Somewhat amazingly, less litigation has occurred than was apparently expected at that early point in the pandemic. However, three main rounds of issues occurred: focusing on the initial shutdown and lack of reimbursement for the subsequent period of remote instruction; mask mandates and general safety concerns; and vaccine requirements.

The first major round of lawsuits concerned institutions' failure to rebate students fully for their interrupted spring 2020 semester. While many schools rebated room and board for the second half of the semester, most did not rebate tuition and fees, apparently on the principle that they were continuing to provide education, albeit through remote means. Following the actual closing of campuses in mid-March 2020, the earliest such filing appears to have been *Dixon v. University of Miami* on April 8, 2020, followed by *Church v. Purdue University & Trustees* on April 9. The majority of such suits were then filed between April and August 2020, but filings continued subsequently, albeit with a big drop-off after the end of 2020, with perhaps the latest suits being those filed in March 2021 against the University of Oregon and Oregon State.[45]

While it is not clear how many tuition lawsuits have been filed— some sites claim over three hundred,[46] but other trackers show around one hundred[47]—the vast majority are similar in nature. They are generally class action suits on behalf of students or a class of students (e.g., undergraduate students or students in a particular graduate school), based on breach of contract and/or educational malpractice. The breach-of-contract suits appear to have been more successful because it is hard to second-guess the quality of higher education; for an accredited institution, the implication is that the institution knows what it is doing.

While many of these lawsuits ran into unsympathetic courts pretty quickly, others have been allowed to proceed, and a number have settled. In December 2020, the motion to dismiss the suit against Rensselaer Polytechnic Institute was denied.[48] In March 2021, Southern New Hampshire University settled for $1.3 million[49] and Barry University settled for $2.4 million;[50] by May 2022, the University of Tampa settled for $3.4 million[51] and Lindenwood University for $1.65 million (about $185 per affected student).[52] In November 2021, Columbia settled its suit for $12.5 million, the largest amount to date.[53] In March 2021, the suit against Quinnipiac University was allowed to proceed, although the parents who were part of the initial suit were not allowed to continue on the grounds that they were not directly affected even if they had provided part of the tuition payment. In this case, the judge pointed out that Quinnipiac had previously been charging less for online courses than for in-person courses, and that it had touted the advantages and additional resources available to on-campus learners, all of which were now not available;[54] the suit was settled in December 2022 for $2.5 million.[55]

In general, suits were more successful if they focused on sections of the IHEs' promotional materials and/or student handbooks that touted the specific advantages of residential learning. In *Barkhordar v. President & Fellows of Harvard Coll.* (D. Mass. Mar. 1, 2022), the court found that marketing statements related to the on-campus experience of students at Harvard College "were too 'vague and generalized'" to be "contractually enforceable," but that "school-specific language from websites, syllabi, course catalogs, and other sources" specific to Harvard's Law School, Graduate School of Education, and School of Public Health were "sufficient to allege a reasonable expectation of in-person instruction and programming" in the spring of 2020.[56] Meanwhile, the university system in Michigan prevailed in February

2022 after going through both appeals and claims courts because the courts found that there was no clear contractual language promising in-person instruction.[57] By the summer of 2023, most cases had been resolved, including several large universities (Colorado, Delaware) creating settlement funds for affected students.[58]

College mask mandates and social distancing requirements received less challenge in court but have been issues in some states between college officials and legislators and/or governors. In August 2021, former governor and current Wisconsin system president Tommy Thompson said that the Wisconsin system would instate mask requirements in defiance of the legislature's requirement that all COVID-19 mitigation measures, such as masking, first be submitted to a legislative committee for review.[59] The Idaho legislature passed a bill in February 2022 prohibiting mask mandates in public entities, including schools and universities.[60] Moving in the other direction, the University of Oregon graduate teaching fellows were concerned about being required to return to in-person teaching in early 2022 even when local COVID-19 prevalence rates were still high, and they filed an unfair labor practice complaint with the state's employment relations board.[61]

A subsequent round of suits was related to the lawfulness of IHEs' vaccine requirements. For example, two students at Santa Clara University sued in March 2022 over the school implementing a vaccine requirement deadline only after tuition was paid for the semester.[62] Fewer of these suits have occurred, with the universities prevailing so far, such as Rensselaer Polytechnic Institute, where a suit brought by three students in January 2022 was dismissed by April.[63] Other suits involved vaccine requirements for university employees; Michigan State University prevailed in one such case, as the judge did not find the argument compelling that persons with natural immunity from a previous infection should be excepted from the policy.[64] As of the pandemic's declared end date of May 11, 2023, few universities were still requiring either original or booster vaccine shots, and the pandemic's official end has made such requirements—and accompanying complaints, including actual and threatened lawsuits—generally moot.

Other governance challenges stemming from the pandemic have related to the restructuring of some IHEs, including dropping numerous adjunct contracts and some terminations of tenured faculty, where the IHEs claimed the restructures were necessary to mitigate the financial impact of the pandemic but did not go through the process of declaring financial exigency and involving faculty in the restructuring decision-making process. As mentioned in Chapter 5, the AAUP investigated eight IHEs, including several of our neighboring schools in upstate New York, and found that they had flouted academic norms, creating serious negative impacts on shared governance at their institutions.[65]

Another trend that numerous commentators predicted at the beginning of the pandemic was that COVID-19 would cause many schools to close, with numbers between one hundred and one thousand mentioned.[66] In fact, between March 2020 and January 2021, only ten colleges closed, several of which had already planned to be taken over by another school before the pandemic began.[67] Indeed, a number of schools that had been running structural deficits for some time found themselves running a surplus for their 2020–21 fiscal year, thanks to the federal government's Coronavirus Aid, Relief, and Economic Security (CARES) Act funding for higher education as well as the paycheck protection plan for smaller employers that led to forgivable loans for employers who kept their workforce on during the pandemic. IHEs could also file for reimbursement from FEMA for a number of their COVID-related expenses, including rental of quarantine space and health center costs. Indeed, it appeared that by the spring of 2022, the higher education labor force, which dipped considerably during the pandemic, had almost recovered to its prepandemic level,[68] somewhat mitigating faculty's employment concerns, if not their concerns over weakened shared governance.

Conclusion: Crises Are to Be Expected and Included in Campus Planning Processes

One of the themes of this chapter is that any college administrator, particularly any president or general counsel, should assume that a significant crisis will occur during their tenure. Indeed, most sitting presidents and general counsels as of this book's writing have had to guide their institution through all or part of the COVID-19 pandemic, and many have experienced other crises during these last few years as well. Some of these crises are somewhat exacerbated by governmental intervention, including requirements for additional paperwork and reporting, but others are somewhat mitigated by governmental financial and logistical support. Some are also amplified by related litigation, which, even if unsuccessful, involves time and effort by both counsel and administrators while the litigation works its way through the legal system.

Much of what is covered in this chapter is very personal to us, as we guided our institution through the pandemic. We also experienced a cybersecurity attack as one of the institutions affected by the Accellion data breach (although we managed to avoid paying any ransom or having our files leaked on the dark web, we did have to notify our employees and vendors of the data breach). In addition, we have both experienced many other examples of the crises discussed in this chapter, including accidental deaths and suicides on campus, a live shooter situation with a full campus shutdown (the Wesleyan incident discussed above), and a campus closure due to a storm knocking out power on campus and the surrounding area for days. In each case, we were grateful for the campus crisis protocols and the level heads of those in charge of the campus community.

Given that crises are bound to occur at some point, it behooves counsel to plan for how to manage those situations and be an active partner in on-campus planning processes regarding emergency preparation, management, and recovery. This is a key part of the general set of strategic roles for counsel that we explore further in Part 2 of this book. Similarly, presidents and other college administrators should incorporate counsel in their planning and management processes in anticipation of the need to interpret regulations related to crises and of forestalling or mitigating any crisis-related litigation. As we have seen in this chapter, crisis-related litigation runs a wide gamut, although certain themes emerge, including negligence, privacy, breach of contract, and failure to follow due process. These themes will arise in other areas of the general counsel's purview as well, along with a number of others. We will turn to a fuller articulation of counsel's purview in the following two chapters.

· II ·

THE NEW ERA OF
CAMPUS COUNSEL

The second section of this book considers how the narrative developed in Part I concerning legal developments over the recent past can be addressed proactively. We lay out our understanding of the roles of general counsel and in-house counsel more broadly in addressing and dealing with both the legal and broader systemic and economic trends and challenges discussed in the preceding chapters. We also sketch out a general strategy for understanding how colleges and universities should use legal counsel, as well as tactics for applying that strategy to the evolving legal issues that colleges and universities are likely to face next. Overall, this second section advances the principle of the importance of building a full legal strategy into operations rather than viewing legal matters as somehow separate from fundamental university governance. The rising tide of legal matters and their direct impact on institutional missions necessitates that counsel be more directly integrated.

Chapter 8 examines how colleges and universities might best respond to the legal trends and headwinds facing higher education through the strategic use and deployment of general counsel or in-house counsel more generally. Chapter 9 considers the institution-specific considerations related to using and staffing a campus legal function. In other words, it addresses the question of whether in-house counsel makes sense for a given institution and in so doing discusses the constraints on this choice imposed by factors like institutional resources, professional ethics, and industry-wide best practice. Finally, Chapter 10 is both reflective and forward-looking and considers the tensions exposed in the first half of the book by prognosticating on what is on the legal horizon for colleges and universities and how the multiple legal forces of regulation, legislation, and litigation may cause continued strains as they potentially collide with institutional missions in the years to come.

Chapter 8

Counsel as Strategic Institutional Partner

We have detailed a long list of issues and accompanying laws and regulations that affect institutions of higher education (IHEs) and have made the case that the challenges and costs of dealing with these external forces on IHEs have increased significantly over the past ten to fifteen years. However, our goal in this book is not simply to delineate and substantiate these matters but also to provide a general approach for leaders and counsel of IHEs to follow so they can work to mitigate any negative effects of regulation, legislation, and litigation on their institutions' fundamental missions and amplify positive effects. Toward that end, we argue for a strategic approach based on the appropriate use of in-house (or possibly dedicated outside) counsel.

In what ways are in-house counsel at IHEs in a unique position to aid their IHEs as they navigate the rapidly evolving legal terrain discussed in the first part of this book? What specifically can in-house counsel do at their IHEs to help steward them through such issues? In this brief chapter, we attempt to answer these and related questions.

Throughout this chapter, we hope to show everyone, whether inside or outside higher education, how the role of general counsel actually works so as to demystify this position and illustrate this important part of the day-to-day running of IHEs.

This chapter is written under the presumption that a given campus has made the decision to hire a general counsel and considers how best to use this role. It discusses both the technicalities of what a general counsel is as well as relevant tenets of professional ethics that guide an in-house lawyer. This chapter also addresses the strategy and tactics of deploying in-house counsel to deal with the various issues addressed in this book and facing higher education at large. The question of whether the move to in-house counsel actually makes economic sense for an institution is discussed in greater detail in Chapter 9, along with how to structure such a relationship. By examining the recent contours of the in-house counsel dynamic at IHEs, this chapter builds the case that effective in-house counsel underpins both operational effectiveness and strategic excellence at IHEs of all sizes. Further, this chapter makes the case that for the vast majority of institutions, maintaining an in-house legal function, when possible, is optimal for confronting the challenges facing IHEs in the future.

What Is a General Counsel?

A general counsel is the institution's chief legal officer, the professional tasked with leading and managing legal affairs of the institution. But a general counsel is often much more than simply the "head" of legal affairs. Robert Iuliano, longtime general counsel at Harvard University and now president of Gettysburg College, eloquently describes a general counsel as "an integrator of strategy, law, policy, and values" and as someone who "helps the president see around corners."[1]

A good general counsel, Iuliano says, "takes into account multiple perspectives, not just the law, and integrates issues across a broad domain that includes not only legal advice but also institutional advice" more broadly.[2]

Structurally, a general counsel is a member of the president's cabinet or senior staff and reports directly to the president. By virtue of the standards of professional responsibility and general principles of corporate law, a general counsel may also have a reporting relationship and ethical obligations to board leadership. This relationship may be either formally recognized or simply implied by virtue of these professional standards and legal principles. For our purposes in this chapter, we presume that, consistent with widely adopted practice, general counsel are "in-house." By that, we mean that they are paid directly by the institution as an employee of the institution and do not operate on a fee-for-service basis. As the chief legal officer, a general counsel not only serves as an institution's counsel of record but, practically speaking, functions as the main source of legal counsel and the first point of contact on legal issues for the president and senior leadership. The general counsel may delegate matters to other lawyers who may be used to represent the institution in a particular capacity, either because of specialty area expertise or workflow. The economics and practicality of this outsourcing are discussed in more detail in Chapter 9.

The legal affairs that are overseen and managed by a general counsel are multidimensional. Broadly speaking, "legal affairs" refers to any matters that may give rise or have given rise to liability or risk in a legal sense. On a campus, the matters that constitute legal affairs, as demonstrated by the preceding seven chapters, are almost endless.

Most obviously, the legal affairs of an IHE include threatened and pending litigation. This includes active management of pending cases and strategic decision-making in concert with the client in those cases. It would also include strategic mitigation, prevention, and assuagement of so-called threatened litigation. This includes situations in which an institution receives a formal demand letter, or situations in which the institution is simply dealing with a party that is threatening a lawsuit or invoking legal protections or processes. This area of work includes counseling the client on the path of avoiding litigation of a particular matter. Where litigation is unavoidable or inevitable or has been determined to be the path in the institution's best interest, this work includes counseling on how best to strategically position the institution to defend against potential claims.

Tangential to pending or threatened litigation, an institution's legal affairs also often touch on the various processes for dispute resolution on campuses. This includes both formal avenues for dispute resolution and internal disputes more broadly. Faculty grievance matters, student conduct and disciplinary hearings, Title IX matters, and other process-laden policy-based pathways that involve the settling of differences—either between two members of the IHE community or between a community member and the institution—are areas that potentially give rise to legal liability and thus require the work and guidance of counsel.

These types of matters have multifaceted legal components. On their face, they present plainly as matters subject to possible future litigation and in that sense are of obvious interest to counsel, but under the surface, there is nuance in the various components of potential legal claims that might be at issue. As such, these matters may require policy and process advice to mitigate potential contractual claims, statutory or regulatory compliance advice, or generalized advice meant to help guide the sort of conduct that might be considered reasonable or rational on the part of the institution under the circumstances. In total, this area of the counsel's work—counseling in prelitigation dispute resolution and dispute processes—requires a tremendous amount of sound judgment and comfort in navigating the many gray areas inherent across the substantive areas of law touching on higher education. It also requires an acute awareness of institutional values. While engaging counsel proactively in these areas is of great potential benefit, at many institutions, this is not standard practice, which we touch on further below in our discussion of preventive law practices.

The work of managing and leading legal affairs also encompasses guiding the institution through the legal issues rife within institutional business transactions. This category of matters would encompass the conventionally understood work in this area pertaining primarily to matters of contract. However, for a higher education lawyer, this category of work could be more broadly interpreted as including matters relating to the creation or unwinding of relationships that involve the negotiation of rights, responsibilities, and risks assumed by the institution. On the more conventional side, general counsel on campuses are involved in matters such as real estate deals, bond financings, and negotiation of service or purchasing contracts with large vendors. Moreover, this work corresponds to well-defined substantive areas of legal practice and expertise. However, campus counsel are often pulled into other areas that are less well defined in a legal sense but that nonetheless invoke legal concepts and obligations or liability calculations on the part of the institution. Memoranda of understanding between institutions or schools and departments within the institution, facility use agreements, partnership agreements, creative joint ventures with local or regional municipalities or other institutions, and similar arrangements that speak to the apportionment of responsibility, risk, and obligations among parties may also all heavily involve in-house counsel.

In addition to litigation-related work, dispute resolution more broadly, and so-called transactional legal work, a significant portion of the general counsel's efforts typically includes providing advice and counsel to client-colleagues who may simply be navigating a complex issue or challenge that has legal, regulatory, or risk undertones. This advice and counsel may be tangential or directly related to a specific piece of litigation, formal dispute, or transaction, but often, these consults can be slightly more detached from a specific project or legal task. A general counsel supports their client through this work by providing analytical clarity and strategic guidance on these sorts of "one-off" issues that are couched within a broader backdrop of legal considerations. For example, a client may be struggling with how best to approach an upcoming sensitive conversation with an employee or colleague or may be seeking advice and strategies on aligning with regulatory changes or deviations from stated policy. Colleagues may seek out general counsel for a listening ear and as a proactive and engaged problem-solving partner in dealing with such issues. Brian Casey, a lawyer and president of Colgate University, reflected to us in this regard that "having someone local, someone who knows the place and who you can call for counsel is invaluable."[3]

In many ways, the work of a general counsel at an IHE encompasses giving advice and counsel on matters that may not fit neatly into a specific subject area box when viewed from a traditional legal perspective. The client is often also considering pathways of action that involve weighing the values and mission of the institution alongside varying degrees of legal risk either by implication or hovering in the background. Lawyers, and particularly those in higher education, cannot be blind to the realities that lie beyond the blackletter law. Indeed, the Model Rules of Professional Conduct contemplate this when they instruct that "in rendering advice, a lawyer may refer not only to law but to other considerations such as moral, economic, social and political factors, that may be relevant to the client's situation."[4] Skilled counsel know that an overly simplistic and bifurcated yes or no answer, when one is even possible, can be unhelpful and that clients are often not making decisions in a "vacuum." A skilled general counsel knows their client's industry, understands their client's values, and provides holistic advice within this context.

The Higher Education "Client" and Legal Ethics Considerations

Long-standing general counsel José Padilla has aptly stated that the pace and complexity of the legal issues on campuses require the general counsel to keep their "head on a swivel."[5] General counsel at IHEs may on the same day be providing legal advice to the director of a disability services center about an accommodations request, a provost about an issue related to a tenure case, a procurement coordinator about a contract, or a department chair about a matter related to the conduct of a faculty member in that department. In each case, the general counsel must be clear about who, specifically, is the client.

Who is the general counsel's client, technically speaking, and why should one care? In a purely legal sense, an IHE is not unlike any other client that presents itself in a corporate form. In this regard, the lawyer's rules of professional conduct related to an "organization as client" are instructive.[6] Generally speaking, the organization itself is the lawyer's client. Under the Model Rules of Professional Conduct, the lawyer "represents the organization acting through its duly authorized constituents."[7] So while the organization is the client, the client acts through its duly authorized representatives such as the president, senior leadership, trustees, and sometimes faculty in certain capacities. When these roles are carried out in their official and authorized capacity, they embody the client, with the highest level of the client being the governing board.

Several high-profile legal matters in the last ten or so years illustrate this principle and help draw out some of the tensions it can present. Regarding the situation at the University of Rochester that we discussed briefly in Chapter I, in response to an Equal Employment Opportunity Commission (EEOC) complaint filed by several faculty members related to allegations of sexual harassment by Dr. Florian Jaeger, the university's board of trustees formed a special committee to investigate the allegations against the university in the handling of the matters referenced in the EEOC complaint. The special committee of the board engaged Mary Jo White of Debevoise & Plimpton to conduct an "independent investigation of the allegations."[8] In addition to the underlying allegations in the EEOC complaint against Jaeger and the university, White's investigation was intended to review university policies, procedures, and "any other related matters as the investigation may uncover that, in Ms. White's sole judgment, should be addressed in her report."[9] In this situation, White's client was clearly the University of Rochester. However, in this case, the client manifests through the select, isolated, "special" committee of the university's board of trustees. The university emphasized that White was "entirely independent of the University, the Administration and the Board of Trustees, the complainants and the defendants."[10]

Such assurances of independence, however technically sound, can sometimes be called into question, often by those under investigation, those disappointed by the outcome of an investigation, or the media more generally. This was the case in a similar situation at Baylor University where, in response to allegations of rampant, systemic mishandling of Title IX–related matters, Baylor's board of regents retained an outside law firm to conduct "an independent and external review of [Baylor's] institutional response to Title IX and related compliance issues through the lens of specific cases."[11] The findings of the investigation eventually led to the resignation of Baylor's president, Kenneth Starr, and Baylor's football coach, Art Briles. Baylor's then-athletic director, Ian McCaw, who later took a position at Liberty University, directly attacked the independence of the investigation, accusing several Baylor regents and Baylor's general counsel of touting "skewed" facts that were "misleading" with regard to the overall issues facing the university.[12] The higher education press has similarly scrutinized such investigations.[13] Stories such as these emphasize an ancillary principle familiar to seasoned general counsel: that a sense of independence can be bolstered when a law firm that is hired for a nonroutine, high-stakes investigation does not also represent the institution on other routine matters.

Simple as it may seem, the rule of the institution acting through its duly authorized representatives is nuanced with a few twists specific to institutions of higher education. It is important for the institution's lawyer to clearly identify the institutional actor who is acting as the client for each and every separate matter or issue on which the lawyer is working. Even the smallest higher education institutions by enrollment can be surprisingly vast horizontally and vertically structured enterprises, with a variety of individuals holding dispersed authority over specific pockets and corners of the institution and interacting with different subcontractors and other entities and individuals. Higher education is a world of presidents, vice presidents, and directors—familiar corporate titles. But it is also a world of provosts; deans; department chairs; committee chairs; coaches; clergy and other individuals with professional ethics constraints; an enormous variety of staff and instructors, both full-time and part-time; and many volunteers, some who are alumni and some who are community members. In this institutional climate, the reasons why it is critical to identify who, specifically, embodies the client at a given time are twofold but interrelated.

First, the rules of professional conduct require that a lawyer clarify the identity of the client "when the lawyer knows or reasonably should know" that the institution's interest is adverse to that of the person interacting with the lawyer.[14] For example, though simplistic, in the case of a lawyer involved in an employment matter where an employee's interests are adverse to those of the institution, the lawyer would typically be representing the institution by virtue of authorized representatives in the human resources office or the president or their designee. As such, if the lawyer is having a conversation with the specific employee involved—or those near that employee that may be implicated in the matter—the lawyer should make clear that they represent the institution, through its duly authorized representatives, and not the individual. In the Baylor example above, for example, it is clear that the interests of the football coach or athletic director may have diverged from those of the university overall given the substance of the allegations under review.

The second reason why it is critical to identify the client at all times relates to maintaining what lawyers refer to as "privilege." To encourage transparency between a lawyer and the represented party in service to the lawyer serving their client most effectively, certain communications between a lawyer and client may be deemed "privileged."[15] This means, in general, that the client and the lawyer cannot be compelled to produce the substance of such "privileged" communications by a court of law or other authority.[16]

There are many nuances to the privilege doctrine, but to understand the implications for higher education, a few general principles suffice. Chiefly, to preserve a communication as privileged, it must be conducted between an attorney and their client to obtain (and give) legal advice.[17] Privilege can be deemed by a court to have been waived when the substance of the communication has breached the confines, inadvertently or otherwise, of both the lawyer and the client.[18] Hence the second reason why it is critical for a general counsel to identify at the outset of giving legal advice precisely who is the client: privilege will apply only to communications for purposes of legal advice with the client, and disclosure of the substance of communications—whether written, oral, or other otherwise—could result in a finding that privilege has been waived.

A noteworthy case related to issues of legal privilege in higher education involves the University of Minnesota and a tenure dispute. Dr. Calvin Kobluk was an assistant professor of veterinary medicine whose path to tenure was complicated by multiple complaints of misconduct.[19] The university ultimately denied Kobluk tenure.[20] Following the denial of tenure, Kobluk sought to use a Minnesota statute to compel production of early drafts of his tenure denial letter that had circulated between the university counsel, and their client, the provost.[21] Kobluk argued that these early drafts of the letter were designated as privileged "simply to gain the protection of the privilege," and not because they involved giving and receiving legal advice.[22] The court agreed with Kobluk on the blackletter principle that "an otherwise unprivileged, preexisting document does not become privileged upon delivery by the client to the attorney."[23] Ultimately, however, the court held for Minnesota, finding that the drafts were circulated to give and receive legal advice, and finding no instance in which the assertion of privilege over the draft letters could be said to have been waived.[24] Nevertheless, cases like *Kobluk* are a reminder to in-house counsel and their clients to be wary of allegations that privilege has been waived. Knowing definitively the institutional actor who is the client and reminding the client of the importance of not waiving privilege can be key.

A distinct but related and equally important concept for higher education clients to be aware of is confidentiality. Administrators, faculty leadership, trustees, and others acting in their authorized capacity on behalf of the institution should view their general counsel as a trusted confidant. Not only may conversations related to legal advice be deemed by a court to be privileged but lawyers are also bound by professional ethics rules to keep information shared with them by a client strictly confidential. This means not sharing the information with anyone beyond the person or persons acting on behalf of, or as, the client on the particular matter—no spouse, partner, friend at the watercooler or gym. For a president, board, administrator, or faculty member dealing with a thorny issue with legal implications, having this confidential resource can be invaluable.

The nuances of clearly identifying the client for purposes of preserving privilege and ensuring confidentiality also pertain to matters related to or involving the president of an institution where the formal "client" might be considered the institution's governing board. For example, in the case of alleged misconduct on the part of the president where such allegations require investigation, the general counsel's client becomes the board of trustees. Similarly, though perhaps less obviously, where the institution is negotiating terms of employment related to the president, the lawyer's client is again the board of trustees. The rules of professional conduct governing attorneys provide some direction in both of these circumstances. Both examples are situations where the board is generally the only manifestation of the institution "duly authorized" to take action. Moreover, both of these examples illustrate situations in which the institution's interests may diverge from those of the president.[25] Typically, a board in these situations will act through the board chair, another authorized board officer, or a designated and authorized committee or subcommittee. When only a subset of the board is authorized to deal with a particular matter, privilege and confidentiality issues can become more difficult to navigate. This can be exacerbated in situations that involve a high degree of media attention or public scrutiny, though in such cases, a privileged and confidential briefing for the entire board may be warranted.

Another legal ethics principle worth noting relates to a lawyer's duty to refer matters to a "higher authority" within an organization.[26] To paraphrase, under the model rules of professional conduct, this duty to refer to a higher authority applies in the situation where a lawyer knows that "substantial injury to the organization" is likely to result from an officer, employee, or someone else affiliated with an organization acting or intending to act in a manner that violates a legal obligation to the organization, or otherwise engages in a violation of law that might be imputed to the organization.[27] In such a situation, the lawyer "shall proceed as is reasonably necessary in the best interest of the organization."[28] This includes referring the matter to "higher authority in the organization, including, if warranted by the circumstances, to the highest authority that can act on behalf of the organization as determined by applicable law."[29] This duty to refer the matter remains the lawyer's obligation "unless the lawyer reasonably believes that it is not necessary in the best interest of the organization to do so."[30]

The often-nebulous hierarchies and ubiquitous "fiefdoms" across higher education institutions can make the principles of the model rule related to referring to higher authority difficult to apply in some situations. This is particularly true at larger institutions with multilawyer offices of general counsel where lawyers are integrated into project-based work that may be several levels deep in an institution. In such an environment, discerning the appropriate authority to which to refer, or the appropriate avenues for referring, might be less clear. Moreover, at institutions of all sizes, while reporting up the chain is at times ethically required and must be conducted with the utmost seriousness, it may be interpersonally fraught or politically challenging. The dilemmas for in-house counsel created by this rule at smaller, less hierarchical institutions can be abated somewhat where a single in-house lawyer primarily works directly with the president and other senior leadership, but challenges nonetheless persist.

General Counsel as Institutional "Guardian"

The sum of the ethics principles discussed above, the doctrine of privilege, and the evolving modern role of higher education general counsel as counselor and advisor more broadly equate to the reality that beyond the operational and functional duties of the general counsel, the role also entails serving as a sort of institutional "guardian."[31] That is to say, the general counsel is by virtue of professional responsibility and ethics at all times focused on the best interests of the institution over any of its individual actors by way of the legal and governance backbones of the institution that ensure its perpetuation.

It is not unusual in higher education to see general counsel serving lengthy terms at IHEs. Often, the term of a general counsel will traverse multiple presidential administrations and board chairs. This happens not simply because counsel may "know where the bodies are buried." Primarily, and more precisely, it occurs because the work of general counsel requires stability and consistency, and the person in the job can easily become a sort of institutional glue, the corporate guardian, and, as we argue explicitly and by implication throughout this book, an institutional *steward* that at once can marry pervasive legal and governance concerns to the mission, values, and operational realities of an institution in a fashion that provides stability and consistency over the long term.

The "guardian" concept as applied to the general counsel function appears initially to have been coined by Ben Heineman. Heineman joined General Electric (GE) corporation in 1987 as its first general counsel and is known as one of the "godfathers" of the in-house counsel movement.[32] Based on his years building the in-house function at GE, Heineman argues that the seminal challenge for general counsel "is to reconcile the dual—and at times contradictory—roles of being both a partner to the business leaders and a guardian of the corporation's integrity and reputation."[33] This tension for general counsel, though perhaps less acute, is no different in the world of higher education. Higher education institutions are not immune from institutional actors at all levels who may, under pressure, reasonably look for short-term gains that may come at the expense of the ideals and values of an institution. At the nexus of the president and senior leadership, the governing board, and the broader campus faculty and staff community, general counsel at IHEs must be adroit in identifying and navigating situations that pit short-term gains, real or perceived, against the integrity, reputation, and values of an institution. As the legal and governance resource, general counsel is typically the final backstop. While general counsel must be creative and collaborative problem-solvers, they must also provide crystalline clarity to their client about the boundaries and requirements of the law. Anything less poses near-term risks and longer-term harms to the integrity of the institution.

Heineman's conception of general counsel continues a step further by arguing that general counsel address questions of not only whether a proposed course of action is legal but also whether it is in fact the "right" thing to do more broadly for both the entity and the society at large that the entity is serving.[34] Applying this to higher education and building it out further, general counsel in higher education grapple not only with the question of "is it legal" but also with the question of whether an institutional course of action squares with the institutional mission and higher education's values writ large.[35] This view directly echoes the sentiments of Colgate's President Casey, who shared the view with us that IHEs in today's legal environment cannot allow themselves to get mired in technicalities but should also focus on "adhering to what we think is right to do. That's always the best path."[36]

In our view, when properly engaged, resourced, and deployed, general counsel are in fact key stewards of the educational mission. Much as the faculty are the agents charged with stewarding the academic core's existence forward, so is the general counsel the agent charged with stewarding the institution forward through the broader sea of legal, compliance, and risk challenges facing modern higher education. Where the mission of IHEs is to pursue truth and convey knowledge, it is the job of the general counsel to steward this mission through the many varying legal shoals and risks that may threaten its highest and best manifestation. The first part of this book laid out the legal realities facing IHEs in great detail. Institutions cannot face these realities blindly and cannot do so alone. So, in essence, the general counsel also becomes a guardian of the institution's mission.

Proactively Deploying the General Counsel:
Preventive Lawyering

So how can general counsel serve to keep an IHE on a steady path, given all the challenges ahead? One of the key movements of late in the world of higher education legal practice has been the focus on so-called preventive law. The concept of preventive law, or preventive law practice, is characterized by a focus on proactivity as opposed to reactivity. Preventive law practice seeks to engage campus communities on the potential for various legal and risk matters ideally before such matters become emergent problems for the institution.

The concept of preventive lawyering in higher education was explicated and popularized in a 2003 article in the *Chronicle of Higher Education* by Kathleen Curry Santora and William Kaplin. Citing the ever-expanding legal terrain for IHEs, Santora, longtime CEO of the National Association of College and University Attorneys, and Kaplin, law professor and coauthor of the leading treatise on the law of higher education, articulate their view that preventive lawyering "allows an institution to manage legal issues systematically, without overreacting or shifting to a crisis mode every time a complaint is lodged or a lawsuit is filed."[37] Moreover, preventive law, they argue, "encourages administrators, faculty members, and students to work together, and it reduces the likelihood of adversarial relationships among people both on and off the campus" as well as the likelihood of litigation.[38] Donica Thomas Varner, vice president and general counsel at Cornell University, mentioned in a conversation with us that she sees preventive lawyering as a key feature that assists IHEs in dealing with today's "increased regulatory obligations and compliance obligations" and noted what she perceived as more "appreciation for the role of in-house counsel as a way of proactively managing . . . risks."[39]

In light of the first half of this book and the robust acceleration of legal issues for IHEs in recent years, what does preventive law look like in practice today? Specifics obviously vary among institutions based on size of the institution, strategic priorities, and size and expertise of the legal unit or division, but a few broad principles surely apply.[40] Namely, a general counsel—or their staff attorneys at larger institutions—must stay abreast of current legal developments and provide timely information to members of the campus community about developments that may impact their area. While outside firms and vendors often use such updates as business development opportunities, general counsel are in a unique position to tailor preventive advice to specific institutional actors. Any attorney can write a synopsis of a recent case, but with a detailed understanding of the structure, people, and resources of a client and their campus workings, in-house counsel are in a unique position to relate the nuance and potential impact of a precedent-setting case to those affected on a particular campus in a way those particular institutional actors can meaningfully act on.

Staying abreast of current legal developments also means proactively working to consider how to modify existing policies to address legal, regulatory, and risk developments. An impactful case or new statute may drive changes to practice or behavior, but in-house counsel should also be looking at how these developments affect stated policy and whether changes to stated policy are required or would be meaningful. At smaller institutions, the general counsel is often viewed as the institution's "chief policy officer." Many general counsel, campus paralegals, or other members of the legal team's staff serve as a resource for policy centralization and standardization to the extent possible. General counsel must know which institutional policies apply to a given scenario, how they apply, and the implications. A staff member with a studied view of the institution's policies can reduce overall risk by ensuring policy accessibility and consistency.

Another key aspect of preventive lawyering involves serving as an internal resource for expanded educational opportunities related to legal challenges, risks, and constraints facing the institution. Just as the law is constantly evolving, so, too, do lawyers and their campus partners need to refresh their knowledge of specific legal and regulatory constraints that come to bear on their work. While "trainings" in the broadest sense have largely been delegated to prerecorded training modules, in-house counsel can provide an additional layer of practical pedagogical insight. In-house counsel can meet with specific departments, divisions, or administrative decision-makers in a setting that gives material typically covered in a "training" a more specific and personalized focus.

The reality of today's legal and regulatory climate, as put on full display in the first part of this book, could lead one quite reasonably to believe that the actual work of preventive lawyering is a rainy-day luxury; the "summer project" that is often aspired to but rarely comes to fruition. With today's demands on time and attention and the flurry of legal developments, it can be difficult for in-house counsel to focus adequate energies on preventive lawyering in its highest form. In resource-constrained institutions in particular, this sentiment can perhaps be even more acutely felt. But many IHEs simply cannot afford to make the perfect the enemy of the good, and so they do what they can with what they have. In such a situation, preventive lawyering at its best involves, and indeed requires, a spirit of collaboration, engagement, and partnership with the campus legal function. This often must be proactive on the part of counsel. "One of the things I've been doing," General Counsel Varner told us, "is going to each of our schools and colleges and meeting with the deans and the deans' cabinet and also the major business units and saying, 'what does the future look like for you?'"[41]

As we discuss further in Chapter 9, part of the actual economic value of in-house counsel derives from the fact that campus counsel simply knows their client so well. The corollary of this, hopefully, is that the campus-client knows and fully uses their attorney. Preventive lawyering, at its best, involves proactively engaging with the legal function early and often, not simply to "check the box" but also to ensure that legal issues are considered and, hopefully, mitigated as part of overall institutional strategy.

Conclusion: Use of General Counsel Improves the Likelihood of Safe versus Sorry

While the use of in-house general counsel does not mean that all legal challenges and risks facing the institution will be effectively managed, it does improve the probability. Preventive law in particular holds the promise of mitigating various factors in advance of a crisis situation and reducing the number of lawsuits filed against an institution, as well as reducing the impact, financial and otherwise, of those lawsuits that are filed.

The challenge, of course, is to make sure that prevention does not mean inhibition of those activities on campus that are fundamental to serving the IHE's mission. Prevention cannot be synonymous with bans or the muzzling of challenging voices on campus or activities that carry risks but also have significant promise of adding to the educational function of the IHE. For example, it would be unfortunate if study-abroad activities were significantly curtailed because of the risks involved in travel, or if campus activities for precollege students were dropped because of the risks of having minors on campus. This may be where presidents, provosts, and other academic leaders of the IHE must work carefully in concert with counsel to make sure such functions are supported and that the educational benefits of somewhat risky actions are weighed against the potential costs that can come from unrest or litigation.

The number of IHEs moving to the use of general counsel has increased over the past decade as more schools come around to the view that they are a good institutional investment. As we discuss in Chapter 9, there are many ways in which general counsel can operate, and there are more or less effective ways to implement the general principles articulated in this chapter. Nevertheless, having a strategic legal partner close at hand is becoming an indispensable part of the modern IHE administration's tool kit for managing the many challenges faced on campuses.

Chapter 9

Institutional Considerations for Campus Counsel

We hope that up to this point, our book has confirmed what both casual and expert commentators have observed of late: that the range and complexity of legal issues facing institutions of higher education (IHEs), and in turn their general counsel, have seen remarkable growth and expansion in recent years.[1] The publication *Corporate Counsel* summed up the recent trends for in-house counsel at IHEs by calling them "staggering."[2] Hamilton College president David Wippman, a former law professor and law school dean, shared with us in conversation: "I do think we're in a much more legally sensitive environment than we were even ten or fifteen years ago."[3] The legal and regulatory headwinds facing IHEs led a commentator in the Canadian publication *University Affairs* to remark that in the current climate, "it is difficult to comprehend why boards or leadership teams of organizations as complex as universities would not want to avail themselves of the expert leadership of a [general counsel]."[4] This chapter considers the full contours of this statement related to using and staffing a campus legal function.

More specifically, this chapter addresses the question of whether hiring and retaining in-house counsel makes sense for a given institution from an operational perspective. In so doing, this chapter discusses the parameters of the general counsel function as constrained by factors like institutional resources, the professional ethics principles discussed in Chapter 8, and industry-wide best practices, and examines how these considerations meld with the operations of IHEs. While Chapter 8 focused on how in-house counsel actually operate as lawyers by focusing on the legal ethics and best practices of the role, this chapter considers in more detail how general counsel and in-house lawyers operate within an IHE and how they add value from an institutional operations perspective. While this chapter may seem more like "inside baseball" than the preceding ones, we think it is important to concretize our points and provide clear consideration of the costs and benefits involved in expanding or "in-housing" this role on campus. It also serves to document the increased role of lawyers on campus, even as we are actively advocating for such a role, in large part to counter effectively against outside lawyers who approach the institution either as adversaries or regulators.

The Evolution of the General Counsel Role on Campuses

The creation of general counsel positions at IHEs is a fairly recent phenomenon. While it does appear that attorneys had been hired on campuses in noncentralized and very specific capacities before the 1970s, the first general counsels at American universities seem to have arrived on campuses around 1969–70.[5] Stanford appears to have added its first general counsel in 1969.[6] Harvard's first general counsel, Daniel Steiner, inaugurated the role at Harvard in 1970,[7] followed closely by Princeton in the early 1970s.[8] The University of Pennsylvania hired its first general counsel, Stephen Burbank, in 1975.[9] The noted jurist Hon. Jose Cabranes served as the first general counsel of Yale, also beginning in the mid-1970s, before his appointment to the federal bench.[10] The National Association of College and University Attorneys (NACUA) was founded in 1960, and since many universities did not start adding general counsel until the late 1960s, one can assume that its early membership must have consisted largely of external lawyers working at law firms who counseled IHEs.[11] There is literature suggesting that, before the period beginning around 1960, much of the legal work of IHEs had been done as acts of charity or volunteerism, usually by members of a governing board or friends of the institution who were practicing lawyers.[12]

Interestingly, the proliferation of in-house counsel roles across the corporate sector is also fairly recent, having apparently originated in the 1970s as well.[13] For the corporate sector, according to one observer, the move toward hiring in-house counsel was "a large counterreaction to the dominance of large private law firms."[14] While this is perhaps also the case for many IHEs that added general counsel around this time, the evidence that the addition of general counsel at IHEs was an explicit counterreaction to domineering outside legal advisors is less clear. As we elucidated in this book's introduction, at least one explanation for why IHEs specifically began hiring their own in-house lawyers seems to have been rooted in an amalgam of factors including the expansion of federal legislation bearing on the workings of IHEs: specifically, the increased recognition of civil rights and individual liberties following the civil rights movement and the resulting shifts in relationships between individuals—including students—and IHEs and the proliferation of private rights of action in federal statutes.[15] However, if the addition of general counsel to IHEs was not a direct response to the existing relationships with outside law firms at the time, a resulting implication certainly has been an altering of the relationships between outside law firms and IHEs, as we explore in more detail below.

In the decades since this initial arrival of general counsel at only a few of America's largest and most well-heeled universities in the 1970s, the number of in-house lawyers working at IHEs has significantly increased, with the number increasing even more over the past ten to fifteen years.[16] General counsel—often supported by small armies of attorneys, paralegals, and support staff—can now be found at nearly all large or midsized universities, both public and private. By 1985, the total number of members of NACUA was 2,400.[17] By 1997, that number increased modestly to 2,762.[18] By 2022, the total number of members of NACUA was 5,050, of which 3,849 were exclusively in-house counsel.[19] While a significant but minority percentage of NACUA's members are highly trusted outside counsel who specialize in providing services to IHEs, NACUA's current CEO, Ona Alston Dosunmu, reflected a sentiment that we had also suspected: that while there exist many great higher education lawyers, what NACUA has seen is that more and more institutions "are bringing . . . legal expertise in-house," unless cost or specialization are barriers.[20]

Smaller institutions have also begun hiring general counsel over the past ten to fifteen years, a trend that has been well noted by search firms, hiring consultants, and college presidents.[21] In a January 2020 article on the rise in general counsel positions, the search firm Russell Reynolds observed that it had "seen a spike in top liberal arts colleges starting to consider or actively creating this new role."[22] Another search firm in 2016 noted that, "confronted by the same complex legal, social, risk and safety issues that exist at universities, American colleges are recognizing that it is often essential (and not a luxury) to have an experienced General Counsel as part of the senior leadership team."[23] Hamilton College president David Wippman reiterated a similar sentiment, stating that he thinks adding a general counsel to campus leadership teams will "become more and more common" as "more schools are headed in that direction."[24]

A conversation with Stephen Burbank, Penn's first general counsel and one of the first general counsels at an IHE, added considerable insight to our understanding of the evolution of the general counsel role for IHEs. Burbank opened up about adding a lawyer to the administrative ranks of one of America's elite universities in the mid-1970s. He was hired, as he said, because Penn's president, Martin Meyerson, valued raw intelligence more than he did experience.[25] "It was insane for them to hire me," Burbank added in our conversation with a smile.[26] Burbank's comment is in part self-deprecating charm that belies his impressive credentials: he joined Penn at the youthful age of twenty-eight with impeccable bona fides, including graduating first in his class at Harvard Law School and clerking for, among other distinguished jurists, the chief justice of the United States. But his comment is also suggestive of how much the general counsel role has evolved and how much more specialized and professionalized the field of higher education law practice has become at IHEs. What is now a vast field of higher education law practice with stratified networks of professionals at various levels of their careers seemingly began with a handful of America's elite universities plucking lawyers they trusted from careers elsewhere to help guide their institutions. As Burbank noted in our conversation, early general counsel "didn't have the luxury of being specialized" because they were dealing with all the university's problems singlehandedly in a novel and evolving practice.[27] While certainly possible, it is hard to imagine an expansive and elite university today hiring a lawyer fresh out of a clerkship with no prior experience counseling IHEs as its chief legal officer.

From the conversation with Burbank, one also gets the sense that adding a general counsel to the administrative ranks of the university at the time was a bold move, albeit a much needed one. Burbank recounted that when he arrived at Penn, "lots of problems came tumbling out of the closet," which was likely the case for most universities at the time.[28] This was in part, he indicated, because many administrators were reluctant to seek advice from outside counsel and so were eager to seek advice from their new colleague on campus. Seemingly, campus demand for legal services at the time was swelling, and he was there to address this demand. However, his new accessibility as a resource to administrative colleagues on campus came with its share of mixed perceptions about having a full-time lawyer on campus. When asked about how he was viewed on campus as a new member of the administration, he remarked on being viewed as a new "whipper-snapper" wielding "much perceived power."[29]

Burbank's experience in this regard would likely still ring true today on many campuses. While we obviously contend that any positive benefits of adding campus counsel outweigh any negatives—particularly in light of the legal realities outlined in Part I of this book—we would be remiss if we did not call attention to a set of obvious pinch points worthy of institutional consideration related to adding in-house legal counsel to campuses where the function does not already exist. If not handled adroitly on such campuses, adding a lawyer to campus operations can have significant interpersonal implications among staff colleagues, as with any new position. Given existing stigmas and stereotypes related to the legal profession or skewed perceptions as to the seemingly new need on a campus for a "full-time" lawyer, institutions should also be mindful of related misperceptions among the community at large. What's more, among their new colleagues, new campus counsel no doubt will have to deal with the usual internal obstacles of institutional fiefdoms and various spheres of influence as they seek to embed a preventive legal ethos across the institution. This work sometimes entails a broader cultural shift. In that regard, the disposition and emotional intelligence of the general counsel are important factors.

When integrating into a new campus community, campus counsel must work hard to develop a reputation as a trusted resource and valuable campus partner and should be supported by their institutions in so doing. We should be clear about what general counsel, or in-house lawyers in any form, are not. In-house counsel should never come to be seen simply as an administrative "yes" person or as a simple instrument of the president or governing board. Interestingly, this appears to have been a problem since the first universities started adding general counsel. "The lawyer may be good cover," Burbank said in our conversation, as "they will come to you for cover."[30] General counsel—attorneys writ large—give legal advice. They are not intended to act either as a rubber stamp or as an administratively contrived obstacle to a project or overall institutional progress.

A somewhat confounding phenomenon emerging since the advent of general counsel on campus is that while the range and volume of purely legal issues facing IHEs have increased, so, too, have nonlegal responsibilities accumulated for campus counsel. This is true to the point that general counsel on a number of campuses find themselves wearing "multiple hats," either formally or informally.[31] This trend is not a particularly new one, and its origins were observed by practitioners as early as the 1980s.[32] "When a field of professional specialization expands as ours has," wrote University of Michigan general counsel Roderick Daane, "going from non-existence to a pervasive campus presence in only twenty-five years, some uncertainty about professional roles is inevitable."[33] Across campuses today, general counsel and their offices take on a variety of projects in service to their institutions. As President Wippman observed, a legal background is "really helpful training [for] senior administrative roles . . . it encourages a structured thinking process, you tend not to jump to conclusions, you look for evidence."[34] Marvin Krislov, president of Pace University and former general counsel at the University of Michigan, echoed this sentiment. "Academia places a lot of value on process in its governance," said Krislov in our conversation, "and people with legal training are generally well-prepared to deal with that."[35]

In some instances, campus counsel even formally take on or evolve into other coadministrative roles such as oversight of human resources, strategic initiatives, chief of staff, chief operating officer, executive vice president, or similar functions.[36] These additional roles are not impossible for campus counsel to assume, but they should be taken on with a measure of thoughtfulness and due diligence. In particular, these additional roles should be structured to avoid ethical or conflict issues related to the general counsel's work as an attorney, and to preserve the attorney-client privilege when providing advice.

The Economics of Insourcing Counsel

Before addressing the economics of insourcing legal services head-on, it is useful to note a few points about the legal services industry overall in the past several years. One observation is that while the legal services industry did in fact experience reduced demand following the

Great Recession, which in turn impacted the pricing strategy of law firms, the price for high-quality legal services has steadily continued to increase year after year.[37] Moreover, the COVID-19 pandemic, to the surprise of many early prognosticators, was a time of significant revenue and profit increases at many firms. This is thought to be due in part to a combination of reduced operating expenses and increases in demand across certain practice areas for some firms.[38] Competition for talent at law firms, situated in the environment of heightened profits, has amplified the "salary wars" among law firms, with first-year associate pay—the pay for those with no experience and just out of law school—now topping $215,000 at most of the top firms.[39] All of this is simply to say that legal services are not cheap.

How can an IHE gauge in financial terms whether hiring a general counsel, or insourcing legal operations more broadly, makes sense for the institution? In our view, there are four primary ways to consider this question: (1) an analysis of the cost of insourced legal advice as compared with outsourced legal advice, (2) an analysis of what an IHE is avoiding spending as a result of insourced legal operations, (3) an understanding of savings by large risk avoidance, and (4) understanding of the various efficiencies gained by in-house counsel and outside counsel workflow integration.

Analyzing the actual cost of insourced legal advice as compared to outsourced legal advice is easy to do and has been touted by many observers of the IHE general counsel function for some time as indicative of the value-added of in-house counsel.[40] To get a sense of the cost of in-house legal counsel as compared to outside legal counsel, one need only consider the sum of the cost of the insourced counsel in terms of salary, benefits, administrative support, and other overhead and divide that number by some reasonable amount of hours worked in a year. For example, assume a salary and benefits of

$250,000 for a general counsel; administrative support of some sort (whether the full-time-equivalent of one position or a shared position) to the tune of $75,000; and technology, supplies, continuing legal education and licensing, and other sundry overhead of $25,000, for a total of $350,000. Now, assume the general counsel works forty hours a week for forty-eight weeks throughout the year for a total of 1,920 hours of work. The resulting cost per hour to the institution for the general counsel's time and support is $182. This compares very modestly to the average hourly billing rates of even junior attorneys at most outside law firms, which typically begin in the low $300s.[41] And thus if the institution were to use even half of an outside lawyer's time for a year, it would come out equal or ahead in cost by having a full-time in-house lawyer along with some additional internal administrative support for their service.

To that end, an institution could also look at the economics of insourcing legal services in terms of what it is instead not spending on such outside law firms and is therefore gaining back. To be even more conservative with our estimates, assume again that the general counsel works forty hours a week for forty-eight weeks a year. But let us further assume that of that time worked, only thirteen hundred hours, or just over five hours a day, is spent doing actual legal work that would be considered billable. The rest of the day is spent dealing with administrative and institutional service matters—that, incidentally, are also of value to the institution—such as hiring committees or general staff meetings, billing and insurance matters, community relations issues, and board of trustee matters, or on preventive legal work on which an institution would otherwise be hesitant to spend proactively. If the thirteen hundred hours of billable work were to be handled by an outside law firm using a mix of partners, associates, and paralegals at an average or blended rate of, say, $450, that would amount to a total outlay by the institution of $585,000 for legal fees. The thirteen hundred hours of inside legal work thus result in a net savings of $235,000 if one assumes the $350,000 of costs associated with an insourced legal function as discussed in the preceding paragraph. When one considers this math, it is not difficult to see why even the smallest institutions can end up spending several hundred thousand dollars in legal fees in even a largely uneventful year.

Another way to understand the positive financial impact that could accrue to an IHE by hiring in-house counsel is to consider the various efficiencies that stand to be gained in legal services workflows between and among in-house and outsourced counsel. These efficiencies have been observed and replicated in many sectors. Speaking generally of the legal services sector, the Bureau of Labor Statistics notes that the formerly prevailing model of one large law firm providing top-to-bottom legal services for a client has been replaced by a model "in which the services of a law firm are retained for a narrow, specific purpose, while the remaining legal work is split between the company's in-house attorney."[42] As one might expect, they note further that this model has been adopted "primarily to reduce costs."[43] Tangentially, these specific efficiencies, discussed in more detail below, are among the central reasons why institutions should reexamine relationships with outside firms in which a single firm performs all or most of the legal work for the institution.

The specific efficiencies to be gained when general counsel effectively engage and manage the workflow of outside counsel are numerous. For starters, and most obviously, when a campus's external legal engagements are centralized through general counsel, the general counsel can ensure the institution is outsourcing legal work only when absolutely necessary. To that end, a general counsel with knowledge of the legal services sector can also ensure that an institution is retaining external counsel at the ideal combination of competitive billing rates and level of expertise and skill required for a particular assignment or task. A general counsel can ensure that matters are not being "over-lawyered" and that they are being addressed by counsel with the specific expertise required, including the experience to handle similar matters.

There are also significant cost savings to be realized from efficiently managing active litigation handled by outside counsel. Litigation can be costly both in terms of actual legal fees and in terms of the amount of time and energy it can drain from other important institutional priorities. Centralizing litigation with a general counsel can reduce and more effectively channel this inevitable drain. An effective general counsel can provide proper direction, coordinate internal resources to respond more effectively throughout litigation, and organize internal decision-making at strategic points in the litigation. Rather than these processes burdening a president, provost, CFO, or similar officer, with the aid of general counsel, the internal distractions of litigation can be effectively cabined so that other senior leaders can focus on their "day jobs."

This relates to another operational efficiency of in-house counsel: they know their clients and their inner folkways in a way that can be somewhat impossible for external counsel, no matter how close they are to the institution. To this end, when a strategic decision point arises in litigation, the general counsel can organize the correct assemblage of internal decision-makers or other counselors, like communications professionals, and present these decision-makers with a suite of clear options and potential institutional impacts. Because of their extensive knowledge of the client, general counsel can more effectively tailor and deliver legal advice to the client and their relevant constituent parts.

Finally, we can also understand the value added by general counsel by examining savings to the institution in the form of large costs that are avoided. This notion is generally thought of in terms of litigation avoidance but can also be conceived of more generally. In short, the advice and guidance of in-house counsel in a situation can ideally lead to successfully avoiding escalation to litigation or even prelitigation dispute resolution processes that can be time-consuming and costly. Institutions save money on every iceberg they do not ultimately hit. In this regard, a general counsel or other in-house lawyer can end up paying for themselves several times over. A second way to conceive of cost avoidance, however, is by considering cost reduction over the longer term. Ideally, general counsel bends institutional costs downward over time through their work in reducing overall risk and engendering a more tactful, informed, risk-averse culture through preventive lawyering efforts.

It should be noted that there is an economic angle to the discussion earlier in this chapter related to general counsel or in-house lawyers wearing multiple hats at the institution or sometimes playing an expanded role. All work has its ebbs and flows in demand and times of the year that may be busier or less busy than others. To the extent that demand for legal services on a campus dips—though as of late, this would appear to be exceedingly rare—an institution can task its in-house lawyer with other projects or institutional initiatives, so long as those assignments are not ethically problematic. The optimized general counsel is a fully integrated team player. More broadly, however, in a general counsel, institutions gain yet another professional with highly transferable cross-disciplinary knowledge and skills. By virtue of the work most lawyers do, they gain strong substantive knowledge of other areas of the business and academic enterprise including human resources, finance, the governing board, insurance, risk assessment, student conduct, and myriad others. It is no surprise, then, that, as alluded to above, general counsel often takes on secondary titles related to areas ranging from chief of staff and strategic initiatives work to human resources and board governance. There is no shortage of work on any campus, and the general counsel can be, and often is, called on to fill the gaps.

Integration of an institution's insurance and legal functions can result in efficiencies that also bolster the financial case for insourcing legal counsel. Attorneys are generally not also insurance professionals; indeed, most general counsel will explicitly disclaim that they are giving specific policy coverage advice or opining on insurance as an insurance professional could or would. Such work represents a highly specialized area of practice that is more often than not outsourced to a coverage attorney when necessary. Nonetheless, general counsels need to understand the various insurance policies of an institution and the institution's benefits and responsibilities under such policies. This is important to ensure optimal coverage and to be sure the institution is availing itself of all of the benefits of such coverage. In concert with an institution's risk management office, general counsel should ensure that any benefits such as prelitigation credits or discounts for certain preventive work are being maximized by the institution and are incorporated into budgeting for legal services where possible. Insurers also take a keen interest in the types of matters institutions are dealing with and their status.[44] This is true even well in advance of actual litigation. It behooves general counsel to keep insurers abreast of certain developments as appropriate with the terms of insurance coverage, institutional policy and practice, and professional ethics. Solid working relationships with insurers serve institutions well particularly when an insurer retains the ability to choose outside counsel under a certain policy or when settlement discussions arise.

Conclusion: Insourcing Legal Makes Sense

The result of this chapter's analysis is the conclusion that IHEs would do well to think hard about their overall legal function and its integration with their overall vision: that legal operations will continue to evolve; that the general counsel when managed efficiently are tremendous added value; and, finally, that there are few circumstances under which an IHE would not be well served by hiring a general counsel. Such is the ultimate irony of the lawyerization of higher education: it is easier to join than to beat.

For the vast majority of IHEs, insourcing legal services and advice makes a tremendous amount of sense. An institution can perform some simple "back of the envelope" calculations to analyze the total cost of insourced legal advice as compared with outsourced legal advice on an hourly basis. An institution can also examine what the institution is instead not spending on outside counsel as a result of insourced legal operations on an hourly basis. Both of these measures can be useful as well in scaling the in-house legal operations. The significant savings to be gained by large risk avoidance should also not be ignored. Preventive lawyering and more sophisticated risk management practices integrated throughout campus operations lead to their own forms of savings. Finally, an understanding of the efficiencies to be gained by integrating the workflows of in-house counsel with knowledge of the client and industry and outside counsel with highly specialized narrow expertise is also a significant advantage to institutions. When the skills and experience of the in-house lawyers are appropriately titrated to the needs and financial realities of the institution, the advantages to the institution are significant.

Chapter 10

What to Expect Next

We have now concluded our whirlwind tour of recent trends in higher education and how they intersect with the realm of law. We have argued throughout that the degree of legal intervention into the inner workings of institutions of higher education (IHEs) has increased substantially over the past ten to fifteen years through the mechanisms of more direct governmental legislation and regulation and the growing reach of litigation involving IHEs, whether in the form of actual lawsuits or threats of lawsuits. We see no immediate end to this trend. It may be that increased legal influence and control over higher education was inevitable, given both the overall trends in society and the increased importance of the higher education sector in American life. However, we also consider countervailing forces that may lead to a rollback of some of the regulation and control over the sector.

In this final chapter, we present what we believe will come next for higher education as related to the topics discussed in Part I and our proposed approaches for addressing them through the judicious use of legal counsel as outlined in Chapters 8 and 9. Our discussion herein also includes various issues that we gave short or no shrift to in the preceding nine chapters, generally because little or no direct regulation or case law involving IHEs exists to date in these areas. However, we believe that these are areas in which we will soon see more interplay with our system of laws as they grow in importance, given the number of ways they imply increased liability for IHEs or increased calls for regulation as these areas receive more notice. These areas include increased collaboration with foreign entities, intellectual property disputes (including between foreign jurisdictions), increased private-public and private-private partnerships with non-IHEs on a variety of projects, and increased use of information technology to expand the reach of IHEs across time and space. We also consider the likelihood of significant changes in the degree and nature of governmental regulation and intervention in higher education's inner workings. We close with some thoughts on the theme with which we started this book: how the increased interaction of IHEs with the legal infrastructure affects their abilities to carry out their stated missions in service to the greater public good.

Further Extension of Governmental Control over Higher Education: What We Know That We Do Not Know

The next several years are likely to produce a continuation of the increased role of government control and oversight of matters that relate to the core functioning of IHEs. Specifically, we see future interactions between our system of laws and regulation and the higher education sector as largely being marked by a continued slide in the independence, autonomy, and deference traditionally owed to IHEs. Several, if not all, of the influential higher education and legal minds that we interviewed for this project echoed this theme. The decreased deference is also couched in an environment of "increased calls for accountability or increased interference," as Ona Alston Dosunmu, CEO of the National Association of College and University Attorneys, described it.[1] But whether driven by values and goals of increased accountability, accessibility, equity, transparency, market fairness, or other factors, there is no question that federal, state, and local governments will continue to exert control and shape the conduct of IHEs in the form of legislation and regulation.

While there is much law that is settled as it relates to higher education, there are many questions yet unanswered that we expect and in some cases hope will find resolution in the coming years. What follows is a review of what we know that we do not know, and that will require resolution by courts, policymakers, and IHEs in the future.

Our book began with a look at the legal structures related to civil rights enforcement on campuses. With regard to Title IX regulatory enforcement, the obvious theme in this area is the "pendular" nature of such enforcement's evolution and the possibility that this will continue in future presidential administrations.[2] The codification of more extensive regulations under the Trump administration was a significant step forward in terms of clarifying, with the power of regulation, the expectations of IHEs under Title IX related to sexual harassment. But not all agree on the substance and effectiveness of the regulations, and the proposed revisions to the regulations promulgated by the Biden administration have produced still more change. In the courts, there are several open questions related to nuances of the private right of action under Title IX, including circuit splits related to the deliberate indifference standard as well as questions of notice and

institutional control over the context of harassment as we have discussed in Chapter 3.[3]

Moreover, while *Bostock v. Clayton County* settled many questions
under Title VII with regard to discrimination based on sexual orientation and gender identity, and while these interpretations have been
extended by executive order to Title IX and in the Biden administration's revised Title IX regulations, codification beyond these points is
still unclear.[4] There appears to be increasing conflict between government regulations and religious colleges; for instance, the College of
the Ozarks was instructed to change its accommodations under the
Fair Housing Law to accommodate transgender students, leading to a
lawsuit.[5] State legislation in and around transgender athletic participation may also be poised for conflict with federal Title IX protections. Student activities other than housing and athletics may also be
areas of conflict between IHEs, students, and governments, such as
the 2023 finding against Yeshiva University to compel it to recognize
a student LGBTQ organization; the university canceled all student
club activities rather than comply with the order, leading the club to
pause its activities so as to let the other clubs continue to operate.[6]
Issues regarding transgender student rights as well as the rights of
other gendered (or nongendered) categories of students are likely to
be a significant area of civil rights expansion. Meanwhile, older forms
of discrimination and harassment such as antisemitism continue to
occur and may potentially even be on the upswing, including the complicated relationship of antisemitism to conflicting aspects of support for Israel, support for Palestine, and anti-Zionism.[7]

Regarding the Americans with Disabilities Act (ADA), there are
several areas of continued ambiguity to be grappled with, and potentially resolved, in the coming years. So-called invisible disabilities are
likely to continue to raise nuanced questions related to accommodations

in the classroom. The continued expansion of the use of technology in teaching and remote learning, particularly after the COVID-19 pandemic, will also spawn nuanced questions related to accommodations and accessibility of online programs.[8] The increasing number of states legalizing marijuana for recreational and medicinal purposes may also raise issues in this context, as marijuana remains classified as a Schedule I drug and subject to the Drug-Free Schools and Communities Act (DFSCA), so campuses cannot declare their campuses to be "marijuana friendly."[9] Students may hold prescriptions for marijuana use for the treatment of anxiety disorders, post-traumatic stress disorder, or other conditions that may impact an academic accommodation, which may force institutions to reconcile such use under the ADA with their obligations under the DFSCA. Finally, student mental health concerns are likely to continue to raise novel issues under the ADA[10] as well as with regard to tort liability.[11]

Issues of speech and expression on campuses as discussed in Chapter 2, particularly as they relate to notions of academic freedom, are also likely to continue to evolve. Courts will continue to grapple with the tensions that arise between free speech and federal statutes like Title IX or Title VII[12] as well as with issues created by spotty recognition among the circuits of an "academic exception" to *Garcetti*.[13] Relatedly, the institution of tenure writ large and its nexus to academic freedom is likely to continue to come under increased scrutiny, raising the question of whether now might be an ideal time for the American Association of University Professors to reexamine and perhaps update its standard-bearer 1940 Statement of Principles on Academic Freedom and Tenure.

The impact of newly formed external advocacy organizations related to free speech on campuses and academic freedom on campuses also remains to be seen. Organizations such as the Free Speech Alliance,

Speech First, and the Academic Freedom Alliance are still largely in their infancy but are beginning to emerge as formidable influencers in both the legal and academic debates around free speech and academic freedom and the wider culture wars around these issues. As questions around actions that "chill" speech, cancel culture in academia, and the interface of public (and private) speech with social media and other new technologies for spreading information widely and quickly are further litigated in the courts of law and public opinion, these organizations are likely to have an impact. This may be particularly true given that recent studies have shown an upward trend in faculty, students and others on campus who feel they may not be able fully to speak their mind without fear of reprisal from fellow students, colleagues, or the community at large.[14]

Chapter 3 examined several aspects of student life on campuses through the lens of institutional liability and risk, raising many unsettled questions for the near future. The overarching issue in this area is the seemingly evolving duty of care, which we have come to call the "caretaker era" for IHEs. Courts analyzing the tort liability of institutions in the caretaker era are called on to reconcile highly nuanced questions related to where lines of responsibility, authority, and control end and begin in today's higher education landscape. Where does a physical campus end and where does one begin in a world of increasingly porous campus borders thanks to factors like remote learning, on-site internships, and international study? What are the roles and responsibilities of parents, as opposed to institutions, in the lives of today's students? How do the increasing price of college and the increasing array of wraparound services that institutions offer to their students—ranging from mental health services to internships and career advice to recreational opportunities—change these relationships? The case law demonstrates an increasing likelihood of courts to find that IHEs owe duties of care to their students in light of these evolving facets of student life on campuses.[15] The area of intercollegiate athletics—one of those aspects of student life high-lighted in Chapter 3—is particularly ripe for evolution in coming years, with significant questions related to the status of "student" ath-letes, institutional liability, antitrust concerns, and the ability of stu-dents to profit from their name, image, or likeness, in need of quick resolution.[16]

In Chapter 4, we considered the legal and regulatory issues related to admissions, advancement, and community relations matters at IHEs. For admissions, much will depend on how IHEs react in prac-tice to the 2023 Supreme Court decision in the *Students for Fair Admis-sions* cases in changing their admissions processes and how other branches of government; for example, the Department of Education, craft guidance in response to this key decision. We will also likely see more clarity with regard to certain antitrust concerns related to ad-missions thanks to the pending lawsuit against the so-called Section 568 schools.[17] Legacy admission is also coming under increased scru-tiny, particularly now that affirmative action has been ruled unconsti-tutional, and attempts to ban legacy admissions may raise novel legal questions regarding enforcement, academic deference, and related concepts in the wake of proposed legislation banning such practices.[18]

In the world of fundraising, cryptocurrencies may introduce new questions related to the provenance of gifts as well as ethics given the decentralized anonymity and general lack of oversight that is, at least today, a hallmark of cryptocurrencies. Data security and governance in general—whether of data related to alumni populations or current students and employees—will continue to present novel issues as cybersecurity concerns grow. While the European General Data

Protection Regulation was met with much anxiety by IHEs,[19] as of this writing, the authors are unaware of an enforcement action against an American IHE operating in the European Union, which might raise the question of not if but when.[20]

With regard to community relations, it seems plausible that the increasing economic divide between institutions with thriving endowments and their often economically repressed home communities will exacerbate tensions, affecting matters related to payments in lieu of taxes,[21] perhaps leading to calls to expand the tax on endowments[22] and even having an impact in courts where institutions might come before a local and relatively unsympathetic jury.[23] And, in a topic that spans fundraising, community relations, and university finances, additional concerns regarding the criteria used in investing IHE endowments are likely to increase. While earlier waves of concern, including many on-campus protests, often centered around pressure for IHEs to divest of South African investments during the apartheid era and more recently have focused on divesting from companies involved in fossil fuel extraction, the range of concerns regarding IHE investment composition is now even wider and also involves offsetting concerns from the right about wanting to limit ESG (environmental, social, and governance) investing.[24]

The governance considerations discussed in Chapter 5 are considerably ripe for evolution in the coming years, particularly in light of the interplay with most of the issues discussed in other chapters. Again, in this context, tenure seems likely to come under still more scrutiny. The question of whether tenure remains a legitimate mechanism in service to its stated end goals seems ripe for discourse from an academic-professional perspective. And legislatures seem poised to continue to exert pressure on tenure as a matter of policy, at least at state-affiliated institutions. Obvious tensions between state legislative use of tenure as a means to censor or create noncontent-neutral restrictions on scholarship have yet to be fully tested in the courts, assuming such flamboyant policy proposals prevail.[25] Issues regarding how various such restrictions on content can be implemented will also occur, as with the recent passage of laws limiting, for instance, coverage of diversity, equity and inclusion-related topics on campus and hiring of associated staff, where it may be murky to implement these laws regarding what does or does not count as covered material under the laws.[26]

The focus on the rising costs of college as well as scrutiny of career outcomes postgraduation will likely continue to fuel novel degree, certificate, and course offerings, which in turn may continue to drive an evolution of the professoriate toward more professors of the practice, adjunct faculty, and part-time faculty and cause dilution of the governance role of the faculty. These same financial pressures will likely continue to exacerbate tensions in the traditional governance model as institutions are called on to act more adroitly in addressing financial challenges. While likely to be rare, court challenges brought by students, employees, or even other trustees and fiduciaries to mergers, consolidations, closures, and other strategic endeavors are bound to occur and continue to refine the role of these constituencies in institutional change from a governance perspective.

The continued exertion of control and shaping of conduct are likely to continue to drive the bureaucratization of student life functions on residential campuses. Compliance and its companion of minimizing risk and overall liability require, if nothing else, attention to detail. Mechanisms like increased reporting and attestations of compliance require experts to dedicate time and energy to properly analyze compliance as well as log and file reports. These jobs cannot and should not be taken lightly and require focus and attention to detail. The continued expansion of quasijudicial bodies and committees on campuses and the potential for litigation arising from such bodies and their processes also require dedicated staff or faculty members who are fully competent, trained, and experienced, and change the governance relations on campus.

There will clearly be many developments related to the financial issues that higher education faces, as discussed in Chapter 6. IHEs face significant challenges ahead from demographic shifts, including the dreaded demographic cliff with the drop in the number of college-aged students predicted to hit in 2025. In addition to the domestic cliff, there may well be changing patterns in international student enrollment as other countries modify their higher education systems and undergo their own demographic changes. Overall, some countries may significantly reduce their net outflow of students, while other countries may increase their net outflows; those shifts will affect IHEs differently but may make it hard for IHEs to depend on foreign students to offset declines in domestic enrollment. The enrollment declines are likely to cause in particular a retrenchment at the second-tier level in state systems, with students still choosing to attend flagship institutions but becoming less interested in institutions at the next level down that have weaker brand identities (e.g., the University of Michigan and Michigan State University are still popular, while almost all of the other state universities in Michigan have experienced drops in enrollment).[27] This is likely to cause additional governance issues at the second-tier schools and even flagships in states with lower populations, as faculty will shrink at those institutions and more programs may close completely.[28]

Smaller private schools with smaller per capita endowments will also come under additional pressure to effect mergers with larger, more financially stable institutions, while others, particularly the small, church-affiliated ones in denominations that are also experiencing membership declines, may well close completely. The remaining women's colleges will also likely continue to be under enrollment pressure if they choose to stay single-gendered. Historically Black Colleges and Universities and tribal colleges have come into some increased funding recently,[29] but they continue to struggle financially given their underresourced, low-endowment capital positions and more financially challenged student bodies.

Meanwhile, there will be more pressure on community colleges to be relevant for those students who want to end their education with an associate's degree and those who aim to transfer to four-year institutions. Those two relevancy goals may be in opposition, as community colleges will be hard-pressed to do it all. Meanwhile, there is some concern that the term "community college" is becoming outdated; just as four-year colleges are increasingly rebranding as universities,[30] many two-year colleges may want to rebrand away from that term.[31] Continuing retrenchment in the for-profit sector will likely occur, following on the current weeding-out of weaker schools with lower measured return on investment, but for-profit schools, including fully online institutions, may pick up some of the slack in areas where community colleges are slower to expand or where there is more job growth, with likely expansion into areas like artificial intelligence, coding, and health professions.

Following our discussion of campus crises in Chapter 7, we see better times ahead for IHEs as we put the COVID-19 pandemic further behind us even as we may continue in an endemic phase for quite a while. Overall, schools have generally become better at handling crises, albeit through a trial by fire (including, for some, hurricanes and other weather crises, along with the pandemic). The sector overall demonstrated resilience during the pandemic and the ability to pivot quickly on school policies and procedures as needed. However, IHEs are still battling the effects of the pandemic, including the weaker preparation of new students post-COVID due to disruptions in the K–12 school systems, continued student mental health issues related to pandemic trauma, and continued weaknesses in student preparation for college that were evident even before the pandemic began. Federal government actions during the pandemic set the stage for later sector bailouts, if necessary, and showed that the government can move quickly to deliver funds to affected IHEs if there is the political will to do so.

How can general counsels help their institutions deal with all of these continuing challenges? In large part, through their role in encouraging preventive measures on campuses: helping to anticipate challenges; crafting better internal policies to stave off challenges to IHE processes; and working through anticipated regulatory changes, often in concert with peers at other IHEs and in other sectors of the economy.

Can general counsel be enlisted to help reduce lawyerization on campuses? Perversely, yes. They can reduce the probability of lawsuits, move more cases to quick settlement, and close down nuisance suits faster. Their work both in preventing situations from spiraling out of control and managing audits and lawsuits as routine matters could have the effect of reducing institutional nervousness at having to engage with regulation, including reducing the internal fear of undergoing audits and litigation. General counsel can also help mitigate risks related to new IHE activities by crafting clear paths to using them as part of the strategic process. We give some examples of this below.

New Areas of Emphasis and Concern

While we have tried to cover many topics in this book to give an idea of the range that an IHE general counsel (and a president) has to work across, there were nonetheless many other topics that we did not discuss. These include a number of areas that we believe will become more important to the higher education legal scene over the next decade. While not all IHEs will come across issues in these topic areas, they are likely to affect some IHEs substantially and set the tone for higher education as a sector in the near future.

The current Supreme Court has issued a number of decisions, such as the 2023 Harvard/UNC admissions case and the disallowance of President Biden's student loan forgiveness plan, that will have a profound impact on higher education either directly or indirectly. The possibility of the Court hearing a case challenging aspects of the private right of action under Title IX as discussed in Chapter 3, and the elimination of "emotional distress" damages in cases brought under statutes passed pursuant to the spending clause are two other examples.[32] Another example is a recent decision that involved a speech controversy at Georgia Gwinnett College. While the case was seemingly of interest to the Court because it was focused on the relatively abstract legal concept of "nominal damages," it nonetheless is impactful in terms of IHE policy setting and the impact of changing a policy on future litigation.[33] Finally, the 2022 ruling of the Court in *Dobbs v. Jackson Women's Health Organization,*[34] overturning *Roe* and a woman's constitutional right to abortion, has already created challenges and confusion on college campuses, particularly as it relates to what campus health centers and other on-campus support structures are permitted to do or advise in states that ban abortion.[35]

Unions have had a role on many campuses for decades, as some campuses have fully unionized faculty, and many others have unions covering at least some types of staff positions, and/or adjunct faculty. But a notable trend over the last few years is the extension of academic unionization efforts to groups of students employed on campus, in part due to the National Labor Relations Board's current stance being that both graduate and undergraduate student-employees can unionize, following on their 2016 ruling that Columbia University graduate students were employees.[36] This trend includes graduate students, who are key contributors to the education process, whether as instructors, teaching assistants, graders, lab assistants, or multiple other roles on campus, but also groups of undergraduate students in certain positions, including dining hall workers, admissions workers (including tour guides),[37] and resident assistants for dormitories. The number of unions covering undergraduate employees has risen from one in 2019 (the University of Massachusetts Amherst union of resident assistants and community development assistants, started in 2002)[38] to over twelve by the spring of 2023.[39] There has also been a rise from about thirty-seven graduate-employee unions in 2019 to about sixty by the spring of 2023.[40] Graduate student strikes in particular can bring campus activities to a relative halt and can sometimes be a factor in toppling a college president's reign, as in the 2023 case of Jason Wingard at Temple University.[41] The 2022–23 academic year also saw the largest academic workers' strike in history, when over forty-eight thousand University of California employees—thirty-six thousand graduate student workers and twelve thousand other workers—walked out for forty days from the system's ten campuses.[42] This current trend toward unionization of graduate and undergraduate students signals another aspect of the changing relationship between IHEs and their students as well as the increasing financial pressures that affect them both.[43] Other aspects of national and state labor regulation that are currently in flux, such as changes in overtime work rules and raises in the minimum wage, often have significant financial and organizational effects on IHEs; overtime work rule changes in particular can have significant effects on the academic environment, where many campus members work much more than forty hours a week, whether in laboratories or at home.

While we are unsure about whether we will see a continued high level of foreign students (particularly undergraduates) coming to the United States to study here, we do predict increased foreign collaboration, including foreign operations of US colleges and vice versa. While there have been some notable fails, including the 2021 announced closure of the Yale-NUS (National University of Singapore) collaboration on a liberal arts college in Singapore,[44] numerous international collaborations at many different levels of complexity continue apace and continue to be encouraged by the US government,[45] even as the government also creates hurdles toward cooperation through visa restrictions and other policies, including new concerns regarding the reporting of foreign gifts.[46] NYU has a number of campuses globally, for instance, generally in partnership with local universities and governments.[47]

Intellectual property disputes, including international branding and copyright issues as such laws vary across jurisdictions (notably with China), are likely to increase as the race for profit-making ideas and processes continues internationally. IHEs that run any level of research operation, including involving undergraduate students in those operations, may need to be increasingly vigilant about maintaining financial stakes in projects that begin on their campuses.

Increased interest in entrepreneurship centers and design centers, as well as formal campus incubator facilities, needs to be accompanied by increased clarity regarding who owns the rights to the projects and how any eventual proceeds might be shared across involved entities, including IHEs.

In addition to more and more elaborate collaborations with international partners, we expect to see more elaborate collaborations with partners both inside and outside of academia, including public-private partnerships. Many new college dormitories are being built on campuses using private funds on a lend-lease operation, but this merely skims the surface of the kinds of collaborations that might occur. Other such deals take the college out of the middle entirely when companies build either adjacent to campus or on land leased from the college.[48] Meanwhile, other universities are advertising that they are "open for business" in the form of partnerships with for-profits (or nonprofits), including opening business engagement centers, such as at the University of Rochester.[49] Business schools are, naturally, particularly interested in collaborations, in part to get their students practical experiences and jobs before and after graduation.[50] All of these partnership projects require significant legal input to safeguard the involved parties and handle unforeseen consequences.

While these examples involved either bricks-and-mortar investments here or abroad and/or flows of students (and faculty) across borders, we also anticipate increased use of information technology to extend the reach of the modern university across time and space. Asynchronous classes reduce the problems of running courses across time zones and also allow for reduced instructional costs so as to reach remote corners of the globe where students may have less funds available for college attendance. While the preferred level of internet connectivity is not available everywhere, it is increasingly possible to take classes almost anywhere, including on ships and relatively remote islands. There are still attendant difficulties related to such matters as making sure that students are doing their own work (remote proctors being available but not foolproof), providing sufficient support for students to do well, and offering a sufficiently high-quality level of coursework (where many accreditors are still leery of allowing substantial coursework toward a degree to be done remotely). Again, counsel is needed to consider how to safeguard instructional quality and meet accreditation standards and other distance learning regulations as IHEs attempt to extend their reach further in all directions.[51]

Knowledge generated through academic research also increasingly flows across borders, and the US government required in 2022 that all federally funded publications and supporting data be made publicly available for free, immediately if possible, or no later than December 2025.[52] This policy will have significant effects on the current structure of academic publishing, including for both for-profit and non-profit publishers, and is likely to have ripple effects on IHE finances, including through effects on their library systems.[53] And, yet again, counsel will be intimately involved, potentially including advising various consortia of research institutions and libraries, in how to implement the necessary infrastructure to support an increasingly open-access academic publishing system.

Considerations for Future Policymakers

The issues addressed throughout this book raise a host of considerations for policymakers. As a threshold matter, policymakers should be reminded of the continuing mission of IHEs across the breadth of the sector—to search for fundamental truth and disseminate knowledge to their students and to the broader population—and should be mindful of the impact that varying regulatory and legal strictures have on this mission. There is no doubt that in the face of rising tuition rates, it is easy to be cynical, and there are always outliers and bad actors seeking to game and exploit any system—but it is our plea that policymakers remain cognizant of the well-meaning earnestness of the vast majority of IHEs and the trustees, faculty, students, administrators, and other staff that make up these institutions. IHEs want to follow the letter and spirit of the law, and they want their compliance with the law to support their core mission and serve students.

Moreover, in many areas of the country—including our own in Upstate New York—IHEs are significant economic drivers employing thousands of people across a broad spectrum of job categories and professions. And most people participate in this sector as "consumers" at some point, as the majority of adult Americans (those twenty-five and older) now have at least some college education (63 percent in 2021, with 10.5 percent holding an associate's degree as their highest degree, 23.5 percent holding a bachelor's degree as their highest degree, and 14.4 percent holding a master's, professional, or doctoral degree), with significant increases in higher education degree attainment, including graduate degrees, over just the past decade (37.9 percent had a bachelor's degree or higher in 2021, as contrasted with 30.4 percent in 2011; a 25 percent increase over this decade).[54] Certainly, there is much that makes higher education, particularly today, not unlike nearly any other industry. But the mission of higher education is markedly unique. An industry with a mission like that of higher education, an industry that employs a dynamic and diverse workforce, an industry that contributes significantly to local economies, an industry that advances the national economy, defense, and well-being, should not be regulated haphazardly.

It should come as no surprise to readers that in higher education, many policymaking debates also intersect quite acutely with what are in fact broader cultural or political wars. How much of the debate about legacy admissions, for example, is about creating the best policy for American higher education institutions and the individuals they serve versus really being about riding one or the other side of a mounting political wave? How much of the debate about free speech on campuses today is really just a dog whistle of sorts to incite one or the other particular group on a particular issue or speaker? How much of the debate about student loan reform or cancellation is really about class instead of the economic or inherent value of higher education and our national willingness to invest in this system or correct its shortcomings?

None of this book is intended to diminish passionate feelings or, heaven forbid, passionate *debate*, around any of the policy issues facing higher education. Instead, this book is meant to do the opposite, but moreover, to do it with a passionate plea for embracing nuance. If nothing else, the preceding nine chapters hopefully demonstrate that the legal and regulatory biome of higher education is starkly complicated and interrelated. So complicated and interrelated, in fact, that policymakers would do well to understand their actions, the success of higher education and the students we serve, and that the impact on our nation and democracy's well-being is largely symbiotic.[55]

Collectively, we must move beyond "culture wars" and toward policy nuance. Only then does the generation of more critical and profound policy questions and solutions become possible. This is true across the range of issues covered or alluded to in this book. For example, are private rights of action under Title IX the best way to meet the underlying spirit and goals of the Title IX statute writ large? Are the policy aspirations of equity, as embodied in the Title IX statute, being met through the current regulatory and enforcement structure? Could costs of enforcement or compliance be spread more efficiently to achieve a better result in line with the statute's goals? Similar questions could be asked across the gamut of statutes and regulatory enforcement regimes bearing down on higher education. Should IHEs be required to contribute or spend more in their local communities? Should more than simply the largest university endowments be taxed, and if so, should the taxes flow to the general fund or be redistributed across the sector in order to more broadly and diversely support higher education's mission?[56] Would increasing funding to higher education have a meaningful impact on the student debt crisis? How does attempting to solve these various issues impact the core mission of IHEs and those they serve, and how will proposed solutions give rise to new obligations, be handled by courts, and hinder the ability of institutions to deliver on their mission to the communities they serve while remaining accessible? These are merely a handful of questions among many that must be thoughtfully asked and answered.

Conclusion: A Crucial Time for Higher Education

The next decade is likely to be a crucial one for higher education. IHEs face increased pressures on their cost structures; changing demographics; additional regulations; and a changing landscape with regard to college sports, to name just a few things affecting them. Numerous scholars and commentators have questioned the future viability of traditional colleges and universities, even as others have argued that many if not most of them can adjust to meet these challenges so as to continue to prosper in the future.[57]

But if we go back to what increasingly looks like the heyday of higher education; namely, the post–World War II expansion in the higher education system, fueled by the GI Bills, the baby boom, and the rise in postgraduate degree attainment, it is easy to find other periods of great challenge for higher education. Those institutions that were founded in the eighteenth and nineteenth centuries also went through challenging periods, including the Revolutionary War, the Civil War, prolonged depressions and periods of deflation, and World Wars I and II. Many survived, but their histories often feature periods of retrenchment, mergers with other institutions, physical moves of their campuses, renamings, and testy town-gown relations. At many times, IHEs needed to be nimble, and a bit lucky, to prosper.

Increased federal funding for education would certainly help take some pressure off of the sector; it is no surprise that many IHEs support the current drive to double the Pell Grant amounts. Similarly, levels of state funding have ebbed and flowed over time, and state institutions need to make the case for increased or restored state support. This will depend in part on their ameliorating current tensions between legislatures and governors on the one hand, oversight boards on another hand (who are currently sometimes on tense terms with the legislature and/or governor on the one side, and sometimes on tense terms with the universities they supervise on the other side), and broader state constituencies (i.e., voters) on the third hand.

A big question is whether governmental/legal purview over the higher education sector will extend yet further in the near term, or whether there may be some pendulum swing back to a more hands-off mode. Presidents and other governmental lobbyists are sometimes able to make a strong case that the sector should be left alone regulatorily; that has been less true lately. However, that argument may come back into fashion if presidents and other academic voices are better able to convince governmental officials that they are doing a good job in educating the next generation, including being open to diverse viewpoints, opening their educative doors to a wider range of students (and doing right by them in terms of retention and graduation rates as well as low amounts of debt on graduation), and providing the country with graduates who have the skills the country (and world) needs to be capable and productive.

If IHEs can effectively deliver in line with their stated missions and convince the general public and government officials that their goals and missions are aligned with the overall societal goals, they may be able to reclaim some of the high ground that they have lost over the past two decades. While the liberal arts IHEs have been under particular scrutiny lately, with stated concerns about their practicality, their relevance, their ability to withstand brainwashing of all types, and their return on investment relative to other forms of education, it is still possible to make a strong case for them that counters all these claims. A number of scholars of higher education, including several sitting and former college presidents, have published books recently that lay the groundwork for such a case.[58] This is a case that can be strengthened by understanding the sector's interaction with the country's legal and regulatory structure, what higher education currently can and cannot do, and how IHEs can work in concert with those structures. If the "lawyerization" of our campuses can come into alignment with both shaping and reshaping law and regulation so as to serve the aligned missions of university and society, understanding that some conflict between the university and governmental sectors can be positive while other, more negative conflicts may be reduced, then we may find that the protection that law can afford to campus activities, including free speech and expression, freedom from discrimination, and clarified and effective governance and financial regulations may actually support both missions rather than creating a wedge between them.

NOTES

ACKNOWLEDGMENTS

INDEX

Notes

Introduction

1.   See the compendia produced by *Chronicle of Higher Education* (https://www
.chronicle.com/), *Inside Higher Ed* (https://www.insidehighered.com/), *Diverse: Issues in
Higher Education* (https://www.diverseeducation.com/), and *University Business* (https://
universitybusiness.com/), and also in *The Hechinger Report* (https://hechingerreport
.org/) and *Higher Ed Dive* (https://www.highereddive.com/). In addition to these,
major newspapers and magazines such as *The Atlantic, The Economist, The New York Times,*
and *The Wall Street Journal* publish editorials and cover higher education stories regularly.

2.   *Strategic Plan 2018–24*, Univ. Oxford, https://www.ox.ac.uk/about
/organisation/strategic-plan-2018-24.

3.   *Mission, Vision, & History*, Harvard Univ., https://college.harvard.edu
/about/mission-vision-history.

4.   *UC's Mission*, Univ. Cal., https://www.ucop.edu/uc-mission/.

5.   *University Mission*, Cornell Univ., https://www.cornell.edu/about
/mission.cfm.

6.   *History & Mission*, Johns Hopkins Univ., https://www.jhu.edu/about
/history/.

7.   *Mission of Amherst College*, Amherst Coll., https://www.amherst.edu
/about/president-college-leadership/mission.

8.   A. Bartlett Giamatti (1990), *A Free and Ordered Space: The Real World of the University.* W.W. Norton & Co.: 43.

9.   *Id.*

10.   *See* Barbara Lee (2010), "Fifty Years of Higher Education Law: Turning the Kaleidoscope," Journal of College and University Law, Vol. 36 No. 3. *See also* Michael Olivas (2013), *Suing Alma Mater,* Johns Hopkins University Press 2013: 23 (chronicling the longer-term rise of legal issues facing higher education and writing over ten years ago that "[i]f events continue as in the past, there can be no doubt that higher education will become increasingly legalized, by the traditional means of legislation, regulation, and litigation . . .").

11.   *See Id.* Lee *and* Olivas. *See also* William A. Kaplin & Barbara A. Lee (2013), *The Law of Higher Education, 5th Ed.* Jossey-Bass: 9.

12.   Sean Farhang (2010), *The Litigation State: Public Regulation and Private Lawsuits in the United States.* Princeton: Princeton University Press: Ch. 1.

13.   *Id.*

14.   Amy Rock, *An Updated List of States That Allow Campus Carry,* Campus Safety Magazine (Apr. 7, 2023), https://www.campussafetymagazine.com/university /list-of-states-that-allow-concealed-carry-guns-on-campus/.

15.   Jason Harward, *South Dakota Legislators Move to Ban Drag Shows on College Campuses, Prohibit Minor Attendance,* Mitchell Republic (Jan. 24, 2023), https://www .mitchellrepublic.com/news/south-dakota/south-dakota-legislators-move-to-ban -drag-shows-on-college-campuses.

16.   Emily Hamer, *Records Show Walker Wanted to Change Wisconsin Idea,* The Badger Herald (May 27, 2016), https://badgerherald.com/news/2016/05 /27/records-show-walker-wanted-to-change-wisconsin-idea/.

17.   Virginia Foxx, *The New Era of Regulatory Overreach,* Inside Higher Ed (Apr. 27, 2023), https://www.insidehighered.com/views/2023/04/07/proposed-tps -changes-biden-admin-overreached-opinion.

18.   NAICU, *Department Releases Massive New Regulatory Package* (May 19, 2023), https://www.naicu.edu/news-events/washington-update/2023/may-19 /department-releases-massive-new-regulatory-package.

19.   Alexander C. Kafka, *Liability Everywhere: Why College Lawyers Will Be Working Overtime,* Chronicle of Higher Education (Feb. 16, 2020), https://www .chronicle.com/article/liability-everywhere/.

20.   Credit is due to Donica Varner, vice president and general counsel at Cornell University, for challenging the authors to think about the nexus between their concept of "lawyerization" of higher education and the broader context of politicization of issues and happenings on campuses.

21.   *Dinner Offers Warm Welcome*, Hobart & William Smith Coll. (Aug. 27, 2013), https://www2.hws.edu/article-id-16945/.

22.   American Association of University Professors, *1940 Statement on Principles of Academic Freedom and Tenure*, https://www.aaup.org/report/1940-statement -principles-academic-freedom-and-tenure.

23.   N.L.R.B. v. Yeshiva Univ., 444 U.S. 672, 680 (1980).

24.   Regents of Univ. of California v. Bakke, 438 U.S. 265 (1978).

25.   *Id.*

26.   WayUp, *Top 5 Industries for Workforce Diversity*, https://www.wayup.com /guide/top-5-industries-for-workforce-diversity/ (last accessed Sep. 16, 2023).

27.   Cf, Steven J. Nelson (2016), *The Shape and Shaping of the College and University in America: A Lively Experiment*, Washington, DC: Lexington Books, for an explication of the evolution of higher education in America alongside the birth of the United States since the country's founding.

28.   Ronald J. Daniels, Grant Shreve, & Phillip Spector (2022), *What Universities Owe Democracy*. Baltimore: Johns Hopkins University Press.

1. Civil Rights and Equity on Campus

1.   Martin Luther King Jr., Remaining Awake through a Great Revolution, Speech at the National Cathedral in Washington, D.C. (Mar. 31, 1968) (transcript available at https://seemeonline.com/history/mlk-jr-awake.htm).

2.   Mark D. Gearan, Convocation at Hobart and William Smith Colleges (Aug. 29, 2016) (transcript available at https://www.hws.edu/news/transcripts /16/gearan_convocation.aspx).

3.   *Disability Discrimination*, U.S. Equal Emp. Opportunity Comm'n., https:// www.eeoc.gov/disability-related-resources (last accessed Sep. 16, 2023); *Harassment*, U.S. Equal Emp. Opportunity Comm'n., https://www.eeoc.gov/harassment (last accessed Sep. 16, 2023).

4.   20 U.S.C. §§ 1681 et seq.

5.   34 C.F.R. Part 106.

6.   Letter from Russlynn Ali, Assistant Sec'y for Civil Rights, U.S. Dept. of Educ., to Colleague (Apr. 4, 2011), https://www2.ed.gov/about/offices/list/ocr/letters/colleague-201104.pdf.

7.   Cannon v. University of Chicago, 441 U.S. 677, 688–89 (1979); Franklin v. Gwinnett Cnty. Pub. Schools, 503 U.S. 60 (1992).

8.   Shep R. Melnick (2018), *The Transformation of Title IX: Regulating Gender Equality in Education, 169,* Washington, DC: Brookings Institution Press.

9.   Videotape: *Nominations of Catherine Lhamon to be Assistant Secretary for Civil Rights at the Department of Education, Elizabeth Brown to be General Counsel of the Department of Education, and Roberto Rodriguez to be Assistant Secretary for Planning, Evaluation, and Policy Development of the Department of Education* (July 13, 2021), https://www.help.senate.gov/hearings/nominations-of-catherine-lhamon-to-be-assistant-secretary-for-civil-rights-at-the-department-of-education-elizabeth-brown-to-be-general-counsel-of-the-department-of-education-and-roberto-rodriguez-to-be-assistant-secretary-for-planning-evaluation-and-policy-development-of-the-department-of-education.

10.   S. 1356, Workforce Investment Act of 2013, 113th Cong. 52 (2013).

11.   Letter from Russlynn Ali, Assistant Sec'y for Civil Rights, U.S. Dept. of Educ., to Colleague (Apr. 4, 2011), https://www2.ed.gov/about/offices/list/ocr/letters/colleague-201104.pdf.

12.   2011 DCL.

13.   Davis v. Monroe Cnty. Bd. Of Ed., 526 U.S. 629 (1999); Gebser v. Lago Vista Indep. Sch. Dist., 524 U.S. 274 (1998).

14.   Michael Stratford, *Aggressive Push on Sex Assault,* Inside Higher Ed (April 30, 2014), https://www.insidehighered.com/news/2014/04/30/white-house-calls-colleges-do-more-combat-sexual-assault.

15.   *Id.*

16.   *Not Alone: The First Report of the White House Task Force to Protect Students from Sexual Assault,* White House (Apr. 2014), https://www.justice.gov/archives/ovw/page/file/905942/download.

17.   *Id.*

18.   *Questions and Answers on Title IX and Sexual Violence,* U.S. Dep't Educ. Off. Civ. Rts. (Apr. 29, 2014), https://www2.ed.gov/about/offices/list/ocr/docs/qa-201404-title-ix.pdf.

19.   OMB Bulletin No. 07-02 *Agency Good Guidance Practices*, at 7 (Jan. 18, 2007), https://www.mbda.gov/sites/default/files/omb-bulletin07-02.pdf.

20.   *Questions and Answers on Title IX and Sexual Violence, supra* note 18.

21.   Michael Stratford, *The Government's New List*, Inside Higher Ed (May 2, 2014), https://www.insidehighered.com/news/2014/05/02/us-names -colleges-under-investigation-sexual-assault-cases.

22.   *Id.*

23.   Michael Stratford, *Tufts University, Federal Officials Resolve Title IX Standoff*, Inside Higher Ed (May 9, 2014), https://www.insidehighered.com/quicktakes /2014/05/09/tufts-university-federal-officials-resolve-title-ix-standoff.

24.   Michael Stratford, *Standoff on Sexual Assaults*, Inside Higher Ed (Apr. 29, 2014), https://www.insidehighered.com/news/2014/04/29/us-finds-tufts -violating-rules-sexual-assault-amid-larger-crackdown.

25.   *Id.*

26.   *Id.*

27.   Sara Lipka, *Tufts U. Disputes Finding That It Failed to Comply with Civil Rights Law*, Chronicle of Higher Education (Apr. 29, 2014), https://www.chronicle .com/article/tufts-u-disputes-finding-that-it-failed-to-comply-with-civil-rights -law/.

28.   Stratford, *supra* note 23.

29.   *Id.*

30.   Walt Bogdanich, *A Star Player Accused, and a Flawed Rape Investigation*, New York Times (Apr. 16, 2014), https://www.nytimes.com/interactive/2014/04/16 /sports/errors-in-inquiry-on-rape-allegations-against-fsu-jameis-winston.html.

31.   Eliza Gray, *The Sexual Assault Crisis on American Campuses*, Times Magazine (May 15, 2014), https://time.com/100542/the-sexual-assault-crisis-on-american -campuses/.

32.   *Rape on Campus: Painful Stories Cast Blame on Colleges*, NPR (Apr. 6, 2014), https://www.npr.org/2014/04/06/299521814/students-stories-of-sexual -assault-puts-schools-to-blame-too.

33.   Roberta Smith, *In a Mattress, a Lever for Art and Political Protest*, New York Times (Sep. 21, 2014), https://www.nytimes.com/2014/09/22/arts/design /in-a-mattress-a-fulcrum-of-art-and-political-protest.html. *See also* https://en .wikipedia.org/wiki/Mattress_Performance_(Carry_That_Weight) (last accessed Sep. 16, 2023).

34.   Lucia Graves, *Five Years on, the Lessons from the Rolling Stone Rape Story,* GUARDIAN (Dec. 29, 2019), https://www.theguardian.com/society/2019 /dec/29/rolling-stone-rape-story-uva-five-years.

35.   STRATFORD, *supra* note 24.

36.   STRATFORD, *supra* note 14.

37.   *Id.*

38.   Eugene Volokh, *28 Harvard Law Professors Condemn Harvard's New Sexual Harassment Policy and Procedures,* WASHINGTON POST (Oct. 15, 2014), https://www .washingtonpost.com/news/volokh-conspiracy/wp/2014/10/15/28-harvard-law -professors-condemn-harvards-new-sexual-harassment-policy-and-procedures/.

39.   *Id.*

40.   Eugene Volokh, *Open Letter from 16 Penn Law School Professors about Title IX and Sexual Assault Complaints,* WASHINGTON POST (Feb. 19, 2015), https://www .washingtonpost.com/news/volokh-conspiracy/wp/2015/02/19/open-letter -from-16-penn-law-school-professors-about-title-ix-and-sexual-assault-complaints/.

41.   34 C.F.R. § 106.

42.   Greta Anderson, *U.S. Publishes New Regulations on Campus Sexual Assault,* INSIDE HIGHER ED (May 7, 2020), https://www.insidehighered.com/news /2020/05/07/education-department-releases-final-title-ix-regulations.

43.   34 C.F.R. § 106.45(b)(6)(i) ("If a party or witness does not submit to cross-examination at the live hearing, the decision-maker(s) must not rely on any statement of that party or witness in reaching a determination regarding responsibility. . . .").

44.   Christopher J. Cunio & Brian J. Bosworth, *Department of Education Ceases Enforcement of "Arbitrary and Capricious" Trump-Era Title IX Regulation,* 12 NAT'L L. REV. 237 (Aug. 25, 2021), https://www.natlawreview.com/article/department -education-ceases-enforcement-arbitrary-and-capricious-trump-era-title-ix.

45.   Lauren Camera, *New Sex Assault Rules Favor the Accused,* U.S. NEWS & WORLD REPORT (Nov. 16, 2018), https://www.usnews.com/news/education-news/ articles/2018-11-16/education-departments-sexual-assault-rules-would-bolster -rights-of-accused; Jeannie Suk Gersen, *How Concerning Are the Trump Administration's New Title Regulations?,* THE NEW YORKER (May 16, 2020), https://www.newyorker .com/news/our-columnists/how-concerning-are-the-trump-administrations -new-title-ix-regulations.

46.   *Id.*

47.   *Id.*

48.   Tamara Lave, *The New Title IX Regs Should Be Reformed—Not Rolled Back,* Chronicle of Higher Education (Aug. 23, 2021), https://www.chronicle.com /article/the-new-title-ix-regs-should-be-reformed-not-rolled-back.

49.   *Department of Education's Office for Civil Rights Launches Comprehensive Review of Title IX Regulations to Fulfill President Biden's Executive Order Guaranteeing an Educational Environment Free from Sex Discrimination,* U.S. Dep't Educ. (Apr. 6, 2021), https:// www.ed.gov/news/press-releases/department-educations-office-civil-rights -launches-comprehensive-review-title-ix-regulations-fulfill-president-bidens -executive-order-guaranteeing-educational-environment-free-sex-discrimination.

50.   https://www.govinfo.gov/content/pkg/FR-2022-07-12/pdf/2022 -13734.pdf.

51.   *Id.*

52.   *Id.*

53.   Kate Bellows, *Here's How Title IX Could Change under Biden's Proposed Rule,* Chronicle of Higher Education (June 23, 2022), https://www.chronicle.com /article/heres-how-title-ix-could-change-under-bidens-proposed-rule.

54.   *See a Timing Update on Title IX Rulemaking,* U.S. Dep't Educ. (May 26, 2023), https://blog.ed.gov/2023/05/a-timing-update-on-title-ix-rulemaking/.

55.   42 U.S.C. § 2000e. *Title VII of the Civil Rights Act of 1964,* U.S. Equal Emp. Opportunity Comm'n, https://www.eeoc.gov/statutes/title-vii-civil-rights-act-1964.

56.   *See, e.g.,* Menaker v. Hofstra Univ., No. 18-3089-CV, 2019 WL 3819631, at *7 (2d Cir. Aug. 15, 2019); Doe v. Columbia University, 831 F.3d 46, 56 (2d Cir. 2016) (adopting the same pleading standard as Title VII).

57.   *See* Bostock v. Clayton Cnty., 140 S. Ct. 1731, 1755–56 (2020).

58.   Exec. Order No. 13988, 86 F.R. 7023 (Jan. 20, 2021), https://www .whitehouse.gov/briefing-room/presidential-actions/2021/01/20/executive -order-preventing-and-combating-discrimination-on-basis-of-gender-identity -or-sexual-orientation/.

59.   *Harassment, supra* note 3.

60.   *Questions and Answers on the Title IX Regulations on Sexual Harassment* at 4, U.S. Dep't Educ. Off. Civ. Rts. (July 20, 2021), https://www2.ed.gov/about/offices /list/ocr/docs/202107-qatitleix.pdf.

61.   *Harassment, supra* note 3.

62.   *Id.*

63.   *See, infra,* Chapter 5 discussing the nature of tenure as a matter of contract. *See also, e.g.,* Holm v. Ithaca Coll., 669 N.Y.S. 2d 483 (Sup. Ct. 1998). *See also* William A. Kaplin & Barbara A. Lee, *The Law of Higher Education 5th Ed* (2013) Josey-Bass: 543, discussing in further detail faculty employment contracts.

64.   Colleen Flaherty, *No Closure at Rochester,* INSIDE HIGHER ED (Jan. 12, 2018), https://www.insidehighered.com/news/2018/01/12/independent -investigation-sexual-harassment-rochester-provides-little-closure.

65.   Letter from Richard N. Aslin & Elissa L. Newport to Members of the University of Rochester Board of Trustees (Sep. 1, 2017), https://drive.google .com/file/d/0ByA-RYNiDM7lMHM0cHFXZWY2cEU/view.

66.   Katherine Mangan, *Rochester Professor at Center of Harassment Controversy Will Return to Teaching,* CHRONICLE OF HIGHER EDUCATION (April 5, 2018), https://www .chronicle.com/article/rochester-professor-at-center-of-harassment-controversy -will-return-to-teaching/.

67.   Letter from Richard N. Aslin & Elissa L. Newport, *supra* note 65.

68.   Aslin v. Univ. of Rochester, No.6:17-CV-06847, 2019 WL 4112130 at *1(N.Y. Civ. Ct. Aug. 28, 2020).

69.   Colleen Flaherty, *Rochester Settles Sex Harassment Case for 9.4M,* INSIDE HIGHER ED (Mar. 30, 2020), https://www.insidehighered.com/quicktakes /2020/03/30/rochester-settles-sex-harassment-case-94m.

70.   *Mangan supra* note 66. *See also* https://thejaegercase.com/ (last accessed Sep. 16, 2023).

71.   Stephanie Kirchgaessner, *Prominent Yale Law Professor Suspended after Sexual Harassment Inquiry,* GUARDIAN (Aug. 26, 2020), https://www.theguardian.com /education/2020/aug/26/jed-rubenfeld-yale-law-school-suspended.

72.   Jed Rubenfeld, Mishandling Rape, NEW YORK TIMES (Nov. 15, 2014), https://www.nytimes.com/2014/11/16/opinion/sunday/mishandling-rape.html.

73.   Irin Carmon, *The Tiger Mom and the Hornet's Nest,* NEW YORK MAGAZINE (June 7, 2021), https://nymag.com/intelligencer/2021/06/amy-chua-jed -rubenfeld-yale-law.html.

74.   Ariel H. Kim & Meimei Xu, *Harvard Anthropology Prof. John Comaroff Placed on Leave Following Sexual Harassment, Professional Misconduct Inquiries,* THE HARVARD

CRIMSON (Jan. 21, 2022), https://www.thecrimson.com/article/2022/1/21/comaroff-unpaid-leave/.

75.   Ariel H. Kim & Meimei Xu, *Harvard Is Embroiled in Another Sexual Misconduct Controversy. Here's What You Need to Know,* THE HARVARD CRIMSON (Feb. 11, 2022), https://www.thecrimson.com/article/2022/2/11/Comaroff-What-You-Need-To-Know/; Meimei Xu, *15 Harvard Anthropology Professors Call on Comaroff to Resign Over Sexual Harassment Allegations,* THE HARVARD CRIMSON (Feb. 21, 2022), https://www.thecrimson.com/article/2022/2/21/anthropology-faculty-call-for-comaroff-resignation/.

76.   Anjeli R. Macaranas, *Harvard Title IX Coordinator Apologizes for Statement on Comaroff Lawsuit,* THE HARVARD CRIMSON (Feb. 19, 2022), https://www.thecrimson.com/article/2022/2/19/merhill-apologizes-for-statement/.

77.   20 U.S.C. § 1232(g); 34 C.F.R. § 99.

78.   *See The Jeanne Clery Act,* CLERY CTR., https://clerycenter.org/the-clery-act/.

79.   34 U.S.C. Subchapter III.

80.   *Questions and Answers on the Title IX Regulations on Sexual Harassment, supra* note 60 at 43.

81.   Franklin v. Gwinnett Cnty. Public Schools, 503 U.S. 60, 21 (1992) *citing* Meritor Savings Bank, FSB v. Vinson, 477 U.S. 57, 64, 106 S.Ct. 2399, 2404, 91 L.Ed.2d 49 (1986).

82.   34 C.F.R. § 106.41 (citing athletics as a designated program or activity).

83.   Noram V. Cantú, *Clarification of Intercollegiate Athletics Policy Guidance: The Three-Part Test,* OFF. CIV. RTS. (Jan. 16, 1996), https://www2.ed.gov/about/offices/list/ocr/docs/clarific.html#two.; 34 CFR § 106.41(c)(1).

84.   *Id.*

85.   Chris Burt, *5 Student-Athletes, Stanford Reach Settlement Over Title IX Lawsuit,* UNIV. BUS. (Aug. 27, 2021), https://universitybusiness.com/5-student-athletes-stanford-reach-settlement-over-title-ix-lawsuit/.

86.   *Id.*

87.   Chris Burt, *Title IX: Dartmouth Reverses Course, Reinstates Women's Athletic Teams,* UNIV. BUS. (Feb. 1, 2021), https://universitybusiness.com/title-ix-dartmouth-reverses-course-reinstates-womens-athletic-teams/.

88.   Lazor v. Univ. of Conn., No. 3:21-cv-583, 2021 WL 2138832, at *1 (D. Conn. May 26, 2021).

89.   Lazor, 2021 WL 2138832, at *6.

90.   Letter from Catherine E. Lhamon, Assistant Sec'y for Civ. Rts., U.S. Dep't of Educ. & Vanita Gupta, Principal Deputy Assistant Att'y Gen. for Civ. Rts., U.S. Dep't of Just., to Colleague (May 13, 2016), https://www2.ed.gov /about/offices/list/ocr/letters/colleague-201605-title-ix-transgender.pdf.

91.   Michael Levenson & Neil Vigdor, *Inclusion of Transgender Student Athletes Violates Title IX, Trump Administration Says*, New York Times (May 29, 2020), https:// www.nytimes.com/2020/05/29/us/connecticut-transgender-student-athletes.html.

92.   *See* Bostock v. Clayton Cnty., 140 S. Ct. 1731, 1755–56 (2020).

93.   Kim Chandler, *Alabama Expands Ban on Trans Athletes to Include College Teams*, AP News, (May 30, 2023), https://apnews.com/article/alabama-legislature -transgender-9614faf4a98ea040bb7bf712be4c3dad; Katie Rogers, *Title IX Protections Extend to Transgender Students, Education Dept. Says*, New York Times (June 16, 2021), https://www.nytimes.com/2021/06/16/us/politics/title-ix-transgender -students.html. *See also* Priya Krishnakumar, *This Record-breaking Year for Anti-transgender Legislation Would Affect Minors the Most* (Apr. 15, 2021), https://www.cnn.com/2021 /04/15/politics/anti-transgender-legislation-2021/index.html.

94.   *Board of Governors Updates Transgender Participation Policy*, NCAA (Jan. 19, 2022), https://www.ncaa.org/news/2022/1/19/media-center-board-of -governors-updates-transgender-participation-policy.aspx.

95.   *See FACT SHEET: U.S. Department of Education's Proposed Change to Its Title IX Regulations on Students' Eligibility for Athletic Teams*, U.S. Dep't Educ. Off. Civ. Rts. (April 6, 2023), https://www.ed.gov/news/press-releases/fact-sheet-us-department -educations-proposed-change-its-title-ix-regulations-students-eligibility-athletic-teams.

96.   As of writing the Biden Administration has also sought to extend the protections of Title VI to include discrimination on the basis of shared ancestry or ethnic characteristics or citizenship or residency in a country with a dominant religion or distinct religious identity. *See FACT SHEET: Protecting Students from Discrimination Based on Shared Ancestry or Ethnic Characteristics*, U.S. Dep't Educ. Off. Civ. Rts. (January 2023), https://www2.ed.gov/about/offices/list/ocr/docs/ocr -factsheet-shared-ancestry-202301.pdf.

97.   *See, e.g., New Workplace Discrimination and Harassment Protections*, N.Y. Div. Hum. Rts., https://dhr.ny.gov/new-workplace-discrimination-and-harassment -protections (last accessed Sep. 16, 2023).

98.   *Disability Discrimination: Frequently Asked Questions,* U.S. Dep't Educ. Off. Civ. Rts., https://www2.ed.gov/about/offices/list/ocr/frontpage/faq/disability .html.

99.   42 U.S.C. § 12182(a); 28 C.F.R. § 36.301(a).

100.   Jason Grant & Andrew Denney, *All-Time High Number of ADA Title III Suits Filed in 2021, According to Seyfarth Study,* The New York Law Journal (March 3, 2022), https://www.law.com/newyorklawjournal/2022/03/03/all-time -high-number-of-ada-title-iii-suits-filed-in-2021-according-to-seyfarth-study/.

101.   ADA Amendments Act of 2008, PL 110-325 (S 3406).

102.   Press Release, *Justice Department Revises Regulations to Implement Requirements of ADA Amendments Act of 2008,* U.S. D.O.J. (Aug. 2016), https://www.justice.gov /opa/pr/justice-department-revises-regulations-implement-requirements-ada -amendments-act-2008.

103.   *Id.*

104.   *Id.*

105.   Arne Duncan & Russlynn Ali, *Students with Disabilities Preparing for Postsecondary Education: Know Your Rights and Responsibilities,* U.S. Dep't Educ. Off. Civ. Rts. (Sep. 2011), https://www2.ed.gov/about/offices/list/ocr/transition.html.

106.   S. 3406, *An Act to Restore the Intent and Protections of the Americans with Disabilities Act of 1990,* 110th Cong., at 122 (2008).

107.   Duncan & Ali, *supra* note 106.

108.   *Id.*

109.   Eugene Beresin, *The College Mental Health Crisis: Focus on Suicide,* Psych. Today (Feb. 27, 2017), https://www.psychologytoday.com/us/blog/inside-out-outside -in/201702/the-college-mental-health-crisis-focus-suicide.

110.   *See* Paul Lannon & Elizabeth Sanghavi, *New Title II Regulations Regarding Direct Threat: Do They Change How Colleges and Universities Should Treat Students Who Are Threats to Themselves?,* 10 NACUANOTE 1 (Nov. 1, 2011)), Nat'l Assoc. Coll & Univ. Att'ys: "But for years, colleges and universities have understood—based upon government guidance—that they could nonetheless dismiss or discipline disabled students who are "direct threats" to themselves, without running afoul of federal anti-discrimination laws."

111.   Final Rule: Nondiscrimination on the Basis of Disability in State and Local Government Services, 75 Fed. Reg. 56164, 56206 (Sep. 15, 2010).

112. Paul G. Lannon, *Direct Threat and Caring for Students at Risk for Self-Harm: Where We Stand Now,* 12 NACUANOTE 8 (Sep. 3, 2014), Nat'l Assoc. Coll & Univ. Att'ys.

113. Settlement Agreement under the Americans with Disabilities Act between the United States of America and Brown University (Aug. 10, 2021), https://www.ada.gov/brown_sa.html.

114. National Association of College & University Attorneys (Jan. 26, 2018), *Principles for Students Who Pose a Risk of Self-Harm.*

115. *See also* Carolyn Kuimelis, *Colleges Face More Pressure to Keep Students with Mental-Health Conditions Enrolled,* CHRONICLE OF HIGHER EDUCATION (Dec. 8, 2023), https://www.chronicle.com/article/colleges-face-more-pressure-to-keep-students -with-mental-health-conditions-enrolled (discussing the trend toward a "flexible" and "student-centered" approach).

116. ADA Rehabilitation Act, 29 C.F.R. §§ 1630, 1614.

117. *Id.*

118. *See, e.g.,* Elizabeth Redden, *Who Controls NYU Shanghai?,* INSIDE HIGHER ED (Aug. 25, 2021), https://www.insidehighered.com/news/2021/08/25 /question-nyus-control-over-nyu-shanghai-sits-center-faculty-suit.

119. 28 C.F.R. § 35.104 (2010) (Title II); 28 C.F.R. § 36.104 (2010) (Title III).

120. Notice from John Trasviña, Assistant Sec'y for Fair Hous. & Equal Opportunity (Apr. 25, 2013), https://www.hud.gov/sites/dfiles/FHEO/docume nts/19ServiceAnimalNoticeFHEO_508.pdf; United States v. Univ. of Neb. at Kearney, 940 F.Supp.2d 974, 978 (D. Neb. 2013) (finding that campus dorms are dwellings subject to the Fair Housing Act).

121. *Drug Scheduling and Penalties,* CAMPUS DRUG PREVENTION, https://www .campusdrugprevention.gov/content/drug-scheduling-and-penalties.

122. Janet Elie Faulkner & Phil Catanzano, *Accommodations for Disabilities in the Title IX Grievance Process,* 20 NACUANOTE 1 (Sep. 1, 2021), Nat'l Assoc. Coll & Univ. Att'ys.

123. 28 C.F.R. § 36.304(a).

124. *See* Joint Dear Colleague Letter on Postsecondary Online Accessibility, U.S. DEP'T EDUC. OFF. CIV. RTS. (May 19, 2023), https://www2.ed.gov/about /offices/list/ocr/docs/postsec-online-access-051923.pdf.

125.   Lindsay McKenzie, *50 Colleges Hit with ADA Lawsuits,* INSIDE HIGHER ED (Dec. 10, 2018), https://www.insidehighered.com/news/2018/12/10/fifty-colleges-sued-barrage-ada-lawsuits-over-web-accessibility; see also Jason Grant, *Pointing to Pandemic-Fueled 'Surge,' Research Company Says 70% of ADA Website Accessibility Lawsuits Now Filed in NY,* N.Y. L. J. (Sep. 29, 2020), https://www.law.com/newyorklawjournal/2020/09/29/pointing-to-pandemic-fueled-surge-research-company-says-70-of-ada-website-accessibility-lawsuits-now-filed-in-ny/.

126.   Lindsay McKenzie, *Feds Prod Universities to Address Website Accessibility Complaints,* INSIDE HIGHER ED (Nov. 6, 2018), https://www.insidehighered.com/news/2018/11/06/universities-still-struggle-make-websites-accessible-all.

2. Free Speech and Expression on Campus

1.   U.S. CONST. amend. I.

2.   Colin Lecher, *First Amendment Constraints Don't Apply to Private Platforms, Supreme Court Affirms,* VERGE (June 17, 2019), https://www.theverge.com/2019/6/17/18682099/supreme-court-ruling-first-amendment-social-media-public-forum.

3.   While rare, in some instances, state laws provide a framework to enforce First Amendment principles against private actors. California's "Leonard Law" is a noteworthy example. *See* Cal. Educ. Code Sec. 94367.

4.   Keyishian v. Bd. of Regents of Univ. of State of N.Y., 385 U.S. 589, 603 (1967).

5.   Erwin Chemerinsky & Howard Gillman (2017), *Free Speech on Campus,* Yale Univ. Press: 126 (arguing that the "Berkley Free Speech Movement established the principle that students and faculty have the right . . . to use campus grounds for personal and political expression.").

6.   *See, e.g.,* Richard H. Hiers, *Institutional Academic Freedom or Autonomy Grounded upon the First Amendment: A Jurisprudential Mirage,* 30 HAMLINE L. REV. 1 (2007), http://scholarship.law.ufl.edu/facultypub/742 (tracing and explaining the path of the concept through the Supreme Court).

7.   Walter P. Metzger, *Profession and Constitution: Two Definitions of Academic Freedom in America,* 66 TEX. L. REV. 1265 (1988) (articulating the professional versus constitutional categorization).

8.   *See id.*; David M. Rabban, *A Functional Analysis of "Individual" and "Institutional" Academic Freedom under the First Amendment*, 53 L. & CONTEMPORARY PROBS. 227 (1990).

9.   Louis Guard, *Legal and Governance Considerations in a Time of Pandemic and Systemic Crisis: A Primer on Shared Governance and AAUP Guidance for Private Colleges and Universities*, 19 NACUANOTE 5 (Mar. 17, 2021), Nat'l Assoc. Coll & Univ. Att'ys.

10.   *See* Rabban, *supra* note 8 at 229.

11.   Kathy Zonana, *Freedom and the Farm*, STANFORD MAGAZINE (May 2021), https://stanfordmag.org/contents/freedom-and-the-farm. *See also* the 1913 case of Willard Fisher and Wesleyan University, *His Big Idea Didn't Have a Prayer*, TODAY IN CONNECTICUT HISTORY (Jan. 27, 2022), https://todayincthistory.com/2022/01/27/january-27-his-big-idea-didnt-have-a-prayer-2/.

12.   *Id.*

13.   *Id.*

14.   Am. Ass'n of Univ. Professors, *1940 Statement on Principles of Academic Freedom and Tenure*, Pol'y Documents & Reps. at 14 (11th ed. 2015).

15.   *Id.*

16.   *See* Hiers, *supra* note 6 at 4–5.

17.   Keyishian v. Bd. of Regents of Univ. of State of N.Y., 385 U.S. 589, 603 (1967).

18.   *Id.*

19.   Regents of the Univ. of Cal. v. Bakke, 438 U.S. 265, 311 (1978). *See also* Hiers, *supra* note 6 (discussing the "confusion" that Justice Powell's opinion subsequently caused on this topic).

20.   *Id.*

21.   *See, e.g.,* Donna R. Euben, *Academic Freedom of Professors and Institutions: The Current Legal Landscape*, AAUP (May 2002), https://www.aaup.org/issues/academic-freedom/professors-and-institutions.

22.   *See* Guard, *supra* note 9.

23.   *See also* Michael Bérubé & Jennifer Ruth (2022), *It's Not Free Speech: Race, Democracy, and the Future of Academic Freedom*, Baltimore: Johns Hopkins Univ. Press 2022 (explicating the relationships between academic freedom and the First Amendment and its impact).

24.   Michael H. LeRoy, *How Courts View Academic Freedom*, 42 J. COLL. & UNIV. L. 1, 14 (2016); *but see infra* note 26 (citing circuit courts that purport to recognize an academic freedom exception to *Garcetti v. Ceballos*).

25. Garcetti v. Ceballos, 547 U.S. 410, 425 (2006).

26. *See, e.g.,* Adams v. Trs. of the Univ. of N.C.–Wilmington, 640 F.3d 550, 562 (4th Cir. 2011); Buchanan v. Alexander, 919 F.3d 847, 852–53 (5th Cir. 2019); Demers v. Austin, 746 F.3d 402, 411 (9th Cir. 2014); Meriwether v. Hartop, 992 F.3d 492 (6th Cir. 2021).

27. LeRoy, *supra* note 24 at 4.

28. Rabban, *supra* note 8 at 230.

29. Hiers, *supra* note 6 at 4.

30. Rabban, *supra* note 8 at 230 ("Although courts have identified both [individual and institutional] academic freedom, they have not fully addressed, and certainly have not resolved, the tensions between them.").

31. *See, e.g.,* Bonnell v. Lorenzo, 241 F.3d 800. *See generally* LeRoy, *supra* note 24.

32. *See also* Lawrence White, *Fifty Years of Academic Freedom Jurisprudence,* 36 J. COLL. & UNIV. L. 791 (2010).

33. *See, e.g.,* Len Gutkin, *The Blasphemer,* CHRONICLE OF HIGHER EDUCATION (February 8, 2023), https://www.chronicle.com/article/the-blasphemer; *see also Hamline University Professor Who Lost Job over Muhammad Art Sues,* BBC NEWS (January 18, 2023), https://www.bbc.com/news/world-us-canada-64243344.

34. ACADEMIC FREEDOM ALLIANCE, https://academicfreedom.org/ (last accessed Sep. 16, 2023).

35. *Id.*

36. Chemerinsky & Gillman, *supra* note 5 at 112.

37. *See, e.g.,* Yeasin v. Univ. of Kan., 51 Kan. App. 2d 939, 939, 360 P.3d 423, 424 (2015).

38. *1.1.1 University Code of Conduct,* STANFORD ADMIN. GUIDE (July 23, 2018), https://adminguide.stanford.edu/chapter-1/subchapter-1/policy-1-1-1.

39. *Swarthmore College Official Student Handbook 2023–2024,* SWARTHMORE, https://www.swarthmore.edu/student-handbook (last accessed Sep. 16, 2023).

40. *Florida State University Student Conduct Code 2018,* FLORIDA STATE UNIVERSITY (June 2018) at 3, https://sccs.fsu.edu/sites/g/files/upcbnu1476/files/Student%20Conduct%20Code%20June%202018-c.pdf.

41. https://en.wikipedia.org/wiki/Foundation_for_Individual_Rights_and_Expression (last accessed Sep. 16, 2023); as of 2022, they have expanded their mission to cover defending and promoting "the value of free speech for all Americans in our courtrooms, on our campuses, and in our culture;" see *Mission,* FOUND.

INDIVIDUAL RTS. EXPR., https://www.thefire.org/about-us/mission/ (last accessed Sep. 16, 2023).

42. *Using FIRE's Spotlight Database*, FOUND. INDIVIDUAL RTS. EXPR., https://www.thefire.org/research-learn/using-fires-spotlight-database (last accessed Sep. 16, 2023).

43. *Find a School*, FOUND. INDIVIDUAL RTS. EXPR., https://www.thefire.org/colleges (last accessed Sep. 16, 2023).

44. *The 2021 College Free Speech Rankings*, FOUND. INDIVIDUAL RTS. EDUC., https://www.thefire.org/the-2021-college-free-speech-rankings/; https://www.thefire.org/research-learn/2024-college-free-speech-rankings (both last accessed Sep. 16, 2023).

45. Greg Greubel, *In Meriwether v. Hartop, the Sixth Circuit recognizes an academic exception to restrictions on the First Amendment rights of public employees*, FOUND. INDIVIDUAL RTS. EDUC. (Mar. 2021), https://www.thefire.org/in-meriwether-v-hartop-the-sixth-circuit-recognizes-an-academic-exception-to-restrictions-on-the-first-amendment-rights-of-public-employees/.

46. *History Professor Fired for Criticizing Mike Pence and Her College's COVID-19 Response Online*, FOUND. INDIVIDUAL RTS. EXPR.: FIRE CASE FILES, https://www.thefire.org/cases/collin-college-email-alludes-to-discipline-under-personnel-policies-after-tweets-criticizing-vice-president-pence/ (last accessed Sep. 16, 2023).

47. *University of Tennessee Health Sciences Center: Student Investigated and Punished for Social Media Posts*, FOUND. INDIVIDUAL RTS. EXPR.: FIRE CASE FILES, https://www.thefire.org/cases/university-of-tennessee-health-sciences-center-student-investigated-and-punished-for-social-media-posts/ (last accessed Sep. 16, 2023).

48. *See* Chemerinsky & Gillman, *supra* note 5 at 97–103.

49. *See, e.g.,* Iota Xi Chapter of Sigma Chi Fraternity v. George Mason Univ., 993 F.2d 386, 393 (1993).

50. Whitney v. Cal., 274 U.S. 357, 377 (1927).

51. *Chicago Statement: University and Faculty Body Support*, FOUND. INDIVIDUAL RTS. EXPR., https://www.thefire.org/chicago-statement-university-and-faculty-body-support/ (last accessed Sep. 16, 2023).

52. Report of the Committee on Freedom of Expression, COMM. FREEDOM EXPRESSION, http://provost.uchicago.edu/sites/default/files/documents/reports/FOECommitteeReport.pdf (last accessed Sep. 16, 2023).

53.   *Harassment*, U.S. EQUAL EMP. OPPORTUNITY COMM'N., https://www.eeoc.gov/harassment (last accessed Sep. 16, 2023).

54.   See *infra* Chapter I.

55.   *Frequently Asked Questions: Race and National Origin Discrimination*, U.S. DEP'T EDUC. OFF. CIV. RTS., https://www2.ed.gov/about/offices/list/ocr/frontpage/faq/race-origin.html.

56.   Brett A. Sokolow, Daniel Kast & Timothy J. Dunn, *The Intersection of Free Speech and Harassment Rules*, ABA (Oct. I, 2011), https://www.americanbar.org/groups/crsj/publications/human_rights_magazine_home/human_rights_vol38_2011/fall2011/the_intersection_of_free_speech_and_harassment_rules/.

57.   Kate Hidalgo Bellows, *More Students Endorse an Expansive Definition of 'Harm.' Colleges Aren't So Sure*, CHRONICLE OF HIGHER EDUCATION (May 3, 2023), https://www.chronicle.com/article/more-students-endorse-an-expansive-definition-of-harm-colleges-arent-so-sure.

58.   *Harassment, supra* note 53.

59.   *Questions and Answers on the Title IX Regulations on Sexual Harrassment* at 4, U.S. DEP'T EDUC. OFF. CIV. RTS. (July 2021), https://www2.ed.gov/about/offices/list/ocr/docs/202107-qa-titleix.pdf.

60.   Letter from Gerald A. Reynolds, Assistant Sec'y, U.S. Dep't Educ. Off. Civ. Rts., to Colleague (July 28, 2003), https://www2.ed.gov/about/offices/list/ocr/firstamend.html.

61.   *See* Laura Kipnis, *Sexual Paranoia Strikes Academe*, CHRONICLE OF HIGHER EDUCATION (Feb. 27, 2015), http://laurakipnis.com/wp-content/uploads/2010/08/Sexual-Paranoia-Strikes-Academe.pdf.

62.   *See* Jeannie Suk Gerson, *Laura Kipnis's Endless Trial by Title IX*, NEW YORKER (Sep. 20, 2017), https://www.newyorker.com/news/news-desk/laura-kipniss-endless-trial-by-title-ix; Chemerinsky & Gillman, *supra* note 5 at 15,123 (driving home the point that Kipnis was investigated for harassment on the basis of expressing certain opinions about sexual misconduct investigations).

63.   *2017 Report on Bias Reporting Systems*, FOUND. INDIVIDUAL RTS. EDUC., https://www.thefire.org/research/publications/bias-response-team-report-2017/report-on-bias-reporting-systems-2017/.

64.   *See, e.g., Bias Incident Response*, GEO. WASH. UNIV. OFF. DIVERSITY, EQUITY & CMTY. ENGAGEMENT, https://diversity.gwu.edu/bias-incident-response.

65.   Jeffery Aaron Snyder & Amna Khalid, *The Rise of "Bias Response Teams" on Campus*, New Republic (Mar. 20, 2016), https://newrepublic.com/article/132195/rise-bias-response-teams-campus.

66.   Ryan A. Miller et al., *Bias Response Teams: Fact vs. Fiction*, Inside Higher Ed (June 17, 2019), https://www.insidehighered.com/views/2019/06/17/truth-about-bias-response-teams-more-complex-often-thought-opinion.

67.   Speech First, Inc. v. Schlissel, 939 F.3d 756, 756 (6th Cir. 2019).

68.   *See* Speech First, Inc. v. Killeen, 968 F.3d 628 (7th Cir. 2020).

69.   *See* Schlissel, 939 F.3d at 756; Speech First, Inc. v. Fenves, 979 F.3d 319 (5th Cir. 2020).

70.   Schlissel, 939 F.3d at 765.

71.   Speech First, Inc. v. Sands, No. 7:21-CV-00203, 2021 WL 4315459, at *20, 43–47 (W.D. Va. Sep. 22, 2021).

72.   Madison Park & Kyung Lah, *Berkeley Protests of Yiannopoulos Caused $100,000 in Damage*, CNN (Feb. 2, 2017), https://www.cnn.com/2017/02/01/us/milo-yiannopoulos-berkeley/index.html; Daniel Henninger, *McCarthyism at Middlebury*, Wall Street J. (Mar. 8, 2017), https://www.wsj.com/articles/mccarthyism-at-middlebury-1489016328.

73.   Josh Moody, *Law Students Shout Down Controversial Speakers*, Inside Higher Ed (Mar. 23, 2022), https://www.insidehighered.com/news/2022/03/23/law-student-protests-stifle-speakers-yale-uc-hastings.

74.   *See* Heffron v. Int'l Soc'y for Krishna Consciousness, Inc., 452 U.S. 640, 647 (1981).

75.   *See* Chemerinsky & Gillman, *supra* note 5 at 123.

76.   Dorian S. Abbot & Ivan Marinovic, *The Diversity Problem on Campus*, Newsweek (Aug. 12, 2021), https://www.newsweek.com/diversity-problem-campus-opinion-1618419.

77.   Dorian Abbot, *MIT Abandons Its Mission. And Me.*, Common Sense (Oct. 5, 2021), https://bariweiss.substack.com/p/mit-abandons-its-mission-and-me.

78.   Colleen Flaherty, *At MIT, Controversy over a Canceled Lecture*, Inside Higher Ed (Oct. 6, 2021), https://www.insidehighered.com/print/news/2021/10/06/mit-controversy-over-canceled-lecture.

79.   Abbot, *supra* note 77.

80.   Flaherty, *supra* note 78.

81.   Colleen Flaherty, *A Cancelled Lecture, Revived*, Inside Higher Ed (Oct. 18, 2021), https://www.insidehighered.com/news/2021/10/19/mit-deals-fallout -canceled-lecture.

82.   *Id.*

83.   Jody Feder, *Protection of Free Speech on Campus*, National Association of Independent Colleges and Universities (Mar. 22, 2019), https://www.naicu .edu/news-events/washington-update/2019/march-22,-2019/protection-of -free-speech-on-campus-target-of-pres.

84.   Exec. Order No. 13864, 84 F.R. 11401 (Mar. 21, 2019), https:// trumpwhitehouse.archives.gov/presidential-actions/executive-order-improving-free -inquiry-transparency-accountability-colleges-universities/.

85.   34 C.F.R. 75,76,106, 606, 607, 608, 609 (2019), https://www2 .ed.gov/about/offices/list/ope/freeinquiryfinalruleunofficialversion09092020.pdf.

86.   *Update on the Free Inquiry Rule*, The Official Blog of the U.S. Department of Education (Feb. 21, 2023), https://blog.ed.gov/2023/02/update-on-the -free-inquiry-rule-2/.

87.   *Id.*

88.   Stuart Taylor Jr. & Edward Yingling, *Alumni Unite for Freedom of Speech*, Wall Street J. (Oct. 17, 2021), https://www.wsj.com/articles/alumni-free -speech-viewpoint-diversity-college-academic-freedom-11634496359.

3. Students, Student Life, and Institutional Liability

1.   Alexander C. Kafka, *Liability Everywhere*, Chronicle of Higher Education (Feb. 16, 2020), https://www.chronicle.com/article/liability-everywhere/.

2.   Legal Info. Inst., *Battery*, Cornell L. Sch., https://www.law.cornell.edu /wex/battery (last accessed Sep. 16, 2023).

3.   Legal Info. Inst., *Intentional Infliction of Emotional Distress*, Cornell L. Sch., https://www.law.cornell.edu/wex/intentional_infliction_of_emotional_distress (last accessed Sep. 16, 2023).

4.   Legal Info. Inst., *Negligence*, Cornell L. Sch., https://www.law.cornell .edu/wex/negligence (last accessed Sep. 16, 2023).

5.   See Palsgraf v. Long Island R.R. Co., 162 N.E. 99, 99–100 (N.Y. 1928).

6. Yeasin v. Univ. of Kan., 51 Kan. App. 2d 939, 939, 360 P.3d 423, 424 (2015) (in which the court exercised unlimited review without deference to the interpretation by the University of Kansas of its student code and found that the university had no authority to expel a student).

7. *Id.*

8. *See* Gebser v. Lago Vista Indep. Sch. Dist., 524 U.S. 274, 284 (1998); Davis v. Monroe Cnty. Bd. of Educ., 526 U.S. 629, 643 (1999); United States v. Georgia, 546 U.S. 151, 159, 126 S. Ct. 877, 882, 163 L. Ed. 2d 650 (2006) (in which the Court found that Title II creates a private cause of action for damages against the states for conduct that *actually* violates the Fourteenth Amendment).

9. *Family Educational Rights and Privacy Act,* U.S. Dep't Educ., https://www2 .ed.gov/policy/gen/guid/fpco/ferpa/index.html (last accessed Sep. 16, 2023).

10. 20 U.S.C. § 1232g(a)(4)(A)(i)-(ii).

11. *See* 34 C.F.R. §§ 99.31, 99.36.

12. 34 C.F.R. § 99.31.

13. 34 C.F.R. § 99.37.

14. *About Us,* U.S. Dep't Educ. Protecting Student Priv., https:// studentprivacy.aem-tx.com/about-us (last accessed Sep. 16, 2023).

15. Peter F. Lake, *The Rise of Duty and the Fall of In Loco Parentis and Other Protective Tort Doctrines in Higher Education Law,* 64 Mo. L. Rev. (1999) (providing an expanded explication of this topic); James Keller, *Liability Considerations for Return to Campus in the Age of COVID-19,* 18 NACUANOTE 7 (May 27, 2020), Nat'l Assoc. Coll & Univ. Att'ys.

16. Peter F. Lake, *Private Law Continues to Come to Campus: Rights and Responsibilities Revisited,* 31 J.C. & U.L. 621 (2005).

17. Lake, *supra* note 15 at 2–3. In an even more nuanced approach, Lake also references a "civil rights" phase and another phase that he coins the "duty era" relating to cases from the mid 1980's to late 1990's.

18. Mahanoy Area Sch. Dist. v. B.L., 141 S. Ct. 2038, 2046 (2021).

19. *See* Lake, *supra* note 15.

20. People ex rel. Pratt v. Wheaton Coll., 40 Ill. 186, 186 (1866).

21. *Id.* at 187.

22. *See* Dixon v. Alabama State Bd. of Educ., 294 F.2d 150 (5th Cir. 1961); *see also* William A. Kaplin & Barbara A. Lee, *The Law of Higher Education, 5th Ed.,*

Jossey-Bass: 839 ("The legal status of students in postsecondary institutions changed dramatically in the 1960s.").

23. Lake, *supra* note 16 at 630.

24. *See* Vimal Patel, *The New 'In Loco Parentis'*, Chronicle of Higher Education (Feb. 17, 2019), https://www.chronicle.com/article/why-colleges-are-keeping-a-closer-eye-on-their-students-lives/.

25. Bradshaw v. Rawlings, 612 F.2d 135 (3d Cir. 1979).

26. *Id.* at 137.

27. *Id.*

28. *Id.* at 143.

29. *Id.* at 140.

30. *See, e.g.,* Helfman v. Ne. Univ., 485 Mass. 308, 318 (Mass. 2020) ("Accordingly, we reject the defendants' blanket contention that, necessarily, universities have no special relationship with voluntarily intoxicated students.").

31. *See, e.g.,* Patel, *supra* note 24.

32. *See generally*, Lake, *supra* notes 15 and 16.

33. *Id.*

34. In loco parentis has itself been an evolving concept subject to some confusion by courts. While it at first was considered a pure bar to suit, it later evolved as a means of arguing that IHEs did in fact have a duty of care given the influence they exhibited over their students. *See* Lake, *supra* note 15 at 6; Bradshaw v. Rawlings, 612 F.2d 135, 139 (3d Cir. 1979) ("A special relationship was created between college and student that imposed a duty on the college to exercise control over student conduct and, reciprocally, gave the students certain rights of protection by the college.").

35. Tsialas v. Cornell Univ., Index No. EF2020-0061 (N.Y. Sup. Ct. filed Jan. 28, 2020).

36. *Id.*

37. David Robinson, *Cornell Settled Hazing Lawsuit with Student's Family amid Lingering Questions about his Death,* Pressconnects (Dec. 1, 2020), https://www.pressconnects.com/story/news/local/watchdog/2020/12/01/cornell-settled-antonio-tsialas-hazing-lawsuit-amid-questions-his-death/6470121002/.

38. Bill Schackner, *Penn State Settles with Piazza Family, Which Sues 28 Former Fraternity Members,* Pittsburgh Post-Gazette (Feb. 1, 2019), https://www

.post-gazette.com/news/education/2019/02/01/Penn-State-University-Timothy -Piazza-fraternity-settlement-Greek-hazing-death-college/stories/201902010139.

39.　　John Bacon, *First Jail Terms Issued in Penn State Fraternity Hazing Death of Timothy Piazza*, USA Today (Apr. 3, 2019), https://www.usatoday.com/story /news/nation/2019/04/03/penn-state-timothy-piazza-first-jail-terms-issued -hazing-death/3353467002/.

40.　　Lauren del Valle, *Parents of Timothy Piazza Settle with Penn State, Sue Fraternity Members*, CNN (Feb. 2, 2019), https://www.cnn.com/2019/02/02/us/piazza -penn-beta-theta-pi-wrongful-death-suit/index.html.

41.　　Bacon, *supra* note 39.

42.　　*Id.*

43.　　*Timothy J. Piazza Antihazing Legislation Signed into Pennsylvania Law*, Penn State (Oct. 19, 2018), https://www.psu.edu/news/administration/story/timothy -j-piazza-antihazing-legislation-signed-pennsylvania-law/.

44.　　*Bowling Green Fraternity Pledge Was "Left Alone on the Couch to Die" after Alleged Hazing, Lawsuit Claims*, CBS News (May 13, 2021), https://www.cbsnews.com /news/stone-foltz-bowling-green-hazing-death-lawsuit/; Cassidy McDonald, *Students Indicted on Manslaughter and Hazing Charges after Death of Bowling Green Sophomore*, CBS (Apr. 29, 2021), https://www.cbsnews.com/news/stone-foltz-hazing-death -bowling-green-fraternity-pi-kappa-alpha/; Andrea May Sahouri, *Student Sues Theta Chi, Drake University after Alleged Hazing Incident That Left Him Near Death*, Des Moines Reg. (Feb. 14, 2020), https://www.desmoinesregister.com/story/news/crime -and-courts/2020/02/14/drake-university-hazing-lawsuit-theta-chi-pledge-says -he-forced-drink-until-unconscious/4753743002/; Vanessa Murphy, *I-Team: UNLV Student's Family Calls Fraternity Boxing Match, 'School-Sanctioned Amateur Fight That Cost Him His Life'*, 8 News Now (Nov. 29, 2021), https://www.8newsnow.com/news /local-news/i-team-unlv-students-family-calls-fraternity-boxing-match-school -sanctioned-amateur-fight-that-cost-him-his-life/.

45.　　*See, e.g., Risk Management*, United Educators, https://www.edurisk solutions.org/blogs/.

46.　　*Fraternity and Sorority*, NASPA, https://www.naspa.org/division /fraternity-and-sorority.

47.　　*Piazza Center and National Organization Partner on Webinar Series*, Penn State (Oct. 17, 2021), https://www.psu.edu/news/impact/story/piazza-center -and-national-organization-partner-webinar-series/.

48.　See Kate Hidalgo Bellows, *What to Know about Fraternities Cutting Ties with Their Colleges*, Chronicle of Higher Education (Aug. 23, 2022), https://www .chronicle.com/article/what-to-know-about-fraternities-cutting-ties-with-their -colleges.

49.　*See, e.g.*, Warren Zola, *College Athletics: The Growing Tension between Amateurism and Commercialism*, Oxford Handbook of American Sports Law, edited by Michael A. McCann (Oxford Handbooks Online, Oxford Univ. Press, 2015); Neil King (2016) *Sport Governance: An Introduction*, Routledge; Eddie Comeaux (2015), *Introduction to Intercollegiate Athletics*, Baltimore: Johns Hopkins Univ. Press.

50.　Associated Press, *Jerry Sandusky Sex Abuse Case Has States Re-examining Mandatory Reporter Laws*, OregonLive (June 9, 2012), https://www.oregonlive.com /today/2012/06/jerry_sandusky_sex_abuse.html; Joseph Spector, *NY Coaches Now Required to Report Suspected Abuse*, Democrat & Chronicle (Aug. 6, 2014), https://www.democratandchronicle.com/story/vote-up/2014/08/06/ny -coaches-now-required-to-report-suspected-abuse/13678689/; John Finnerty, *Sandusky Case Spurred Major Changes to Beef Up Reporting of Suspected Abuse*, CNHI News (Sep. 24, 2021), https://www.cnhinews.com/pennsylvania/article_0045af7e -1d6d-11ec-9189-f32e908ccfa9.html.

51.　Abby Kloppenburg, *Top Football Schools Review Policies in Penn State's Wake*, USA Today (Sep. 4, 2013), https://www.usatoday.com/story/news/nation /2013/09/04/football-schools-make-new-rules-after-sandusky/2764603/.

52.　*Penalties for Failure to Report and False Reporting of Child Abuse and Neglect*, Children's Bureau, https://www.childwelfare.gov/pubPDFs/report.pdf.

53.　*Id.* at 2.

54.　Nell Gluckman, *The Long Shadow of Jerry Sandusky*, Chronicle of Higher Education (Nov. 4, 2021), https://www.chronicle.com/article/ the-long-shadow-of-jerry-sandusky.

55.　*Id.*; Scott Jaschik, *Did Michigan State Look the Other Way?*, Inside Higher Ed (Nov. 27, 2017), https://www.insidehighered.com/news/2017/11/27 /guilty-plea-former-team-doctor-renews-scrutiny-michigan-state.

56.　Gluckman, *supra* note 54.

57.　*Id.*; Steve Marowski, *University of Michigan Officials Could Have Stopped Abuse by Late Athletic Doctor, Report Finds*, Michigan Live (May 11, 2021), https://www.mlive .com/news/ann-arbor/2021/05/university-of-michigan-officials-could-have -stopped-abuse-by-late-athletic-doctor-report-finds.html.

58. *See also* Spector, *supra* note 50.

59. *See, e.g.,* Ben Baby, *Former TCU Player Sues School, Gary Patterson for Negligence, Being 'Threatened' to Return from Injury,* DALLAS MORNING NEWS (Feb. 1, 2018), https://www.dallasnews.com/sports/tcu-horned-frogs/2018/02/01/former
-tcu-player-sues-school-gary-patterson-for-negligence-being-threatened-to-return
-from-injury/; Dana O'Neil, *Former Seton Hall Star Myles Powell Suing School, Coach over Knee Injury,* ATHLETIC (July 15, 2021), https://theathletic.com/news/former-seton
-hall-star-myles-powell-suing-school-coach-over-knee-injury/ZY9r4JzKZ9vg/;
Fecke v. Bd. of Supervisors of L.A. State Univ. & Agric. & Mech. Coll., 180 So.3d
326 (La. Ct. App. 2015).

60. *See, e.g.,* Marek Mazurek, *Former Notre Dame Football Player Sues School, NCAA for Negligence in Concussion Education,* SOUTH BEND TRIBUNE (Sep. 16, 2021), https://
www.southbendtribune.com/story/news/2021/09/16/notre-dame-football
-richard-morrison-ncaa-lawsuit-school-concussions-cte/8364665002/; Chao
Xiong, *Former University of Minnesota Football Player Sues School for Head Injuries Sustained as Student Athlete,* STAR TRIBUNE (Aug. 27, 2021), https://www.startribune.com
/university-of-minnesota-josh-campion-concussion-lawsuit-painkillers
/600091699/; Ben Bolch, *Three Former UCLA Football Players Sue School and Coach Jim Mora over Alleged Mishandling of Injuries,* L.A. TIMES (May 30, 2019), https://www
.latimes.com/sports/ucla/la-sp-ucla-football-lawsuit-jim-mora-20190530-story
.html.

61. In re: National Collegiate Athletic Association Student-Athlete
Concussion Injury Litigation (MDL No. 2494/ Master Docket No. 1:13-cv
-09116 (N.D. Ill.)) (Arrington Matter); *see also Arrington Class Settlement Information,*
NCAA, https://www.ncaa.org/about/arrington-class-settlement-information.

62. Email from Scott Bearby, Vice President Legal Affs. & Gen. Couns.,
NCAA (available at http://image.mail2.ncaa.com/lib/fe5715707d6d067e7c1c
/m/5/1a96786d-64dd-4c4f-9d54-fcc5fc031bc0.pdf).

63. Schweyen v. Univ. of Montana-Missoula, CV 21-138-M-DLC
(D. Mont. Nov. 18, 2021).

64. Alex Seats, *Report: Former LSU OL Coach James Cregg Sues University for Breach of Contract,* 24/7 SPORTS (Aug. 19, 2021), https://247sports.com/Article/LSU
-football-James-Cregg-suing-university-for-breach-of-contract-NCAA-rule
-violation-Ed-Orgeron-Scott-Woodward-169374369/.

65.   Micheal McCann, *WSU Fires Unvaccinated Coaches as School Claims 'Just Cause'*, Sportico (Oct. 19, 2021), https://www.sportico.com/law/analysis/2021 /rolovichs-anti-vax-firing-not-immune-from-litigation-1234644326/.

66.   *Id.*

67.   Memorandum from Jennifer A. Abruzzo, Gen. Couns., to All Regional Directors, Officers-in-Charge, & Resident Officers at 3 (Sep. 29, 2021) (available at https://www.nlrb.gov/guidance/memos-research/general-counsel-memos).

68.   *Id.* at 4.

69.   Alston, 141 S. Ct. at 2147.

70.   *Id.*

71.   Elizabeth Redden, *Study Abroad and a $41.5 Million Verdict*, Inside Higher Ed (Aug. 24, 2017), https://www.insidehighered.com/news/2017/08/24/415m -verdict-student-who-fell-ill-school-trip-china-has-implications-study-abroad.

72.   Munn v. Hotchkiss Sch., 326 Conn. 540, 165 A.3d 1167 (2017).

73.   Alexa Lardieri, *State Department Rolls Out Revamped Travel Warning System*, U.S. News & World Report (Jan. 11, 2018), https://www.usnews.com/news/best -countries/articles/2018-01-11/state-department-rolls-out-revamped-travel -warning-system.

74.   Boston Univ., *Depression, Anxiety, Loneliness Are Peaking in College Students*, ScienceDaily (Feb. 19, 2021), https://www.sciencedaily.com/releases/2021/02 /210219190939.htm.

75.   *See, e.g.,* Kelly Field, *'Heart-Pounding' Conversations: Professors Are Being Trained to Spot Signs of Mental-Health Distress*, Chronicle of Higher Education (Sep. 28, 2021), https://www.chronicle.com/article/heart-pounding-conversations-professors-are -being-trained-to-spot-signs-of-mental-health-distress.

76.   Dzung Duy Nguyen v. Mass. Inst. of Tech., 96 N.E.3d 128, 147 (2018).

77.   *Id.*

78.   *See, e.g.,* Helfman v. Ne. Univ., 149 N.E.3d 758 (Mass. 2020).

79.   Thomas J. Weber, *Family of UF Grad Student Who Died by Suicide Files Legal Claim against University*, The Gainesville Sun (Aug. 13, 2021), https://www.gainesville.com /story/news/education/campus/2021/08/13/family-uf-grad-student-suicide -files-claim-against-university-huixiang-chen-tao-li/8121082002/.

80.   Aaditi Lele & Katerine Oung, *Parents of Former Vanderbilt Student Brian Adams File Wrongful Death Lawsuit against University*, The Vanderbilt Hustler (Jan. 26, 2023),

https://vanderbilthustler.com/2023/01/26/parents-of-former-vanderbilt
-student-brian-adams-file-wrongful-death-lawsuit-against-university/.

81.　　Tang v. President and Fellows of Harvard College, et al., Middlesex
Superior Court, C.A. No. 1881CV02603 (Dec. 20, 2022) (Tingle, J.), https://
www.hklaw.com/-/media/files/insights/publications/2023/01/tangvharvard
decision.pdf.

82.　　Regents of Univ. of Cal. v. Superior Ct., 413 P.3d 656 (2018).

83.　　*Id.*

84.　　*Id.*

85.　　*Id.* at 660.

86.　　Weber, *supra* note 79.

87.　　Roe v. Ne. Univ., No. 16-03335-C, 2019 WL 1141291 (Mass. Super.
Mar. 8, 2019).

88.　　*See, e.g.,* Doe v. R.I. Sch. of Design, 432 F. Supp. 3d 35, 37 (D.R.I. 2019).

89.　　*See, e.g.,* Feibleman v. Trs. of Columbia Univ. in N.Y., No. 19-CV-4327,
2020 WL 882429 (S.D.N.Y. Feb. 24, 2020).

90.　　*See* Courtney Joy McMullan, *Flip It and Reverse It: Examining Reverse Gender
Discrimination Claims Brought under Title IX,* 76 Wash. & Lee L. Rev. 1825 (2019). In a
novel legal development that is sure to have further ramifications, the Connecticut
Supreme Court recently held that because of nuances in Yale University's Title IX
policies, a respondent in a Title IX proceeding could bring a defamation suit
against a complainant who made allegations against the respondent in that
proceeding. *See* Saifullah Khan v. Yale University et al., Sup. Ct. of Conn. SC20705
(June 27, 2023).

91.　　Davis v. Monroe Cnty. Bd. of Educ., 526 U.S. 629 (1999).

92.　　*See* Kollaritsch, 944 F.3d 613 (6th Cir.); Shank v. Carleton Coll., 993
F.3d 567, 576 (8th Cir. 2021); Escue v. N. Okla. Coll., 450 F.3d 1146, 1155–56
(10th Cir. 2006); Reese v. Jefferson Sch. Dist. No. 14J, 208 F.3d 736, 740 (9th
Cir. 2000); *see also* Fitzgerald v. Barnstable Sch. Comm., 504 F.3d 165, 172–73 (1st
Cir. 2007), rev'd and remanded on other grounds, 555 U.S. 246 (2009); Williams
v. Bd. of Regents of the Univ. Sys. of Ga., 477 F.3d 1282 (11th Cir. 2007).

93.　　*See* Fairfax Co. School Bd. v. Jane Doe, 1 F.4th 257 (4th Cir. 2021) and
10 F.4th 406 (4th Cir. 2021) (denying School Board's petition for rehearing en
banc).

94.   Cummings v. Premier Rehab Keller, P.L.L.C., No. 20-219 (Roberts, C.J.).

95.   Feibleman, 2020 WL 882439, at *16-17 (S.D.N.Y. Feb. 24, 2020) ("The Second Circuit has recognized two general ways in which a plaintiff can "attack[] a university disciplinary proceeding on grounds of gender bias": an erroneous outcome claim and a selective enforcement claim.").

96.   *Id.* at 17.

97.   *Id.*

98.   *See, e.g.*, Roe v. Ne. Univ., No. 16-03335-C, 2019 WL 1141291 (Mass. Super. Mar. 8, 2019); Feibleman v. Trs. of Columbia Univ. in N.Y., No. 19-CV-4327, 2020 WL 882429 (S.D.N.Y. Feb. 24, 2020).

99.   Roe, 2019 WL 1141291; Helfman v. Ne. Univ., 485 Mass. 308, 315 (Mass. 2020); Doe v. R.I. Sch. of Design, 516 F.Supp.3d 188 (D. R.I. Feb. 2, 2021); Doe v. Hobart & William Smith Colls., 6:20-CV-06338, 2021 WL 2603400 (W.D.N.Y. June 25, 2021).

100.   Mallika Kallingal & Jennifer Henderson, *University of Utah Settles with Family of Murdered Student Lauren McCluskey and Renames Its Violence Prevention Center in Her Honor,* CNN (Oct. 23, 2020), https://www.cnn.com/2020/10/23/us/lauren-mccluskey -university-of-utah-settlement/index.html; Darran Simon & Madeline Holcombe, *Parents of a University of Utah Student Who Was Killed after Weeks of Harassment Sue the School,* CNN (June 27, 2019), https://www.cnn.com/2019/06/27/us/lauren-mccluskey -murder-parents-sue-trnd/index.html.

101.   *Id.*

102.   *Id.*

103.   Christine Hauser, *Family of Lauren McCluskey Agrees to $13.5 Million Settlement in Daughter's Death,* New York Times (Oct. 22, 2020), https://www.nytimes.com /2020/10/22/us/lauren-mccluskey-death-settlement.html.

104.   Kallingal & Henderson, *supra* note 100.

105.   Katherine Mangan, *The Lethal Consequences of Dropping the Ball on Dating Violence,* Chronicle of Higher Education (July 20, 2022), https://www.chronicle .com/article/the-lethal-consequences-of-dropping-the-ball-on-dating-violence.

106.   Taylor Randall, *Letter from President Randall on the Death of Zhifan Dong,* The University of Utah (July 19, 2022), https://attheu.utah.edu/facultystaff /statement-from-president-randall-on-the-death-of-zhifan-dong/.

107.   Claire Wang, *Univ. of Utah to Pay $5 Million to Parents of Slain International Student Zhifan Dong*, NBC News (Feb. 23, 2023), https://www.nbcnews.com/news/asian-america/univ-utah-pay-5-million-parents-slain-international-student-zhifan-don-rcna72057.

4. Admissions, Advancement, and Community Relations

1.   Abigail Johnson Hess, *Fewer Than 1 in 5 Americans Think the College Admissions Process Is Fair*, CBS (Mar. 20, 2019), https://www.cnbc.com/2019/03/20/under-20percent-of-americans-think-the-college-admissions-process-is-fair.html.

2.   *Id.*

3.   *See, e.g.,* Aaron Carroll, *To Be Sued Less, Doctors Should Consider Talking to Patients More*, New York Times (June 1, 2015), https://www.nytimes.com/2015/06/02/upshot/to-be-sued-less-doctors-should-talk-to-patients-more.html.

4.   Ronald J. Daniels (2021), *What Universities Owe Democracy*, Baltimore: Johns Hopkins Univ. Press: 9.

5.   Bakke, 438 U.S. at 311; *See supra* Chapter 2.

6.   *See, e.g.,* Powers v. St. John's Univ. Sch. of Law, 32 N.E.3d 371, 372 (2015); *See also* Kaplin & Lee at 880–81.

7.   Powers, 32 N.E.3d at 372.

8.   *Id.* at 375.

9.   *Id.*

10.   42 U.S.C. § 2000(d).

11.   U.S. Const. amend. XIV, §1.

12.   *See* Students for Fair Admissions, Inc. v. President and Fellows of Harvard College and Students for Fair Admissions, Inc. v. University of North Carolina, et al., Nos. 20-1199 and 21-707, 600 U.S. ____ (2023). Hereafter SFA.

13.   *Id.*

14.   Fisher v. Univ. of Tex. at Austin, 579 U.S. 365 (2016)

15.   Fisher v. Univ. of Tex. at Austin, 570 U.S. 297, 310 (citing Grutter v. Bollinger, 539 U.S. 306, 326 (2003)).

16.   *Id.* (citing Regents of Univ. of Cal. v. Bakke, 438 U.S. 265, 311–12 (1978)).

17.   Grutter, 539 U.S. at 325.

18.   Fisher, 570 U.S. at 310.

19.   SFA, at 22.

20.   Fisher v. Univ. of TX at Austin, 570 U.S. 297; Fisher v. University of Texas at Austin, 579 U.S. 365 (2016).

21.   Fisher v. Univ. of Tex. at Austin, 579 U.S. 365 (2016).

22.   Regents of Univ. of Cal. v. Bakke, 438 U.S. 265, 307 (1978); Grutter v. Bollinger, 539 U.S. 306, 330 (2003).

23.   *See* DeFunis v. Odegaard, 416 U.S. 312 (1974); Bakke, 438 U.S. at 265; Brown v. Bd. Of. Educ., 345 U.S. 972 (1953).

24.   539 U.S. 244 (2003).

25.   Grutter, 539 U.S. at 337.

26.   Grutter, 539 U.S. at 337–39.

27.   *Id.*; *See* Fisher v. Univ. of Tex. at Austin, 570 U.S. 297, 334 (Ginsburg, J., dissenting).

28.   Fisher v. Univ. of Tex. at Austin, 645 F.Supp. 2d 587, 608 (W.D. Tex. 2009).

29.   Fisher v. Univ. of Tex. at Austin, 579 U.S. 365 (2016).

30.   Grutter v. Bollinger, 539 U.S. 306, 326 (2003).

31.   Fisher v. Univ. of Tex. at Austin, 570 U.S. 297, 312 (2003).

32.   Fisher, 570 U.S. at 335 (Ginsburg, J., dissenting).

33.   Fisher, 579 U.S. at 365.

34.   Scott Jaschik, *UNC Wins Affirmative Action Case, for Now,* Inside Higher Ed (Oct. 25, 2021), https://www.insidehighered.com/admissions/article/2021/10 /25/unc-wins-affirmative-action-case.

35.   *See* SFA.

36.   *Id.* at 39.

37.   *Id.*

38.   Off. Pub. Affs., *Justice Department Sues Yale University for Illegal Discrimination Practices in Undergraduate Admissions,* U.S. Dep't Just. (Oct. 8, 2020), https://www .justice.gov/opa/pr/justice-department-sues-yale-university-illegal-discrimination -practices-undergraduate.

39.   *Id.*

40.   Anemona Hartocollis, *Justice Dept. Sues Yale, Citing Illegal Race Discrimination,* New York Times (Oct. 8, 2020), https://www.nytimes.com/2020/10/08/us/yale -discrimination.html.

41.   Rachel Treisman, *Justice Department Drops Race Discrimination Lawsuit against Yale University*, Nat'l Pub. Radio (Feb. 3, 2021), https://www.npr.org/2021/02/03/963666724/justice-department-drops-race-discrimination-lawsuit-against-yale-university.

42.   Anthony Depalma, *Ivy Universities Deny Price-Fixing but Agree to Avoid It in the Future*, New York Times (May 23, 1991), https://www.nytimes.com/1991/05/23/us/ivy-universities-deny-price-fixing-but-agree-to-avoid-it-in-the-future.html.

43.   *Id.*

44.   Scott Jaschik, *Justice Department Investigates Early-Decision Admissions*, Inside Higher Ed (Apr. 9, 2018), https://www.insidehighered.com/admissions/article/2018/04/09/justice-department-starts-investigation-early-decision-admissions.

45.   Scott Jaschik, *Department of Justice Probes Admissions Ethics Code*, Inside Higher Ed (Jan. 10, 2018), https://www.insidehighered.com/news/2018/01/10/department-justice-investigating-antitrust-issues-regard-nacacs-ethics-code.

46.   *Id.*

47.   Scott Jaschik, *Justice Department Sues, Settles with NACAC*, Inside Higher Ed (Dec. 16, 2019), https://www.insidehighered.com/admissions/article/2019/12/16/justice-department-sues-and-settles-college-admissions-group.

48.   *Id.*

49.   Henry v. Brown Univ., No. 1:2022CV00125 (N.D. Ill. filed Jan. 9, 2022).

50.   Improving America's Schools Act of 1994 § 568 (2015), https://www.naicu.edu/docLib/20150803_Antitrust_legislation.pdf.

51.   *Id.*

52.   Henry v. Brown Univ., No. 1:2022CV00125 (N.D. Ill. filed Jan. 9, 2022).

53.   https://www.reuters.com/legal/litigation/u-chicago-first-settle-financial-aid-price-fixing-claims-us-court-2023-04-20/.

54.   34 C.F.R. § 668.14(b)(22)(i).

55.   34 C.F.R. § 668.14(b)(22)(i)(A).

56.   Elizabeth Redden, *New Law Threatens International Recruiting Model*, Inside Higher Ed (Oct. 25, 2021), https://www.insidehighered.com/admissions/article/2021/10/25/veterans-ed-law-could-impact-international-recruitment.

57.   *THRIVE Act Veterans Benefits Provision Poses Unexpected Challenge to Use of Incentive-Based Agents for International Student Recruitment*, NAFSA (Dec. 21, 2021),

https://www.nafsa.org/regulatory-information/thrive-act-veterans-benefits
-provision-poses-unexpected-challenge-use.

58.　Scott Jaschik, *Bill Would Dent Aid to Colleges with Legacy Admissions*, Inside Higher Ed (Feb. 7, 2022), https://www.insidehighered.com/admissions/article /2022/02/07/bill-would-cut-student-aid-colleges-legacy-preferences.

59.　Scott Jaschik, *Attacking Legacy and Early-Decision Admissions*, Inside Higher Ed (Mar. 14, 2022), https://www.insidehighered.com/admissions/article /2022/03/10/new-york-bill-would-ban-legacy-admissions-and-early-decision.

60.　http://edreformnow.org/wp-content/uploads/2021/12/Legacy -groups-letter.pdf.

61.　*See* Frank LoMonte, *The First Amendment, Social Media and College Admissions*, Inside Higher Ed (Dec. 13, 2021), https://www.insidehighered.com/admissions /views/2021/12/13/admissions-officials-need-pay-attention-first-amendment-opinion; *Kaplan Survey: Percentage of College Admissions Officers Who Visit Applicants' Social Media Pages on the Rise Again*, KAPLAN (Jan. 13, 2020), https://www.kaptest.com/blog /press/2020/01/13/kaplan-survey-percentage-of-college-admissions- officers-who -visit-applicants-social-media-pages-on-the-rise-again.

62.　Frank D. LoMonte & Courtney Shannon, *Admissions against Pinterest: The First Amendment Implications of Reviewing College Applicants' Social Media Speech*, 49 Hofstra L. Rev. 773, 798 (2021).

63.　*Investigations of College Admissions and Testing Bribery Scheme*, U.S. Att'y's Off. Dist. Mass., https://www.justice.gov/usao-ma/investigations-college-admissions -and-testing-bribery-scheme.

64.　Anemona Hartocollis, *2 Parents Are Convicted in the Varsity Blues Admissions*, *Trial*, New York Times (Oct. 9, 2021), https://www.nytimes.com/2021/10/08 /us/varsity-blues-trial-wilson-abdelaziz.html.

65.　*Varsity Blues Scandal*, Wikipedia, https://en.wikipedia.org/wiki/Varsity _Blues_scandal (last accessed Sep. 17, 2023).

66.　*Georgetown Father Found Not Guilty in Final Trial of "Varsity Blues" College Admissions Scandal*, AP News (June 16, 2022), https://www.cbsnews.com/news/georgetown -father-amin-khoury-not-guilty-final-trial-varsity-blues-college-admissions-scandal/.

67.　Anemona Hartocollis, *2 Parents Are Convicted in the Varsity Blues Admissions Trial*, New York Times (Oct. 9, 2021), https://www.nytimes.com/2021/10/08 /us/varsity-blues-trial-wilson-abdelaziz.html.

68.   Benjamin Wallace-Wells, *The Stanford Sailing Coach's Defense in the Varsity Blues Case*, New Yorker (Oct. 22, 2021), https://www.newyorker.com/news/annals-of-inquiry/the-stanford-sailing-coachs-defense.

69.   *Lawsuit Says 16 Elite Colleges Are Part of Price-Fixing Cartel*, New York Times (Jan. 14, 2022), https://www.nytimes.com/2022/01/10/us/financial-aid-lawsuit-colleges.html.

70.   See Wallace-Wells, *supra* note 68, ("raises questions about the admissions practices at elite universities and colleges—including the Operation Varsity Blues scandal, in which wealthy and well-connected donors were shown to have bought their children's admission to college.").

71.   *See, e.g., Gift Acceptance, Counting and Reporting Policy*, Carnegie Mellon Univ. (Jan. 2022), https://www.cmu.edu/policies/administrative-and-governance/gift-acceptance.html.

72.   *See also* Bert Feuss, *Bitcoin Basics for NFPs: Accepting and Valuing Crypto Asset Gifts*, AICPA (2021), https://www.aicpa.org/resources/article/bitcoin-basics-for-nfps-accepting-and-valuing-crypto-asset-gifts.

73.   Francie Diep, *The Sacklers Gave Millions to Higher Ed. Here's How Scholars on One Campus Feel about Taking the Money*, Chronicle of Higher Education (Oct. 9, 2019), https://www.chronicle.com/article/the-sacklers-gave-millions-to-higher-ed-heres-how-scholars-on-one-campus-feel-about-taking-the-money/.

74.   Francie Diep, *Universities Are Facing Criticism for Taking Dirty Money. Do Their Donor Policies Protect Them?*, Chronicle of Higher Education (Oct. 30, 2019), https://www.chronicle.com/article/universities-are-facing-criticism-for-taking-dirty-money-do-their-donor-policies-protect-them/.

75.   *Gift Acceptance Policy*, Brown Univ. (Oct. 26, 2019), https://policy.brown.edu/policy/gift-acceptance.

76.   Brian Mann, *The Sacklers, Who Made Billions from OxyContin, Win Immunity from Opioid Lawsuits*, NPR (Sep. 1, 2021), https://www.npr.org/2021/09/01/1031053251/sackler-family-immunity-purdue-pharma-oxycontin-opioid-epidemic.

77.   Jonah S. Berger, *Activists Call on Harvard to Strip Art Museum of Sackler Name*, The Harvard Crimson (Jan. 21, 2019), https://www.thecrimson.com/article/2019/1/21/somerville-mayor-condemns-harvard-sackler-ties/.

78.   *Board Action on School of Law Name*, UNIVERSITY OF RICHMOND (Sep. 23, 2022), https://trustees.richmond.edu/naming/.

79.   For the original text of the letter, see https://www.realclearmarkets.com /articles/2023/02/01/the_woke_ingrate_university_of_richmond_leadership_should _give_the_money_back_879007.html#google_vignette (last accessed Sep. 16, 2023).

80.   Christina Guessferd, *Former Governor Douglas Sues Middlebury College over Chapel Name*, WCAX (Mar. 24, 2023), https://www.wcax.com/2023/03/25 /former-gov-douglas-sues-middlebury-college-over-chapel-name/; Rachel Lu & Lily Jones, *College Files Motion to Dismiss Mead Lawsuit, Considers Education Efforts*, THE MIDDLEBURY CAMPUS (May 11, 2023), https://www.middleburycampus.com /article/2023/05/college-files-motion-to-dismiss-mead-lawsuit-considers -education-efforts; Riley Board, Lucy Townend, & Abigail Chang, *Mead Chapel Name Removed in Acknowledgement of Its Namesake's Role in Eugenics*, THE MIDDLEBURY CAMPUS (Sep. 27, 2021), https://www.middleburycampus.com/article/2021/09/mead -chapel-name-removed-in-acknowledgement-of-its-namesakes-role-in-eugenics.

81.   Karen Sloan, *Former 'Hastings' Law School Loses Appeal to Block Suit over Name Change*, REUTERS (June 6, 2023), https://www.reuters.com/legal/government /former-hastings-law-school-loses-appeal-block-suit-over-name-change-2023 -06-06/; *Serranus Clinton Hastings*, WIKIPEDIA, https://en.wikipedia.org/wiki /Serranus_Clinton_Hastings (last accessed Sep. 16, 2023).

82.   *Facilitating Respectful Return*, NAT'L PARK SERV. (Nov. 22, 2019), https:// www.nps.gov/subjects/nagpra/index.htm.

83.   Sage Alexander, *Grave Robbing at UC Berkeley: A History of Failed Repatriation*, DAILY CALIFORNIAN (Dec. 5, 2020), https://www.dailycal.org/2020/12/05/grave -robbing-at-uc-berkeley-a-history-of-failed-repatriation/.

84.   Cara J. Chang, *Harvard Holds Human Remains of 19 Likely Enslaved Individuals, Thousands of Native Americans, Draft Report Says*, THE HARVARD CRIMSON (June 1, 2022), https://www.thecrimson.com/article/2022/6/1/draft-human-remains-report/.

85.   Ed Pilkington, *Ivy League University Set to Rebury Skulls of Black People Kept for Centuries*, THE GUARDIAN (Aug. 7, 2022), https://www.theguardian.com/us-news /2022/aug/07/us-university-plans-repatriation-black-american-remains.

86.   Macrina Wang, *The Restitution Question*, YALE DAILY NEWS (May 21, 2019), https://yaledailynews.com/blog/2019/05/21/the-restitution-question/.

87.   Daniel Grant, *Lawsuit Filed to Block University's Sale of Georgia O'Keeffe Painting to Fund Dormitory Renovations,* THE ART NEWSPAPER (Apr. 25, 2023), https://www .theartnewspaper.com/2023/04/25/lawsuit-valparaiso-university-deaccession -georgia-okeeffe.

88.   *Brandeis, Plaintiffs Settle Rose Art Museum Lawsuit,* BRANDEIS TODAY (June 30, 2011), https://www.brandeis.edu/now/2011/june/rose.html.

89.   Chase Sutton & Celia Kreth, *A Fair Fare Affair,* DAILY PENNSYLVANIAN (July 7, 2020), https://www.thedp.com/article/2020/07/penn-pilots-taxes-exempt -nonprofit-protest-defund-police-philly-schools; Kevin Kiley, *A Fair Fare Affair,* INSIDE HIGHER ED (Feb. 10, 2012), https://www.insidehighered.com/news /2012/02/10/brown-dispute-questions-whats-fair-payment-lieu-taxes.

90.   Jim Shelton, *With New $140+ Million Yale Pledge, Yale, New Haven Promote Growth, Economy,* YALE NEWS (November 17, 2021), https://news.yale.edu /2021/11/17/new-140-million-yale-pledge-yale-new-haven-promote -growth-economy.

91.   Ginsburg v. City of Ithaca, 5 F.Supp.3d 243, 247-49 (N.D.N.Y. 2014).

92.   Compl., Gibson Bros., Inc. v. Oberlin Coll., No. 17-CV-193761 (Ct. Com. Pl. Lorain Cnty. Nov. 7, 2017); Anemona Hartocollis, *Oberlin Helped Students Defame a Bakery, a Jury Says. The Punishment: $33 Million,* N.Y. TIMES (June 14, 2019), https://www.nytimes.com/2019/06/14/us/oberlin-bakery-lawsuit.html.

93.   *Id.*

94.   *Bakery Litigation: 10 Key Facts,* OBERLIN, https://www.oberlin.edu/news -and-events/bakery-litigation/10-key-facts.

95.   Compl., *Gibson Bros., Inc.* (No. 17-CV-193761).

96.   Oyin Adedoyin, *Oberlin's Aid to Student Protestors Led to a $32-Million Judgment. The College Appealed, and Lost.* CHRONICLE OF HIGHER EDUCATION (Apr. 1, 2022), https://www.chronicle.com/article/oberlins-aid-to-student-protestors-led -to-a-32-million-judgment-the-college-just-lost-its-appeal.

97.   Anemona Hartocollis, *Oberlin Helped Students Defame a Bakery, a Jury Says. The Punishment: $33 Million,* N.Y. TIMES (June 14, 2019), https://www.nytimes.com/ 2019/06/14/us/oberlin-bakery-lawsuit.html.

98.   *See also* the case of Michael McAlear and Wesleyan University, with FIRE commenting: "The court generally got things right here . . . that universities and colleges should not be responsible, legally, for the speech of their constituents."

Hannah Reale, *Judge Rules against Professor McAlear, Closing Defamation Case against Wesleyan*, The Wesleyan Argus (March 3, 2020), http://wesleyanargus.com/2020/03/03/wesleyan-wins-defamation-case-against-professor-mcalear/.

99.   *Official Statements Regarding the Gibson's Litigation: May 13, 2019*, Oberlin, https://www.oberlin.edu/news-and-events/bakery-litigation/official-statements.

100.   Thomas M. Boyd, *Oberlin College Loses Its Appeal*, The Wall Street Journal (Apr. 1, 2022), https://www.wsj.com/articles/oberlin-college-loses-appeal-ohio-gibsons-bakery-v-woke-pc-cancel-culture-crt-critical-race-theory-libel-emotional-distress-racial-profiling-higher-education-11648829090.

101.   Dave DeNatale & Lindsay Buckingham, *Gibson's Bakery Receives Complete Payment of $36.50 Million from Oberlin College in Defamation Suit*, AP Press (Dec. 16, 2022), https://www.wkyc.com/article/news/local/lorain-county/oberlin-college-completes-payment-gibsons-bakery-defamation-case/95-ff4da16c-37d1-433f-bc1b-3e1ee219da29.

5. Governance and Oversight

1.   *Corporate Governance*, Black's Law Dictionary (11th ed. 2019).

2.   *See, e.g.*, Penn State University, Corporate Charter of the Pennsylvania State University, https://trustees.psu.edu/charter-bylaws-standing-orders/ (last accessed Sep. 16, 2023).

3.   Rick Bell, *A Brief History of Colonial Harvard*, https://legacy.sites.fas.harvard.edu/~hsb41/Inventing_Harvard/colonial_harvard.html; *History of William and Mary*, WM. & Mary: Student Handbook, https://www.wm.edu/offices/deanofstudents/services/communityvalues/studenthandbook/history_of_william_and_mary/index.php (both last accessed Sep. 16, 2023).

4.   *Cornell's Land-Grant Mission Serves New York State*, Cornell: Land Grant, https://landgrant.cornell.edu; *Rutgers, the Land-Grant University of New Jersey*, Rutgers, https://njaes.rutgers.edu/extension/history/land-grant.php (both last accessed Sep. 16, 2023).

5.   *See Fiduciary Behavior*, AGB (Mar. 2013), https://agb.org/trusteeship-article/fiduciary-behavior-whats-the-responsible-trustee-to-do-and-not-do/ ("The concept of fiduciary traces to the Latin term *fiduciarius*, meaning to hold in trust or in faith.").

6.   *Harvard Corporation*, Harvard University, https://www.harvard.edu/about /leadership-and-governance/harvard-corporation/ (last accessed Sep. 16, 2023).

7.   *See e.g., Right from the Start: Responsibilities of Directors of Not-For-Profit Corporations*, Off. N.Y. State Att'y Gen. Charities Bureau (May 15, 2015), https:// www.charitiesnys.com/pdfs/Right-From-the-Start.pdf.

8.   *See e.g., id.*

9.   *Id.*

10.   N.Y. Not-For-Profit Corp. Law § 715 (McKinney 2021).

11.   For a study in the use of institutional bylaws to narrow the scope of faculty governance purview, *see* Colleen Flaherty, *Oberlin's Board Seeks to Limit Faculty Power* (Oct. 6, 2022), https://www.insidehighered.com/news/2022/10/07/oberlins -board-seeks-limit-faculty-power; and Colleen Flaherty, *Oberlin Board Votes to Limit Faculty Power* (Oct. 9, 2022), https://www.insidehighered.com/quicktakes/2022/10/10 /oberlin-board-votes-limit-faculty-power.

12.   Paraphrased from the Bylaws of Hobart and William Smith Colleges.

13.   *See, e.g., The Faculty Handbook: The Faculty and the Senate*, Cornell Univ., https:// theuniversityfaculty.cornell.edu/the-new-faculty-handbook/appendix-2-opuf/#IX.

14.   Sections of this chapter draw heavily from Louis Guard, *Legal and Governance Considerations in a Time of Pandemic and Systemic Crisis: A Primer on Shared Governance and AAUP Guidance for Private Colleges and Universities*, 19 NACUANOTE 5 (Mar. 17, 2021), Nat'l Assoc. Coll & Univ. Att'ys.

15.   *See* Erwin Chemerinsky & Howard Gillman (2017), *Free Speech on Campus*, Yale Univ. Press, 53–58.

16.   *Id.* at 56.

17.   NLRB v. Yeshiva Univ., 444 U.S. 672, 680 (1980).

18.   *Id.*

19.   This image is colorfully portrayed by a quote from Henry Wadsworth Longfellow, who wrote of the American university in the early nineteenth century that it was primarily "two or three large brick buildings,—with a chapel, and a President to pray in it!" Chemerinsky & Gillman, *supra* note 15 at 54.

20.   Yeshiva, 444 U.S. at 681.

21.   Chemerinsky & Gillman, *supra* note 15 at 59.

22.   *Id.*; American Association of University Professors' volume of "Policy Documents and Reports" (commonly referred to and hereinafter referred

to as the *"Redbook"*), "1940 Statement on Principles of Academic Freedom and Tenure."

23.   The fact that administrative structures and campus operations became more complex over the arc of the twentieth century is largely a truism, but for a brief general discussion of the expansion of regulation affecting higher education during this time period, *see* Barbara A. Lee, *Fifty Years of Higher Education Law: Turning the Kaleidoscope*, 36 J. Coll. & Univ. L. 650 (2010).

24.   *See supra* note 22, *Redbook*, "Statement on Government of Colleges and Universities."

25.   *Id.*

26.   *Id.*

27.   *Id.*

28.   *See, e.g.,* Middle States Commission on Higher Education, *Standards for Accreditation and Requirements of Affiliation Thirteenth Edition* (2015), Requirement 15 ("The institution has a core of faculty (full-time or part-time) and/or other appropriate professionals *with sufficient responsibility to the institution to assure the continuity and coherence of the institution's educational programs.*") (emphasis added), https://www.msche.org/standards/thirteenth-edition/#requirements.

29.   *See, e.g.,* 8 CRR-NY 52.2, "Standards for the Registration of Under-graduate and Graduate Curricula" at §52.2(b)(3) ("the institution shall designate a body of faculty who, with the academic officers of the institution, shall be responsible for setting curricular objectives, for determining the means by which achievement of objectives [is] measured, for evaluating the achievement of curricular objectives and for providing academic advice to students.").

30.   The AAUP does however have a Collective Bargaining Congress that serves as an umbrella organization for certain labor unions. See https://www.aaup.org/NR/rdonlyres/60EDE364-88EA-4494-8CBC-7CC6907428EC/0/c5 Constitution.pdf.

31.   Bylaws of Cornell University (Oct. 9, 2020), https://cpb-us-e1.wpmucdn .com/blogs.cornell.edu/dist/5/9068/files/2020/12/20-10-bylaws-w-TC.pdf.

32.   *See, e.g.,* Holm v. Ithaca College, 669 N.Y.S.2d 483 (Sup. Ct. 1998); *Faculty Handbooks as Enforceable Contracts: A State Guide,* Am. Assoc. Univ. Professors (2009), https://www.aaup.org/sites/default/files/files/Faculty-Handbooks-as -Enforceable-Contracts.pdf.

33. *Recommended Institutional Regulations on Academic Freedom and Tenure,* Am. Assoc. Univ. Professors (2018), https://www.aaup.org/report/recommended -institutional-regulations-academic-freedom-and-tenure.

34. *Id.*

35. *Faculty Handbooks as Enforceable Contracts: A State Guide, supra* note 30.

36. Jacobs v. Mundelein Coll., 628 N.E.2d 201 (Ill. App. Ct. 1993).

37. Waring v. Fordham Univ., 640 F. Supp. 42 (S.D.N.Y. 1986).

38. *See, e.g.,* Katz v. Georgetown Univ., 246 F.3d 685 (D.C. Cir. 2001).

39. *Special Report: COVID-19 and Academic Government,* Am. Assoc. Univ. Professors (May 2021), https://www.aaup.org/file/Special-Report_COVID -19-and-Academic-Governance.pdf.

40. *Id.*

41. *Id.*

42. *Id.*

43. *Id.; Redbook, supra* note 22, Regulation 4(c)(1).

44. *Id.,* Regulation 4(d).

45. The relevant provisions related to financial exigency or program elimination can be found in the AAUP's model regulation "Recommended Institutional Regulations on Academic Freedom and Tenure," https://www.aaup.org/report/recommended -institutional-regulations-academic-freedom-and-tenure (last accessed Sep. 16, 2023).

46. In addition to requiring faculty participation in the process through a duly authorized faculty body or committee, Regulation 4, *supra* note 43, generally requires that a faculty body have its own chance to "render an assessment in writing of the institution's financial condition" and requires access to certain data for decision-making.

47. *Redbook,* Regulation 4c (4)-(5); Regulation 8.

48. *See, e.g.,* Sean Ray, *Allegheny College to Reduce Faculty Staffing, Academic Programs over Next Three Years,* Meadville Tribune (Feb. 7, 2022), https://www.meadvilletribune .com/news/local_news/allegheny-college-to-reduce-faculty-staffing-academic -programs-over-next-three-years/article_9497962a-87a2-11ec-9109-3bbd7dc 78825.html.

49. IN RE: Yvonne Chavez HANSBROUGH et al., Respondents, v. The COLLEGE OF SAINT ROSE et al., Appellants, No. 534551 (N.Y. Sup. Ct. 3d Dept. 2022).

50. Editorial Board, *Academic Tenure Is in Desperate Need of Reform*, Boston Globe (May 9, 2021), https://www.bostonglobe.com/2021/05/09/opinion /academic-tenure-is-desperate-need-reform/.

51. Emma Pettit, *Tenure without Teeth*, Chronicle of Higher Education (Feb. 11, 2022), https://www.chronicle.com/article/tenure-without-teeth.

52. Fernanda Zamudio-Suarez, *Missouri Lawmaker Who Wants to Eliminate Tenure Says It's 'Un-American,'* Chronicle of Higher Education (Jan. 12, 2017), https:// www.chronicle.com/article/missouri-lawmaker-who-wants-to-eliminate-tenure -says-its-un-american/.

53. Aaron Sullivan, *Dan Patrick's Plan to End Tenure Has Yet to Come to Fruition, but Some Texas Lawmakers Are Targeting Class Curriculum*, The Daily Texan (Feb. 12, 2023), https://thedailytexan.com/2023/02/12/dan-patricks-plan-to-end-tenure-has-yet -to-come-to-fruition-but-some-texas-lawmakers-are-targeting-class-curriculum/; *see also* Jenn Selva, *Texas Lieutenant Governor Wants to End Tenure for New University Instructors in Attempt to Stop the Teaching of Critical Race Theory*, CNN (Feb. 18, 2022), https://www .cnn.com/2022/02/18/us/texas-university-tenure-critical-race-theory/index.html.

54. Pettit, *supra* note 51.

55. Jeremy Bauer-Wolf, *5 State Plans to Restrict Tenure You'll Want to Watch*, Higher Ed Dive (Mar. 13, 2023), https://www.highereddive.com/news/5-state-plans-to -restrict-faculty-tenure-youll-want-to-watch/643880/; Michael T. Nietzel, *North Dakota Senate Votes Down Controversial College Tenure Bill*, Forbes (Apr. 3, 2023), https:// www.forbes.com/sites/michaeltnietzel/2023/04/03/north-dakota-senate-votes -down-controversial-college-tenure-bill/.

56. Alcino Donadel, *A Regulation Targeting Tenure in Florida Gains Approval, Big Win for DeSantis*, University Business (Mar. 30, 2023), https://universitybusiness.com /a-regulation-targeting-tenure-in-florida-gains-approval-big-win-for-desantis/.

57. John Warner, *End Tenure, Before It's Too Late*, Inside Higher Ed (Feb. 17, 2017), https://www.insidehighered.com/blogs/just-visiting/end-tenure-its-too -late; *see also* Richard Vedder, *Tenure Is Dying*, Forbes (Apr. 13, 2020), https://www .forbes.com/sites/richardvedder/2020/04/13/academic-tenure-rip/.

58. Bill Schackner, *Chatham University Faculty Members Overwhelmingly Vote to Return to Tenure System*, Pittsburgh Post-Gazette (Feb. 22, 2022), https://www.post -gazette.com/news/education/2022/02/22/chatham-university-tenure-faculty -vote-aaup-professors-college-enrollment-pittsburgh/stories/202202220077.

59.   Meimei Xu, *15 Harvard Anthropology Professors Call on Comaroff to Resign over Sexual Harassment Allegations,* HARVARD CRIMSON (Feb. 21, 2022), https://www .thecrimson.com/article/2022/2/21/anthropology-faculty-call-for-comaroff -resignation/.

60.   Ariel Kim & Meimei Xu, *Harvard Anthropology Prof. John Comaroff Placed on Leave following Sexual Harassment, Professional Misconduct Inquiries,* HARVARD CRIMSON (Jan. 21, 2022), https://www.thecrimson.com/article/2022/1/21/comaroff -unpaid-leave/.

61.   Isabella Cho & Ariel Kim, *Lawsuit Alleges Harvard Ignored Sexual Harassment Complaints against Prof. John Comaroff for Years,* HARVARD CRIMSON (Feb. 9, 2022), https://www.thecrimson.com/article/2022/2/9/comaroff-lawsuit/.

62.   Xu, *supra* note 59.

63.   *Id.*

64.   Colleen Flaherty, *Academic Freedom Above All?,* INSIDE HIGHER ED (Feb. 6, 2022), https://www.insidehighered.com/news/2022/02/07/philosophers -comments-pedophilia-lead-his-suspension.

65.   Scott Jaschik, *Is Penn Going to Punish Amy Wax?,* INSIDE HIGHER ED (July 18, 2022), https://www.insidehighered.com/news/2022/07/19/penn-going -punish-amy-wax.

66.   *Id.*

67.   *See* Isaac Avilucea, *Where Penn's Disciplinary Case against Professor Amy Wax Stands,* AXIOS PHILADELPHIA (Mar. 23, 2023), https://www.axios.com/local /philadelphia/2023/03/23/penn-law-school-amy-wax-hearings-disciplinary -case.

68.   Anemona Hartocollis, *Princeton Fires Tenured Professor in Campus Controversy,* NEW YORK TIMES (May 23, 2022), https://www.nytimes.com/2022/05/23/us /princeton-fires-joshua-katz.html.

69.   Emma Whitford, *Virginia AG Rattles Higher Ed,* INSIDE HIGHER ED (Feb. 3, 2022), https://www.insidehighered.com/news/2022/02/03/virginias-new-ag -has-made-big-changes-state-colleges.

70.   *Id.*

71.   Elizabeth Redden, *Changed Political Winds in Virginia Shift Vaccine Policy,* INSIDE HIGHER ED (Jan. 31, 2022), https://www.insidehighered.com/news/2022/01/31 /virginia-ag-says-colleges-cant-mandate-covid-vaccines.

72.   Elizabeth Redden, *Virginia Public Colleges Lift COVID Vaccine Mandates,* INSIDE HIGHER ED (Feb. 1, 2022), https://www.insidehighered.com/quicktakes/2022 /02/01/virginia-public-colleges-lift-covid-vaccine-mandates/.

73.   Emma Whitford, *Politics Prevail in Search for Georgia Chancellor,* INSIDE HIGHER ED (Feb. 16, 2022), https://www.insidehighered.com/news/2022 /02/16/georgia-regents-tap-sonny-perdue-system-chancellor.

74.   *Id.*

75.   *Id.*

76.   Sam Sachs, *Florida Law Hides ID of University President Search Candidates from Public Record,* WFLA (Mar. 16, 2022), https://www.wfla.com/news/education /florida-law-hides-id-of-university-president-search-candidates-from-public -record/; see also Chelsea Long, *Florida Bill May Shield University Presidential Searches from the Public,* CHRONICLE OF HIGHER EDUCATION (Feb. 1, 2022), https://www.chronicle .com/article/florida-bill-may-shield-university-presidential-searches-from-the -public.

77.   Jason Garcia, *Ron DeSantis Plotted an All-Out Assault on Public Universities,* SEEKING RENTS (June 1, 2022), https://jasongarcia.substack.com/p/ron -desantis-plotted-an-all-out-assault.

78.   Divya Kumar, *DeSantis Signs Bill Limiting Tenure at Florida Public Universities,* TAMPA BAY TIMES (Apr. 19, 2022), https://www.tampabay.com/news/education /2022/04/19/desantis-signs-bill-limiting-tenure-at-florida-public-universities/.

79.   Garcia, *supra* note 77.

80.   Andrew Atterbury, *New College Scores Millions in Florida's Budget amid DeSantis Revamp,* POLITICO (May 4, 2023), https://www.politico.com/news/2023/05/04 /lawmakers-are-on-board-with-desantis-overhaul-of-new-college-00095442; Michelle Goldberg, *This Is What the Right-Wing Takeover of a Progressive College Looks Like,* NEW YORK TIMES (Apr. 29, 20223), https://www.nytimes.com/2023/04/29 /opinion/new-college-florida-republican-desantis.html.

81.   Kyla Calvert-Mason & Parth Shah, *UW Regents Approve Tenure Changes,* WIS. PUB. RADIO (Mar. 10, 2016), https://www.wpr.org/uw-regents-approve-tenure -changes; Rebecca Schuman, *The End of Research in Wisconsin,* SLATE (Mar. 21, 2016), https://slate.com/human-interest/2016/03/university-of-wisconsin-and-the -aftermath-of-destroying-professor-tenure.html.

82.   *Id.*

83.   Hallie Busta, *Iowa Lawmakers Advance Bills That Would Kill Tenure at Public Universities,* HIGHER ED DIVE (Feb. 16, 2021), https://www.highereddive.com /news/iowa-lawmakers-advance-bills-that-would-kill-tenure-at-public-universities /595158/; Mark Drozdowski, *Tenure under Attack Nationwide,* BEST COLLS. (Dec. 7, 2021), https://www.bestcolleges.com/news/analysis/2021/12/07/tenure -under-attack-nationwide/.

84.   Special Report, *Nikole Hannah-Jones and the Politicization of Higher Ed Governance,* CHRONICLE (2022), https://www.chronicle.com/package/nikole -hannah-jones-and-the-politicization-of-university-governance.

85.   *See* Jack Stripling, *'Look Us in the Eye,'* CHRONICLE OF HIGHER EDUCATION (July 1, 2021), https://www.chronicle.com/article/look-us-in-the-eye; *see also* the special report and compendium of articles at *Nikole Hannah-Jones and the Politicization of Higher Ed Governance,* CHRONICLE OF HIGHER EDUCATION (2022), https://www .chronicle.com/package/nikole-hannah-jones-and-the-politicization-of-university -governance.

86.   Colleen Flaherty, *'A New Low' in Attacks on Academic Freedom,* INSIDE HIGHER ED (Feb. 21, 2022), https://www.insidehighered.com/news/2022/02/21/texas -lt-govs-pledge-end-tenure-over-crt-new-low.

87.   *S.D. House Passes Gov. Kristi Noem's Bills Aiming to Ban 'Divisive Concepts.'* UNIVERSITY BUSINESS (Feb. 16, 2022), https://universitybusiness.com /s-d-house-passes-gov-kristi-noems-bills-aiming-to-ban-divisive-concepts/; *DeSantis' 'Stop Woke Act' Faces Court Test as Universities Become Targets,* UNIVERSITY BUSINESS (June 17, 2022), https://universitybusiness.com/desantis-stop-woke-act-faces -court-test-as-universities-become-targets/.

88.   https://crtforward.law.ucla.edu (last accessed Sep. 16, 2023).

89.   *Id.*

90.   *See, e.g.,* Honeyfund.com, Inc. v. DeSantis (N.D. Fla. Aug. 18, 2022) (challenging the "STOP WOKE Act").

91.   Lindsey Ellis, Jack Stripling & Dan Bauman, *Partisan College Governance: 5 Takeaways,* CHRONICLE OF HIGHER EDUCATION (Sep. 25, 2020), https://www .chronicle.com/article/partisan-college-governance-5-takeaways; *see also* Brian O'Leary, Lindsay Ellis, Jack Stripling, & Dan Bauman, *Public-College Boards and State Politics,* CHRONICLE OF HIGHER EDUCATION (Sep. 25, 2020), https://www.chronicle .com/article/public-college-boards-and-state-politics.

92.   Daniel Golden & Kirsten Berg, *The Red State University Blues*, CHRONICLE OF HIGHER EDUCATION (June 29, 2022), https://www.chronicle.com/article/the-red-state-university-blues.

93.   *Id.*

94.   Megan Zahneis, *Diversity Statements Are under Fire*, CHRONICLE OF HIGHER EDUCATION (Mar. 7, 2023), https://www.chronicle.com/article/diversity-statements-are-under-fire-heres-what-they-are-and-how-theyre-used.

95.   Christopher F. Rufo, Ilya Shapiro, & Matt Beienburg, *Abolish DEI Bureaucracies and Restore Colorblind Equality in Public Universities*, MANHATTAN INSTITUTE ISSUE BRIEF (January 2023), https://media4.manhattan-institute.org/sites/default/files/model_dei_legislation013023.pdf.

96.   *DEI Legislation Tracker*, Chronicle of Higher Education (updated July 4, 2023), https://www.chronicle.com/article/here-are-the-states-where-lawmakers-are-seeking-to-ban-colleges-dei-efforts.

97.   Natalia Mayorga, *Did You Know? College Closures and Mergers Since 2016*, THE JAMES G. MARTIN CENTER FOR ACADEMIC RENEWAL (Aug. 26, 2021), https://www.jamesgmartin.center/2021/08/did-you-know-college-closures-and-mergers-since-2016/.

98.   Higher Ed. Dive Team, *A Look at Trends in College Consolidation since 2016*, HIGHER ED DIVE (Feb. 2, 2022), https://www.highereddive.com/news/how-many-colleges-and-universities-have-closed-since-2016/539379/.

99.   Michelle Robertson, *Mills College Alumnae Sue School over Pending Shutdown, Merger*, SF GATE (July 8, 2021), https://www.sfgate.com/education/article/Mills-College-alumnae-lawsuit-school-shutdown-16301579.php.

100.   *Id.*

101.   Molly Callahan, *Northeastern University and Mills College Finalize Historic Merger*, CHRONICLE OF HIGHER EDUCATION (Sep. 14, 2021), https://news.northeastern.edu/2021/09/14/mills-college-northeastern-university-merger/#_ga=2.8345653.689487314.1645801036-641940826.1645801036.

102.   First Amended Compl. for Damages & Equitable Relief, Alumnae Assoc. of Mills Coll. v. Hillman, No. RG21101875 (Cal. Super. Ct. Alameda Cnty. 2021).

103.   *Id.*

104.   Ord. Granting Plaintiffs' *Ex Parte* Application for Temp. Restraining Ord. & Ord. to Show Cause Re: Preliminary Injunction, Nakka-Cammauf v. Hillman, No. RG21101875 (Cal. Super. Ct. Alameda Cnty. 2021).

105.   Cross-Compl., *Nakka-Cammauf,* No. RG21101875.

106.   *Brief Overview of AAMC v. Mills College,* https://static1.squarespace.com
/static/60de4f4aa25e053fedb84faa/t/61e51d17963af533b3ef8362/1642405
144033/011122+-+Brief+Overview+of+AAMC+vs+Mills+College.pdf.

107.   Alumnae Association of Mills College, *Alumna Trustees Sue Mills for
Information They Need to Help Decide the College's Future,* ALUMNAE ASSOC. MILLS COLL.
(Aug. 6, 2021), https://www.aamc-mills.org/lawsuit.

108.   Squeri v. Mount Ida Coll., 954 F.3d 56 (1st Cir. 2020).

109.   *Id.*

110.   *Id.* at 67.

111.   Dana Poleski, *Defining Leadership: Five Years after the Saving Sweet Briar Effort,*
SWEET BRIAR COLL. (Mar. 3, 2020), https://sbc.edu/news/defining-leadership/;
Bill Donahue, *Can Antioch College Return from the Dead Again?,* NEW YORK TIMES (Sep.
16, 2011), https://www.nytimes.com/2011/09/18/magazine/can-antioch
-college-return-from-the-dead-again.html.

6. The Higher Education Business Model

1.   *See* Robert Kelchen, *An Exploration of Nonresident Student Enrollment and
Institutional Finances at Public Universities,* JOURNAL OF POSTSECONDARY STUDENT SUCCESS
(2021) Vol. 1, No. 1, https://journals.flvc.org/jpss/article/view/121539; *and see*
Aaron Klein & Ariel Gelrud Shiro, *The Great Student Swap,* BROOKINGS MOUNTAIN
WEST POLICY BRIEF (Aug. 31, 2021), https://digitalscholarship.unlv.edu
/brookings_policybriefs_reports/7/.

2.   *See* Goldie Blumenstyk (2014), *American Higher Education in Crisis? What
Everyone Needs to Know,* Oxford University Press.

3.   See *Big Ideas for Reforming College,* BROOKINGS (Oct. 2015), https://www
.brookings.edu/series/big-ideas-for-reforming-college/.

4.   W. Bentley MacLeod & Miguel Urquiola, *Why Does the United States Have
the Best Research Universities? Incentives, Resources, and Virtuous Circles,* JOURNAL OF ECO-
NOMIC PERSPECTIVES (2021) Vol. 35, No. 1: 185–206.

5.   *Census Bureau Releases New Educational Attainment Data* US BUREAU OF THE
CENSUS (Feb. 16, 2023), Press Release Number CB23-TPS-21, https://www
.census.gov/newsroom/press-releases/2023/educational-attainment-data.html.

6.   https://www.newyorkfed.org/research/college-labor-market/index#
/unemployment (last accessed Sep. 16, 2023).

7.   https://www.newyorkfed.org/research/college-labor-market/index#
/wages (last accessed Sep. 16, 2023).

8.   Douglas Holtz-Eakin & Tom Lee, *The Economic Benefits of Educational Attainment*,
American Action Forum (June 4, 2019), https://www.americanactionforum.org
/project/economic-benefits-educational-attainment/.

9.   *Ranking 4,500 Colleges by ROI (2022)*, Georgetown University Center
on Education and the Workforce (2022), https://cew.georgetown.edu/cew
-reports/roi2022/.

10.   *Id.*

11.   *Digest of Education Statistics*, National Center for Education Statistics
(2022), Table 330.10, https://nces.ed.gov/programs/digest/d22/tables/dt22
_330.10.asp.

12.   *Id.*

13.   Jennifer Ma & Matea Pender (2022), *Trends in College Pricing and Student Aid
2022*, New York: College Board: 41; Bureau of Economic Analysis, Table 1.15.
Gross Domestic Product (last revised June 29, 2023).

14.   Ma & Pender (2022), *op cit.*: 43.

15.   Ma & Pender (2022), *op cit.*: 37.

16.   Ma & Pender (2022), *op cit.*: 26.

17.   *Education Department Releases Proposed Regulations to Protect Veterans and Service
Members, Increase College Oversight, and Increase College Access for Incarcerated Individuals*,
Dept of Education (July 26, 2022), https://www.ed.gov/news/press-releases
/education-department-releases-proposed-regulations-protect-veterans-and-service
-members-increase-college-oversight-and-increase-college-access-incarcerated
-individuals.

18.   Erica Blom, *What Can We Learn about College and University Finances?*, Urban
Institute (July 2021), https://www.urban.org/sites/default/files/publication
/104622/what-can-we-learn-about-college-and-university-finances.pdf.

19.   Bernal v. Burnett, 793 F. Supp. 2d 1280 (D. Colo. 2011); the Westwood
College case.

20.   Pension Tr. Fund for Operating Engineers v. DeVry Educ. Grp., Inc.,
Nol 16 C 5198, 2017 WL 6039926, at *1 (N.D. Ill. Dec. 8, 2017).

21. See also In re ITT Educ. Servs., Inc. Sec. & S'holder Derivatives Litig., 859 F. Supp. 2d 572 (S.D.N.Y. 2012); Oklahoma Firefighters Pension & Ret. Sys. v. Capella Educ. Co., 873 F. Supp. 2d 1070 (D. Minn. 2012); Karam v. Corinthian Colleges, Inc., No. CV 10-6523-GHK PJWX, 2012 WL. 8499135. at *1 (C.D. Cal. Aug. 20, 2012); Ross v. Career Educ. Corp., No. 12 C 276, 2012 WL 5363431, at *1 (N.D. III. Oct. 30, 2012).

22. *Zovio,* WIKIPEDIA, https://en.wikipedia.org/wiki/Zovio (last accessed Sep. 15, 2023).

23. Sara Weissman, *Lawsuit against Ashford University and Zovio Prevails,* INSIDE HIGHER ED (Mar. 7, 2022), https://www.insidehighered.com/quicktakes /2022/03/08/lawsuit-against-ashford-university-and-zovio-prevails.

24. Dan Bauman, *Two Years after Promising a 'Transformational Partnership, the U. of Arizona and Zovio Part Ways,'* CHRONICLE OF HIGHER EDUCATION (Aug. 1, 2022), https://www.chronicle.com/article/two-years-after-promising-a-transformational -partnership-the-u-of-arizona-and-zovio-part-ways.

25. Sarah Brown, *U.S. Cancels $5.8 Billion in Student Loans, the Most Ever,* CHRONICLE OF HIGHER EDUCATION (June 1, 2022), https://www.chronicle.com /article/u-s-cancels-5-8-billion-in-student-loans-the-most-ever.

26. *Education Department Approves $415 Million in Borrower Defense Claims Including for Former DeVry University Students,* US DEPT OF EDUCATION (Feb. 16, 2022), https:// www.ed.gov/news/press-releases/education-department-approves-415-million -borrower-defense-claims-including-former-devry-university-students.

27. *Duke Paying $19M to Its Own, UNC-Chapel Hill Faculty to Settle Antitrust Lawsuit,* WRAL NEWS (Oct. 25, 2021), https://www.wral.com/story/duke-paying-19m-to -its-own-unc-chapel-hill-faculty-to-settle-antitrust-lawsuit/19943462/.

28. *Guide to Ethical Practice in College Admission,* NATIONAL ASSOCIATION FOR COLLEGE ADMISSION COUNSELING (Sep. 2020): 1, https://www.nacacnet.org /advocacy--ethics/NACAC-Guide-to-Ethical-Practice-in-College-Admission/.

29. *Id.*

30. *NACAC Removes Recruiting Rules from Code of Ethics and Professional Practices in Light of DOJ Investigation and Potential Litigation and Signs Consent Decree,* LIEBERT CASSIDY WHITMORE (Mar. 4, 2020), https://www.lcwlegal.com/news/nacac-removes -recruiting-rules-from-code-of-ethics-and-professional-practices-in-light-of-doj -investigation-and-potential-litigation-and-signs-consent-decree/.

31.   Complaint at 3, *Department of Justice v. National Association for College Admission Counseling*, Document 1, (D.D.C. 2019)(Case 1:19-cv-03706).

32.   LIEBERT ET AL, *supra* note 30.

33.   https://www.highpoint.edu/admissions/early-decision-benefits-in-action/ (last accessed Sep. 15, 2023).

34.   Judith Eaton, *Will Regional Accreditation Go National?*, INSIDE HIGHER ED (Mar. 16, 2022), https://www.insidehighered.com/views/2020/03/17/pros-and-cons-having-regional-accreditors-go-national-opinion.

35.   Indeed, Hobart & William Smith was one of the first colleges to switch to an accreditor outside its region; *see* Emma Whitford, *Looking for a New Accreditor,* INSIDE HIGHER ED (Mar. 20, 2022), https://www.insidehighered.com/news/2022/03/21/colleges-seek-accreditation-outside-their-region; the college successfully completed the process as of early 2023.

36.   For example, Wells College was placed on probation by the MSCHE in 2019 for lack of compliance with the planning, resources, and institutional improvement standard and then returned to good standing in 2021 (Emma Whitford, *Wells College off Probation*, INSIDE HIGHER ED (July 8, 2021), https://www.insidehighered.com/quicktakes/2021/07/09/wells-college-probation). Colleges can also be put on probation for nonmonetary reasons: the Higher Learning Commission placed Southwest Baptist University on probation in 2021 for being out of compliance with accreditation criteria regarding academic freedom, governance, and effective leadership (Elizabeth Redden, *In Conflict over Theology and Governance, an Accreditor Steps In*, INSIDE HIGHER ED (Nov. 8, 2021), https://www.insidehighered.com/news/2021/11/10/accreditor-places-southwest-baptist-probation).

37.   Isabel Soto & Tom Lee, *Options for Innovation and Reform in Higher Education*, AMERICAN ACTION FORUM (Nov. 12, 2019), https://www.americanactionforum.org/research/options-for-innovation-and-reform-in-higher-education/.

38.   Matt Reed, *No More Regional Accreditors*, INSIDE HIGHER ED (Sep. 15, 2020), https://www.insidehighered.com/blogs/confessions-community-college-dean/no-more-regional-accreditors.

39.   Eric Kelderman, *'A Mandate for Musical Chairs': Florida Bill Would Require Colleges to Change Accreditors*, CHRONICLE OF HIGHER EDUCATION (Feb. 4, 2022), https://www.chronicle.com/article/a-mandate-for-musical-chairs-florida-bill-would-require-colleges-to-change-accreditors.

40.   Emma Whitford, *Education Department Warns Florida about Accreditation Bill,* INSIDE HIGHER ED (Mar. 13, 2022), https://www.insidehighered.com/quicktakes /2022/03/14/education-department-warns-florida-about-accreditation-bill.

41.   Meghan Brink, *Ed Dept. Clarifies Guidelines on Switching Accreditors,* INSIDE HIGHER ED (July 20, 2022), https://www.insidehighered.com/quicktakes /2022/07/21/ed-dept-clarifies-guidelines-switching-accreditors.

42.   Arman Kyaw, *Florida Gov. Ron DeSantis Sues Education Department over Higher Ed Accreditation Process,* DIVERSE (June 23, 2023), https://www.diverseeducation .com/leadership-policy/article/15541187/florida-gov-ron-desantis-sues-education -department-over-higher-ed-accreditation-process.

43.   *Will Regional Accreditation Go National?,* INSIDE HIGHER ED (Mar. 16, 2020), https://www.insidehighered.com/views/2020/03/17/pros-and-cons-having -regional-accreditors-go-national-opinion.

44.   Doug Lederman, *Midwest Accreditor to Explore Differences by Sector,* INSIDE HIGHER ED (Mar. 17, 2021), https://www.insidehighered.com/quicktakes /2021/03/18/midwest-accreditor-explore-differences-sector.

45.   REED, *supra* note 38.

46.   Eric Kelderman, *Why Are Trump and DeSantis Talking about Accreditation?,* CHRONICLE OF HIGHER EDUCATION (May 31, 2023), https://www.chronicle.com /article/why-are-trump-and-desantis-talking-about-accreditation; Katherine Knott, *Trump's 'Secret Weapon'? College Accreditation,* INSIDE HIGHER ED (May 4, 2023), https:// www.insidehighered.com/news/government/2023/05/04/trumps-secret-weapon -college-accreditation.

47.   The accreditor had gone through several waves of being threatened with final closure; *see* Eric Kelderman, *Federal Panel Votes to Shut Down an Accreditor Blamed for Failures of For-Profit Higher Ed,* CHRONICLE OF HIGHER EDUCATION (June 24, 2016), https://www.chronicle.com/article/federal-panel-votes-to-shut-down-an-accreditor -blamed-for-failures-of-for-profit-higher-ed/; Eric Kelderman, *DeVos Gives Controversial Accreditor a New Chance and More Time,* CHRONICLE OF HIGHER EDUCATION (Apr. 3, 2018), https://www.chronicle.com/article/devos-gives-controversial -accreditor-a-new-chance-and-more-time/; and, possibly finally: Cindy Marten, *In the Matter of Accrediting Council for Independent Colleges and Schools,* DEPT. OF EDUCATION (Aug. 19, 2022), https://www2.ed.gov/documents/acics/materials/depsecretary -order-matter-of-accrediting-council-for-independent-colleges-schools.pdf.

48.   https://collegecost.ed.gov/ (last accessed Sep. 16, 2023).

49.   https://collegecost.ed.gov/net-price (last accessed Sep. 16, 2023).

50.   https://collegescorecard.ed.gov/ (last accessed Sep. 16, 2023).

51.   https://collegecost.ed.gov/affordability (last accessed Sep. 16, 2023).

52.   Scott Jaschik, *House Approves College Transparency Act*, INSIDE HIGHER ED (Feb. 6, 2022), https://www.insidehighered.com/news/2022/02/07/house -passes-college-transparency-act.

53.   *Department of Education Releases Proposed Rules on Accountability for Certificate and For-Profit Programs and Transparency into Unaffordable Student Debt*, DEPT. OF EDUCATION (May 17, 2023), https://content.govdelivery.com/accounts/USED/bulletins /35ad17e.

54.   Philip Mousavizadeh, *A 'Proliferation of Administrators': Faculty Reflect on Two Decades of Rapid Expansion*, YALE DAILY NEWS (Nov. 10, 2021), https://yaledailynews .com/blog/2021/11/10/reluctance-on-the-part-of-its-leadership-to-lead-yales -administration-increases-by-nearly-50-percent/.

55.   Michael Delucchi, Richard B. Dadzie, Erik Dean & Xuan Pham, *What's That Smell? Bullshit Jobs in Higher Education*, REVIEW OF SOCIAL ECONOMY (June 17, 2021): Table 1, https://www.tandfonline.com/doi/full/10.1080/00346764.2021.1940255.

56.   David Faris, *A New Theory of Rising College Costs*, THE WEEK (Dec. 22, 2021), https://theweek.com/education/1007974/a-new-theory-of-rising-college-costs.

57.   *The Cost of Federal Regulatory Compliance in Higher Education: A Multi-Institutional Study*, VANDERBILT UNIVERSITY (Oct. 2015), https://news.vanderbilt.edu/files/Cost -of-Federal-Regulatory-Compliance-2015.pdf.

58.   Joseph McNicholas & Patrick Hogan, *Calculating the Cost of Compliance at a Predominantly Undergraduate Institution of Higher Education*, ASSOCIATION OF COLLEGE & UNIIVERSITY AUDITORS (Nov. 1, 2019), https://acua.org/College-and-University -Auditor-Journal/Fall-2017/Calculating-the-Cost-of-Compliance-at-a -Predominan.

59.   DELUCCHI ET AL, *supra* note 55.

60.   Wendy Fischman & Howard Gardner (2022), *The Real World of College: What Higher Education Is and What It Can Be*, Cambridge: MIT Press.

61.   Susan H. Greenberg, *'Earning Is More Important Than Learning,'* INSIDE HIGHER ED (Mar. 7, 2022), https://www.insidehighered.com/news/2022/03/08 /authors-discuss-how-higher-education-has-lost-its-way.

62. Scott Jaschik, *'The Evidence Liberal Arts Needs,'* Inside Higher Ed (Nov. 17, 2021), https://www.insidehighered.com/news/2021/11/18/author-discusses-his-book-evidence-value-liberal-arts.

63. Richard A. Detweiler (2021), *The Evidence Liberal Arts Needs: Lives of Consequence, Inquiry, and Accomplishment,* Cambridge: MIT Press.

64. Parthenon E-Y Practice (2016), *Strength in Numbers: Strategies for Collaborating in a New Era for Higher Education.*

65. Robert Zemsky, Susan Shaman, & Susan Campbell Baldridge (2020), *The College Stress Test: Tracking Institutional Futures across a Crowded Market,* Baltimore: Johns Hopkins University Press.

66. Abigail Johnson Hess, *Harvard Business School Professor: Half of American Colleges Will Be Bankrupt in 10 to 15 Years,* CNBC (Aug. 30, 2018), https://www.cnbc.com/2018/08/30/hbs-prof-says-half-of-us-colleges-will-be-bankrupt-in-10-to-15-years.html. Specifically, Christensen stated in 2017 at a conference that "50 percent of the 4,000 colleges and universities in the U.S. will be bankrupt in 10 to 15 years." Christensen made similar predictions at various other points as well, including stating at another conference in April 2017: "I might bet that it takes nine years rather than 10" (*see* Doug Lederman, *Clay Christensen, Doubling Down,* Inside Higher Ed (Apr. 28, 2017), https://www.insidehighered.com/digital-learning/article/2017/04/28/clay-christensen-sticks-predictions-massive-college-closures).

67. Clayton M. Christensen & Michael B. Horn, *Innovation Imperative: Change Everything,* New York Times (Nov. 1, 2013), https://www.nytimes.com/2013/11/03/education/edlife/online-education-as-an-agent-of-transformation.html.

68. Michael B. Horn, *Will Half of All Colleges Really Close in the Next Decade?,* Forbes (Dec. 13, 2018), https://www.forbes.com/sites/michaelhorn/2018/12/13/will-half-of-all-colleges-really-close-in-the-next-decade/.

69. Sarah Butrymowicz & Pete D'Amato, *Analysis: Hundreds of Colleges and Universities Show Financial Warning Signs,* The Hechinger Report (Aug. 4, 2020), https://hechingerreport.org/analysis-hundreds-of-colleges-and-universities-show-financial-warning-signs/.

70. Jon Marcus, *The Colleges That Won't Die,* The Hechinger Report (Feb. 23, 2022), https://hechingerreport.org/the-colleges-that-wont-die/.

71. Scott Carlson, *Surviving among the Giants,* Chronicle of Higher Education (Sep. 21, 2021), https://www.chronicle.com/article/surviving-among-the-giants.

72.   Robert Kelchen, *Examining the Feasibility of Empirically Predicting College Closures*, Brookings Economics Studies (Nov. 2020), https://www.brookings.edu/research/examining-the-feasibility-of-empirically-predicting-college-closures/.

73.   Robert H. Brown & Richard Ortner, *Berklee and Boston Conservatory Merge*, Berklee College of Music (Jan. 9, 2016), https://college.berklee.edu/berklee-boston-conservatory.

74.   Jeffrey R. Young, *2U Buys edX for $800M, in Surprise End to Nonprofit MOOC Provider Started by MIT and Harvard*, EdSurge (June 29, 2021), https://www.edsurge.com/news/2021-06-29-2u-buys-edx-for-800m-in-surprise-end-to-nonprofit-mooc-provider-started-by-mit-and-harvard.

75.   Mary L. Churchill & David J. Chard (2021), *When Colleges Close: Leading in a Time of Crisis*, Baltimore: Johns Hopkins University Press.

76.   Elizabeth Redden, *A Cross-Town Acquisition*, Inside Higher Ed (July 1, 2021), https://www.insidehighered.com/news/2021/07/02/delaware-state-university-finalizes-acquisition-neighboring-wesley-college.

77.   Esteban Parra, *Was Delaware State University Takeover of Wesley a 'Sham' to Avoid Debt as Lawsuit Claims?*, Delaware Online (Feb. 6, 2022), https://www.delawareonline.com/story/news/2022/02/03/delaware-state-university-sued-wesley-college-merger-debt/9282839002/.

78.   Natalia Alamdari, *Faculty Members Sue Wesley College as Completion of DSU Acquisition Draws Near*, Delaware Online (May 26, 2021), https://www.delawareonline.com/story/news/2021/05/26/wesley-faculty-members-sue-school-dsu-acquisition-approaches/7436015002/.

79.   *Feds Complicate College Mergers, With Possible Unintended Consequences*, Inside Higher Ed (Aug. 21, 2023), https://www.insidehighered.com/news/government/2023/08/21/new-federal-rules-college-mergers-cause-delays-concerns; Aaron Marbone, *Paul Smith's College Won't Be Acquired by Fedcap: Request Withdrawn After State Education Dept. Required More Revisions*, Adirondack Daily Enterprise (July 15, 2023), https://www.adirondackdailyenterprise.com/news/local-news/2023/07/psc-wont-be-acquired-by-fedcap/.

80.   Rob Polansky, *CT's Community Colleges to Become a Single Institution*, WFSB (Mar. 8, 2022), https://www.wfsb.com/2022/03/08/cts-community-colleges-become-single-institution.

81.   Emma Whitford, *Merger Approved for 5 Minnesota Community Colleges,* INSIDE HIGHER ED (Mar. 16, 2022), https://www.insidehighered.com/quicktakes /2022/03/17/merger-approved-5-minnesota-community-colleges.

82.   Sara Weissman, *'Audacious' Merger or 'One-Size-Fits-All' Mistake?,* INSIDE HIGHER ED (Mar. 8, 2022), https://www.insidehighered.com/news /2022/03/09/accreditor-approves-connecticut-community-colleges-merger.

83.   Emma Whitford, *Pennsylvania's Plans to Consolidate 6 State Universities,* INSIDE HIGHER ED (Apr. 6, 2021), https://www.insidehighered.com/news/2021/04 /27/pennsylvania-higher-ed-system-releases-consolidation-plans.

84.   Emma Whitford, *Middle States Approves Northeast Pennsylvania Merger,* INSIDE HIGHER ED (Mar. 15, 2022), https://www.insidehighered.com/quicktakes/2022 /03/16/middle-states-approves-northeast-pennsylvania-merger.

85.   Susan H. Greenberg, *Castleton Faculty Fight Merger of Vermont State Colleges,* INSIDE HIGHER ED (Nov. 4, 2021), https://www.insidehighered.com/quicktakes /2021/11/05/castleton-faculty-fight-merger-vermont-state-colleges.

86.   Katherine Mangan, *Could Alaska's Diverse Campuses Survive a Forced Marriage?,* CHRONICLE OF HIGHER EDUCATION (Sep. 19, 2019), https://www.chronicle.com /article/could-alaskas-diverse-campuses-survive-a-forced-marriage/; Katherine Mangan, *Alaska Board Suspends Consideration of Controversial Merger,* CHRONICLE OF HIGHER EDUCATION (Oct. 7, 2019), https://www.chronicle.com/article/alaska -board-suspends-consideration-of-controversial-merger/.

87.   Emma Whitford, *Can Public Colleges Stave Off Closures?,* INSIDE HIGHER ED (Apr. 21, 2020), https://www.insidehighered.com/news/2020/04/22/financial -peril-prompting-calls-close-some-public-college-campuses-systems-can-often.

88.   James Page, *The System's Role in Saving Weakened Public Colleges,* INSIDE HIGHER ED (May 21, 2020), https://www.insidehighered.com/views/2020/05/22/how -state-university-systems-can-save-weakened-campuses-opinion.

89.   https://www.claremont.edu/ (last accessed Sep. 16, 2023).

90.   https://gmhec.org/ (last accessed Sep. 16, 2023).

91.   https://www.fivecolleges.edu/ (last accessed Sep. 16, 2023).

92.   *Five New Mexico Colleges Join Forces to Transform and Improve the Higher Education Experience,* CISION (Mar. 31, 2021), https://www.prnewswire.com/news-releases /five-new-mexico-colleges-join-forces-to-transform-and-improve-the-higher-education -experience-301259864.html.

93.   *A Collaboration among North Central College, Three Other Midwest Institutions, Receives a Total of $10 Million in Grant Funding from Lilly Endowment, Inc.,* North Central College (Mar. 25, 2021), https://www.northcentralcollege.edu/news/2021/03/25/collaboration-among-north-central-college-three-other-midwest-institutions-receives.

94.   Emma Whitford, *Judson College Will Close,* Inside Higher Ed (May 6, 2021), https://www.insidehighered.com/news/2021/05/07/judson-college-closing-amid-enrollment-and-debt-woes.

95.   Emma Whitford, *Closing Becker College to Lay Off More Than 300,* Inside Higher Ed (May 3, 2021), https://www.insidehighered.com/quicktakes/2021/05/04/closing-becker-college-lay-more-300.

96.   https://www.minerva.edu/ (last accessed Sep. 16, 2023).

97.   https://www.uaustin.org/ (last accessed Sep. 16, 2023); *see* Nicholas Reimann, *Here's What We Know about the University of Austin—The Self-Proclaimed Anti-Censorship Institution,* Forbes (Nov. 8, 2021), https://www.forbes.com/sites/nicholasreimann/2021/11/08/heres-what-we-know-about-the-university-of-austin-the-self-proclaimed-anti-censorship-institution/?sh=34f1640451a8; *and see* Derek Robertson, *It's the University of Austin against Everyone—Including Itself,* Politico (Nov. 17, 2021), https://www.politico.com/news/magazine/2021/11/17/university-austin-bari-weiss-pinker-culture-politics-522800 regarding subsequent controversy.

7. Crisis Comes to Campus

1.   Zach Myers, *Taylor University Remembers Case of Mistaken Identity 10 Years Later,* IndyStar (Apr. 25, 2016), https://www.indystar.com/story/news/2016/04/25/taylor-university-remembers-case-mistaken-identity-10-years-later/83522446/.

2.   *College Campus Shootings,* VOA News (June 1, 2021), https://projects.voanews.com/mass-shootings/english/locations/college.html.

3.   Rachel Mipro, *Grambling State University Has Had at Least One Shooting Per Year over the Last Five Years,* IndyStar (Nov. 22, 2021), https://lailluminator.com/2021/11/22/grambling-university-has-had-at-least-one-shooting-per-year-over-the-last-five-years/.

4.   *2022 University of Virginia shooting,* Wikipedia, https://en.wikipedia.org/wiki/2022_University_of_Virginia_shooting (last accessed Sep. 15, 2023).

5.   *2023 Michigan State University shooting,* WIKIPEDIA, https://en.wikipedia.org /wiki/2023_Michigan_State_University_shooting (last accessed Sep. 15, 2023).

6.   *Prof Wrongly ID'd as Wesleyan Suspect Files Suit,* NBC NEWS (Dec. 4, 2009), https://www.nbcnews.com/id/wbna34275272; Bea Lomongo Paterno, *Dr. Stephen L. Morgan Sues Univ. over False Accusations of Murder,* WESLEYAN ARGUS (Dec. 11, 2009), http://wesleyanargus.com/2009/12/11/dr-stephen-l-morgan-sues-univ-over -false-accusations-of-murder/.

7.   Daniel Greenberg, *Cornell Professor's Lawsuit against University Settled,* WESLEYAN ARGUS (Apr. 30, 2012), http://wesleyanargus.com/2012/04/30 /cornell-professors-lawsuit-against-university-settled/.

8.   *University of Alabama in Huntsville Shooting,* WIKIPEDIA, https://en.wikipedia. org/wiki/University_of_Alabama_in_Huntsville_shooting (last accessed Sep. 15, 2023).

9.   John Brackin, *Ala. High Court Affirms Shooting Case Dismissal,* COURTHOUSE NEWS SERVICE (Feb. 6, 2015), https://www.courthousenews.com/ala-high-court -affirms-shooting-case-dismissal/.

10.   *Virginia Tech Shooting,* WIKIPEDIA, https://en.wikipedia.org/wiki/Virginia _Tech_shooting (last accessed Sep. 15, 2023).

11.   Allie Grasgreen, *Virginia Tech Ruling Reversed,* INSIDE HIGHER ED (Nov. 1, 2013), https://www.insidehighered.com/news/2013/11/01/va-supreme-court -rules-virginia-tech-not-liable-shooting-deaths.

12.   https://lis.virginia.gov/cgi-bin/legp604.exe?ses=231&typ=bil&val= sb910.

13.   Elizabeth Redden, *Hurricane Ida's Impact,* INSIDE HIGHER ED (Aug. 31, 2021), https://www.insidehighered.com/news/2021/08/31/many-colleges-idas -path-remain-closed.

14.   *Wildlife Resources,* UNIV. OR., https://www.uoregon.edu/wildfire.

15.   Emma Whitford, *Spared from Tornado Damage, Colleges Help Rebuild,* INSIDE HIGHER ED (Dec. 14, 2021), https://www.insidehighered.com/news/2021/12 /14/colleges-help-rebuild-after-tornadoes-rip-through-midwest.

16.   *How Schools and Higher Ed Institutions Can Access FEMA's Public Assistance Program,* READINESS & EMERGENCY MGMT. SCHS., https://rems.ed.gov/docs/Public AssistanceProgramWebinar [1].pdf.

17.   *List of Costliest Atlantic Hurricanes,* WIKIPEDIA, https://en.wikipedia.org/wiki /List_of_costliest_Atlantic_hurricanes (last accessed Sep. 15, 2023).

18.	*History*, Univ. New Orleans, https://www.uno.edu/about-uno/history (last accessed Sep. 15, 2023).

19.	*New Orleans Post-Katrina: Dillard University Students Start School in Luxury*, Diverse Issues in Higher Education (Jan. 11, 2006), https://www.diverse education.com/students/article/15081554/new-orleans-post-katrina-dillard -university-students-start-school-in-luxury.

20.	*Effect of Hurricane Katrina on Tulane University*, Wikipedia, https://en .wikipedia.org/wiki/Effect_of_Hurricane_Katrina_on_Tulane_University (last accessed Sep. 15, 2023).

21.	Robert M. O'Neil et al., *Report of an AAUP Special Committee: Hurricane Katrina and New Orleans Universities*, Am. Assoc. Univ. Professors (May 2007), https://www.aaup.org/NR/rdonlyres/6BBEDF23-3FA6-4BBB-85BA-73424 C41B5B3/0/KatrinaReportt.pdf.

22.	Scott Cowen & Betsy Seifter (2018), *Winnebagos on Wednesdays: How Visionary Leadership Can Transform Higher Education*, Princeton: Princeton University Press.

23.	*Hurricane Maria*, Wikipedia, https://en.wikipedia.org/wiki/Hurricane _Maria (last accessed Sep. 15, 2023).

24.	Andrea Widener, *Puerto Rico's Universities Are on the Road to Recovery*, Chem. & Eng'g News (Sep. 17, 2018), https://cen.acs.org/education/Puerto-Ricos -universities-road-recovery/96/i37.

25.	Collin Binkley, *FBI Investigating 6 Suspects after Bomb Threats at Black Colleges*, PBS News Hour (Mar. 17, 2022), https://www.pbs.org/newshour/education /fbi-investigating-6-suspects-after-bomb-threats-at-black-colleges.

26.	Briefing Room, *FACT SHEET: Biden-Harris Administration Announces Resources for Historically Black Colleges and Universities That Have Recently Experienced Bomb Threats*, White House (Mar. 16, 2022), https://www.whitehouse.gov/briefing-room/statements -releases/2022/03/16/fact-sheet-biden-harris-administration-announces-resources -for-historically-black-colleges-and-universities-that-have-recently-experienced-bomb -threats/.

27.	Lindsay McKenzie, *Secure File Sharing Compromises University Security*, Inside Higher Ed (Apr. 7, 2021), https://www.insidehighered.com/news/2021/04 /07/accellion-data-security-breach-latest-hit-universities.

28.	Carly Page, *Ukrainian Police Arrest Multiple Clop Ransomware Gang Suspects*, TechCrunch (June 16, 2021), https://techcrunch.com/2021/06/16 /ukrainian-police-arrest-multiple-clop-ransomware-gang-suspects/.

29.   Sarah Coble, *Accellion Reaches $8.1m Data Breach Settlement,* INFOSECURITY (Jan. 17, 2022), https://www.infosecurity-magazine.com/news/accellion-reaches -81m-data-breach/.

30.   Catalin Cimpanu, *University of Utah Pays $457,000 to Ransomware Gang,* ZDNET (Aug. 20, 2020), https://www.zdnet.com/article/university-of-utah-pays -457000-to-ransomware-gang/.

31.   Suzanne Smalley, *2 More Community Colleges Targeted by Ransomware,* INSIDE HIGHER ED (Nov. 30, 2021), https://www.insidehighered.com/news/2021 /11/30/butler-county-lewis-and-clark-community-colleges-hacked.

32.   Sam P. K. Collins, *Howard University Gradually Bounces Back from Ransomware Attack,* WASH. INFORMER (Sept. 15, 2021), https://www.washingtoninformer.com /howard-university-gradually-bounces-back-from-ransomware-attack/.

33.   Scott Jaschik, *College Closes after 157 Years,* INSIDE HIGHER ED (Apr. 1, 2022), https://www.insidehighered.com/news/2022/04/01/lincoln-college -illinois-close.

34.   *The State of Ransomware in the US: Report and Statistics 2022,* EMSISOFT (Jan. 2, 2023), https://www.emsisoft.com/en/blog/43258/the-state-of-ransomware -in-the-us-report-and-statistics-2022/.

35.   *Increasing Higher Education Cyberattacks Add to Financial Pressures,* FITCH RATINGS (May 5, 2022), https://www.fitchratings.com/research/us-public -finance/increasing-higher-education-cyberattacks-add-to-financial-pressures -05-05-2022.

36.   Gabriel Rogers, *Hope College Faces New Lawsuit over Data Breach,* FOX17 (Feb. 2, 2023), https://www.fox17online.com/news/local-news/michigan/hope-college -faces-new-lawsuit-over-data-breach; Rich Egger, *More Lawsuits Filed over Knox College Data Breach from Ransomware Attack,* TRI STATES PUBLIC RADIO (Feb. 6, 2023), https:// www.tspr.org/tspr-local/2023-02-06/more-lawsuits-filed-over-knox-college-data -breach-from-ransomware-attack; Natalie Schwartz, *At Least 3 Class-Action Lawsuits Filed over Mercer University's Recent Data Breach,* HIGHER ED DIVE (June 6, 2023), https://www.highereddive.com/news/class-action-mercer-university-data-breach /652251/.

37.   https://www.helpfightmeningitis.com/meningitis-college-outbreaks/ (last accessed Sep. 15, 2023).

38. *Outbreaks on U.S. College Campuses,* NATIONAL MENINGITIS ASSOC. (2016), https://nmaus.org/nma-disease-prevention-information/serogroup-b -meningococcal-disease/outbreaks-on-u-s-college-campuses/.

39. Karen Farkas, *Ohio University Pays $1 Million to Settle Lawsuit after Freshman from Cleveland Heights Dies of Bacterial Meningitis,* CLEVELAND (Feb. 10, 2015), https:// www.cleveland.com/metro/2015/02/ohio_university_p.html.

40. Reeve Hamilton, *Battle Brewing over Mandatory Meningitis Vaccine,* TEXAS TRIBUNE (Feb. 23, 2011), https://www.texastribune.org/2011/02/23/battle -brewing-over-mandatory-meningitis-vaccine/.

41. *Texas Minimum State Vaccine Requirements for College Entry,* TEX. HEALTH & HUM. SERVS. (Aug. 9, 2021), https://www.dshs.texas.gov/immunize/school/college -requirements.aspx.

42. Hugh Sun, *Jamie Dimon's Warning for the U.S. Economy—Nobody Knows What Comes Next,* CNBC (July 18, 2020), https://www.cnbc.com/2020/07/18/jamie -dimons-warning-for-the-us-economy.html.

43. *COVID-19 Pandemic in New York (State), Government Response,* WIKIPEDIA, https://en.wikipedia.org/wiki/COVID-19_pandemic_in_New_York_(state) #Government_response (last accessed Sep. 15, 2023).

44. James Keller, *Liability Considerations for Return to Campus in the Age of COVID-19,* 18 NACUANOTE 1 (May 27, 2020) Nat'l Assoc. Coll & Univ. Att'ys, https://www.acuho-i.org/Portals/0/doc/liability-considerations-NACUA .pdf?ver=2020-07-15-102118-623.

45. Jordyn Brown, *University of Oregon, Oregon State University Sued over Charging Full-Price Tuition in 2020, Despite Shutdowns,* REG. GUARD (Mar. 23, 2021), https:// www.registerguard.com/story/news/2021/03/23/university-oregon-state -university-students-lawsuits-full-price-tuition-pandemic-covid-19/6958818002/.

46. Doug Lederman, *Courts Skeptical on COVID-19 Tuition Lawsuits,* INSIDE HIGHER ED (May. 6, 2021), https://www.insidehighered.com/news/2021 /05/06/courts-view-covid-19-tuition-refund-lawsuits-skeptically.

47. *Class Action Litigation Related to COVID-19: Filed and Anticipated Cases in 2020, Education,* PIERCE ATWOOD LLP (Mar. 9, 2021), https://www.pierceatwood.com /alerts/class-action-litigation-related-covid-19-filed-and-anticipated-cases -2020#Education.

48.   *Coronavirus Refund of College Tuition and Fees*, DREYER BOJAJIAN, https://www
.dreyerboyajian.com/class-action-college-tuition-coronavirus-refund/ (last accessed
Sep. 15, 2023).

49.   Hailey Konnath, *Southern New Hampshire Inks $1.3M Deal in Virus Refund Suit*,
LAW360 (Mar. 4, 2021), https://www.law360.com/articles/1361592/southern
-new-hampshire-inks-1-3m-deal-in-virus-refund-suit.

50.   Julie Steinberg, *Barry University $2.4 Million Covid Tuition Deal Gets Final Nod*,
BLOOMBERG LAW (Sep. 8, 2021), https://news.bloomberglaw.com/coronavirus
/barry-university-2-4-million-covid-tuition-deal-gets-final-nod.

51.   Holly Barker, *University of Tampa Agrees to $3.4 Million Covid-19 Tuition Deal*,
BLOOMBERG LAW (May 26, 2022), https://news.bloomberglaw.com/coronavirus
/university-of-tampa-agrees-to-3-4-million-covid-19-tuition-deal.

52.   Katie Kull, *Lindenwood U. to Pay $1.65 Million to Settle Claim Online Classes
'Subpar,'* ST. LOUIS POST-DISPATCH (May 11, 2022), https://www.stltoday.com/news
/local/crime-and-courts/lindenwood-u-to-refund-students-1-1-million-for-subpar
-online-classes-during-covid/article_5d251402-a1ae-5c5d-88df-3a9fe77bc766
.html.

53.   Josh Moody, *Columbia Settles COVID-19 Refund Case*, INSIDE HIGHER ED
(Nov. 29, 2021), https://www.insidehighered.com/quicktakes/2021/11/29
/columbia-settles-covid-19-refund-case.

54.   Metzner v. Quinnipiac Univ., 528 F.Supp.3d 15 (D. Conn. 2021).

55.   Chatwan Mongkol, *Quinnipiac University Reaches $2.5M Settlement in Remote
Learning Tuition Refund Case*, NEW HAVEN REGISTER (Dec. 12, 2022), https://www
.nhregister.com/news/article/Quinnipiac-University-reaches-2-5M-settlement
-in-17648675.php.

56.   Barkhordar v. President & Fellows of Harv. Coll., 2022 WL 605820, at
*2-3 (D. Mass. Mar. 1, 2022).

57.   Scott Jaschik, *Michigan Appeals Court: Refunds on Tuition, Housing Not Required*,
INSIDE HIGHER ED (Feb. 14, 2022), https://www.insidehighered.com/quicktakes
/2022/02/15/michigan-appeals-court-refunds-tuition-housing-not-required.

58.   *University of Colorado Settles $5 Million Class Action Lawsuit*, CBSNEWS (Apr.
19, 2023), https://www.cbsnews.com/colorado/news/university-colorado-settles
-5-million-class-action-lawsuit/; Randall Chase, *University of Delaware Agrees to Settle
Class-Action Suit over COVID Campus Shutdown*, AP (June 14, 2023), https://apnews

.com/article/covid-university-delaware-lawsuit-settlement-d2b647ee1923d79
cd011b1ac6fddd3d2.

59.   Sara Weissman, *Wisconsin System Clashes with Republican State Lawmakers*, Inside Higher Ed (Aug. 25, 2021), https://www.insidehighered.com/quicktakes/2021 /08/25/wisconsin-system-clashes-republican-state-lawmakers.

60.   Kelcie Moseley-Morris, *House Passes Bill Prohibiting Mask Mandates in Idaho*, Idaho Capital Sun (Feb. 21, 2022), https://idahocapitalsun.com/2022/02/21 /house-passes-bill-prohibiting-mask-mandates-in-idaho/.

61.   Meerah Powell, *UO Graduate Employee Union Files Complaint against University over COVID-19 Policy*, Or. Pub. Broad. (Jan. 11, 2022), https://www.opb.org /article/2022/01/11/uo-graduate-employee-union-files-complaint-against -university-over-covid-19-policy/.

62.   Scott Jaschik, *2 Students Sue Santa Clara U over Vaccines*, Inside Higher Ed (Mar. 10, 2022), https://www.insidehighered.com/quicktakes/2022/03/10 /2-students-sue-santa-clara-u-over-vaccines.

63.   John Cropley, *Ex-Upstate NY Students Lose Vaccine Mandate Lawsuit*, AuburnPub.Com (July 9, 2022), https://auburnpub.com/ex-upstate-ny-college -students-lose-vaccine-mandate-lawsuit/article_b067015a-765c-5f31-a8f1 -8a25373c08e4.html.

64.   David Eggert, *Judge Tosses Rest of Lawsuit Challenging MSU Vaccine Mandate*, Associated Press (Feb. 23, 2022), https://apnews.com/article/coronavirus -pandemic-health-education-lawsuits-michigan-96ba29f00f6c38e6f4f6b5a 729a90340.

65.   *Special Report: COVID-19 and Academic Governance*, Am. Assoc. Univ. Professors (May 2021), https://www.aaup.org/special-report-covid-19-and -academic-governance.

66.   Cf, Jessica Dickler, *Will Pandemic Force Your College to Go Bankrupt?*, CNBC (May 27, 2020), https://www.cnbc.com/2020/05/27/a-growing-number -of-colleges-could-close-for-good-post-pandemic.html, quoting Hafeez Lakhani: "In a year or two years I expect to see something north of 100 colleges on the brink of financial ruin"; Richard Vedder, *Why the Coronavirus Will Kill 500–1,000 Colleges*, Forbes (April 7, 2020), https://www.forbes.com/sites /richardvedder/2020/04/07/500-1000-colleges-to-disappear-survival-of-the -fittest/.

67.   Rebecca Natow, *Why Haven't More Colleges Closed?*, CHRONICLE OF HIGHER EDUCATION (Mar. 4, 2021), https://www.chronicle.com/article/why-havent -more-colleges-closed?.

68.   Dan Bauman, *Higher Ed's Labor Force Is Nearly Back to Full Strength. Thank the Bureau of Labor Statistics*, CHRONICLE OF HIGHER EDUCATION (Mar. 28, 2022), https://www.chronicle.com/article/higher-eds-labor-force-is-nearly-back -to-full-strength-thank-the-bureau-of-labor-statistics.

8. Counsel as Strategic Institutional Partner

1.   Interview with Robert Iuliano, June 14, 2022.

2.   *Id.*

3.   Interview with Brian Casey, July 20, 2022.

4.   MODEL RULES OF PRO. CONDUCT r. 2.1 (AM. BAR ASS'N).

5.   Katherine Mangan, *Roommate Tiff, Title IX Dispute: The General Counsel Sees It All*, CHRONICLE OF HIGHER EDUCATION (July 19, 2015), https://www.chronicle .com/article/roommate-tiff-title-ix-dispute-the-general-counsel-sees-it-all/.

6.   MODEL RULES OF PRO. CONDUCT r. 1.13 (AM. BAR ASS'N).

7.   *Id.*

8.   Sara Miller, *Message from the Board of Trustees Special Committee* (Oct. 11, 2017), https://www.rochester.edu/newscenter/message-board-trustees-special-committee/.

9.   *Id.*

10.   *Id.*

11.   Baylor University Board of Regents, *Findings of Fact* (2015), https://www .baylor.edu/thefacts/doc.php/266596.pdf.

12.   Sarah Brown, *How Independent Are Those 'Independent' Investigations into Campus Sexual-Assault Scandals?*, CHRONICLE OF HIGHER EDUCATION (July 5, 2018), https:// www.chronicle.com/article/how-independent-are-those-independent-investigations -into-campus-sexual-assault-scandals/.

13.   *Id.*, Eric Kelderman, *Independent Investigators Seek to Save Colleges from Themselves*, CHRONICLE OF HIGHER EDUCATION (May 26, 2016), https://www.chronicle.com /article/independent-investigators-seek-to-save-colleges-from-themselves/.

14.   MODEL RULES OF PRO. CONDUCT r. 1.13(f) (AM. BAR ASS'N).

15.   MODEL RULES OF PRO. CONDUCT r. 1.6(a) (AM. BAR ASS'N).

16. *Id.*

17. *Id.*

18. *Id.*

19. Kobluk v. Univ. of Minn., 574 N.W.2d 436 (Minn. 1998).

20. *Id.*

21. *Id.*

22. *Id.*

23. *Id.*

24. *Id.*; *see also* State ex rel. Or. Health Scis. Univ. v. Haas, 942 P.2d 261 (Or. 1997) (holding that no waiver of privilege occurred where a statement about an investigative report was made by a department chair during a faculty meeting).

25. *See* MODEL RULES OF PRO. CONDUCT r. 1.13(f) (AM. BAR ASS'N).

26. MODEL RULES OF PRO. CONDUCT r. 1.13(b) (AM. BAR ASS'N).

27. *Id.*

28. *Id.*

29. *Id.*

30. *Id.*

31. *See* Ben W. Heineman Jr. (2016), *The Inside Counsel Revolution: Resolving the Partner-Guardian Tension, 2nd Ed.* American Bar Association Publishing.

32. *Id.* at 8.

33. *Id.* at 55.

34. *Id.* at 3.

35. *Id.*

36. Interview with Brian Casey, July 20, 2022.

37. Kathleen Curry Santora & William A. Kaplin, *Preventive Law: How Colleges Can Avoid Legal Problems*, CHRONICLE OF HIGHER EDUCATION (Apr. 18, 2003), https://www.chronicle.com/article/preventive-law-how-colleges-can-avoid -legal-problems/.

38. *Id.*

39. Interview with Donica Thomas Varner, July 21, 2022.

40. *See also* John Kroger, *How to Use Lawyers*, INSIDE HIGHER ED (Feb. 9, 2020), https://www.insidehighered.com/blogs/leadership-higher-education /how-use-lawyers.

41. Interview with Donica Thomas Varner, July 21, 2022.

9. Institutional Considerations for Campus Counsel

1.   *See, e.g.,* Alexander C. Kafka, *Liability Everywhere,* CHRONICLE OF HIGHER EDUCATION (Feb. 16, 2020), https://www.chronicle.com/article/liability-everywhere/.

2.   Rebekah Mintzer, *Tough Times for Lawyers on Campus,* CORP. COUNS. (Jan. 22, 2015), https://www.smu.edu/~/media/Site/Provost/EmergingLeader/Materials/2015/Tough%20Times%20for%20Lawyers%20on%20Campus%20_%20Corporate%20Counsel.ashx.

3.   Interview with David Wippman, June 16, 2022.

4.   Cheryl Foy, *All Universities Should Have a General Counsel,* UNIV. AFFS. (Aug. 29, 2019), https://www.universityaffairs.ca/opinion/in-my-opinion/all-universities-should-have-a-general-counsel/.

5.   *Iris Brest Leaves Stanford after 24 Years,* STANFORD UNIV. NEWS SERV. (Apr. 25, 1995), https://news.stanford.edu/pr/95/950425Arc5270.html.

6.   Obituary of James V. Siena, WASH. POST (Jan. 5, 1988), https://www.washingtonpost.com/archive/local/1988/01/05/associate-postmaster-general-fletcher-f-acord-56-dies/8dbcb62f-87fd-4c84-bd45-3ff9158e045f/.

7.   Aditi Banga, *Harvard's First General Counsel Passes Away at 72,* HARV. CRIMSON (June 16, 2006), https://www.thecrimson.com/article/2006/6/16/harvards-first-general-counsel-passes-away/.

8.   *Thomas H. Wright '62,* PRINCETON ALUMNI WKLY. (Jan. 28, 2004), https://www.princeton.edu/~paw/archive_new/PAW03-04/07-0128/prezpage.html.

9.   Greg Johnson, *Q&A with Penn Law's Stephen Burbank, the System Arbitrator of the NFL,* PENN TODAY (Nov. 14, 2018), https://penntoday.upenn.edu/news/qa-penn-laws-stephen-burbank-system-arbitrator-nfl.

10.   Jose A. Cabranes, *American Higher Education and the Law: Some Reflections on NACUA'S Silver Anniversary,* 12 J.C. & U.L. 261 (1985).

11.   *See generally* William A. Kaplin, *Celebrating Twenty-Five Years of Law and Higher Education,* 12 J. COLL. & UNIV. L. 269 (1985).

12.   *See* Peter H. Ruger, *The Practice and Profession of Higher Education Law,* 27 STETSON L. REV. 175, 176 (1997).

13.   Ben Heineman (2016), *The Inside Counsel Revolution: Resolving the Partner-Guardian Tension.* ABA Books: 8.

14. *Id.*

15. *See infra*, Introduction, citing Barbara Lee, *Fifty Years of Higher Education Law: Turning the Kaleidoscope*, 36 J. Coll. & Univ. L. 649 (2009); William A. Kaplin & Barbara A. Lee (2013), *The Law of Higher Education, 5th ed.* Jossey-Bass: 9; Sean Farhang (2010), *The Litigation State: Public Regulation and Private Lawsuits in the United States,* Princeton: Princeton University Press: Ch. 1.

16. *See infra*, Introduction, referencing chart; Alexander C. Kafka, *Liability Everywhere,* Chronicle Of Higher Education (Feb. 16, 2020), https://www.chronicle.com/article/liability-everywhere/.

17. *See* Ruger, *supra* note 12, at 175. While NACUA membership at this time surely included counsel employed at outside firms, by 2022, the total number of attorneys working in-house had exceed the total membership of NACUA in 1985.

18. *Id.*

19. Email exchange with Holly Peterson, Assoc. Dir. Legal Res., NACUA, Apr. 25, 2022.

20. Interview with Ona Alston Dosunmu, Aug. 5, 2022.

21. *See* Michael T. Nietzel, *Small Colleges Are Lawyering Up, Here's Why*, Forbes (Mar. 9, 2020), https://www.forbes.com/sites/michaeltnietzel/2020/03/09/small-colleges-are-lawyering-up-heres-why/.

22. Anne Coyle, *The Rise of the General Counsel*, Russell Reynolds (Jan. 21, 2020), https://www.russellreynolds.com/en/insights/articles/the-rise-of-the-general-counsel.

23. *Is Your College Ready to Hire Its First General Counsel?*, Princeton Legal Search Grp., LLC (Nov. 13, 2016), https://www.princetonlegal.com/blog/is-your-college-ready-to-hire-its-first-general-counsel/#.YkdZOC-cb5m.

24. Interview with David Wippman, June 16, 2022.

25. Interview with Stephen Burbank, Jan. 14, 2022.

26. *Id.*

27. *Id.*

28. *Id.*

29. *Id.*

30. *Id.*

31. *See generally* Madelyn Wessel & Stephen Dunham, *Making Sure the Hat Fits: Juggling the Many Roles of the General Counsel*, Conference Presentation

Materials, NACUA General Counsel Institute (Feb. 2019), https://www.nacua.org/docs/default-source/legacy-doc/conference/february2019/07_19-01-08.pdf.

32. Roderick K. Daane, *The Role of University Counsel*, 12 J. COLL. & UNIV. L. 399 (1985).

33. *Id.*

34. Interview with David Wippman, June 16, 2022.

35. Interview with Marvin Krislov, October 25, 2022.

36. Another continuing and well-documented trend personified by Marvin Krislov, Bob Iuliano, Jonathan Alger, and many others is the evolution from general counsel to college or university president. For a detailed explication on lawyers as college presidents more generally, *see* Patricia Salkin (2022), *May It Please the Campus: Lawyers Leading Higher Education,* Touro University Press.

37. Joseph Valentine, *Producer Prices in the Legal Services Industry after the Great Recession,* MONTHLY LAB. REV. (Nov. 2019), https://www.bls.gov/opub/mlr/2019/article/producer-prices-in-the-legal-services-industry-after-the-great-recession.htm.

38. David Thomas, *Richest Law Firms Saw Profits Soar as Pandemic Tamped Down Expenses,* Thomson Reuters WESTLAW TODAY (Feb. 1, 2021), https://today.westlaw.com/Document/Idb1a593064d911eba5aed72132589a0f/View/FullText.html.

39. Staci Zaretsky, *Salary Wars Scorecard: Firms That Have Announced Raises (2022),* ABOVE L. (Jan. 21, 2022), https://abovethelaw.com/2022/01/biglaw-raise-tracker-2022/.

40. *See* Jonathan Peri, *The Wisdom of Employed General Counsel in Higher Education,* 18 WIDENER L.J. 191 (2008). *See also* Lawrence White, *Managing Your Campus Legal Needs: An Essential Guide to Selecting Counsel,* NACUA (June 2008), https://www.acenet.edu/Documents/Managing-your-Campus-Legal-Needs-An-Essential-Guide-to-Selecting-Counsel.pdf.

41. Susan Kostal, *Solo and Small Firm Hourly Rates: Winners and Losers, by State and Practice Area,* ATT'Y WORK (Feb. 3, 2021), https://www.attorneyatwork.com/solo-and-small-firm-lawyer-hourly-rates/.

42. Valentine, *supra* note 36.

43. *Id.*

44. *See* UNITED EDUCATORS (2022), *Large Loss Report 2022,* https://www.ue.org/globalassets/global/large-loss-report-2022.pdf.

10. What to Expect Next

1. Interview with Ona Alston Dosunmu, August 5, 2022.

2. Keeley B. Gogul, *The Title IX Pendulum: Taking Student Survivors Along for the Ride*, University of Cincinnati Law Review, Vol. 90 Issue 3 (March 2022), https://scholarship.law.uc.edu/cgi/viewcontent.cgi?article=1440&context=uclr (coining the term "pendulum swing" in describing Title IX).

3. *See, e.g.,* Doe v. Fairfax Cty. Sch. Bd., 1 F.4th 257 (4th Cir. 2021); Kollaritsch v. Michigan State University Board of Trustees, 944 F.3d 613 (6th Cir. 2019); Shank v. Carleton Coll., 993 F.3d 567, 576 (8th Cir. 2021); Escue v. N. Okla. Coll., 450 F.3d 1146, 1155–56 (10th Cir. 2006); Reese v. Jefferson Sch. Dist. No. 14J, 208 F.3d 736, 740 (9th Cir. 2000); Fitzgerald v. Barnstable Sch. Comm., 504 F.3d 165, 172–73 (1st Cir. 2007), *rev'd and remanded on other grounds,* 555 U.S. 246 (2009); Williams v. Bd. of Regents of the Univ. Sys. of Ga., 477 F.3d 1282 (11th Cir. 2007).

4. Joseph J. Biden Jr., *Executive Order on Preventing and Combating Discrimination on the Basis of Gender Identity or Sexual Orientation,* The White House (Jan. 20, 2021), https://www.whitehouse.gov/briefing-room/presidential-actions/2021/01/20/executive-order-preventing-and-combating-discrimination-on-basis-of-gender-identity-or-sexual-orientation/.

5. Elizabeth Redden, *Christian College Sues to Keep LGBTQ+ Housing Policy,* Inside Higher Ed (Sep. 7, 2021), https://www.insidehighered.com/news/2021/09/08/christian-college-sues-over-biden-fair-housing-act-directive.

6. Jo Yurcaba, *LGBTQ Student Group Strikes Deal with Yeshiva University Allowing Other Clubs to Operate,* NBC News (Sep. 22, 2022), https://www.nbcnews.com/nbc-out/out-news/lgbtq-student-group-strikes-deal-yeshiva-university-allowing-clubs-ope-rcna49040.

7. *See* the Department of Education's 2023 Dear Colleague Letter regarding antisemitic harassment: https://www2.ed.gov/about/offices/list/ocr/docs/antisemitism-dcl.pdf; Douglas Belkin, *Antisemitism Is Rising at Colleges, and Jewish Students Are Facing Growing Hostility,* Wall Street Journal (Dec. 14, 2022), https://www.wsj.com/articles/antisemitism-is-rising-at-colleges-and-jewish-students-are-facing-growing-hostility-11671027820.

8. Kristen Clarke & Catherine Lhamon, *Dear Colleague,* US Dept. of Education Office for Civil Rights (May 19, 2023), https://www2.ed.gov/about/offices/list/ocr/docs/postsec-online-access-051923.pdf.

9.   September Johnson, *Cannabis on Campus? Not Allowed*, Campus Drug Prevention, https://www.campusdrugprevention.gov/content/cannabis-campus-not-allowed (last accessed Sep. 15, 2023).

10.   Susan H. Greenberg, *Accommodating Mental Health*, Inside Higher Ed (May 2, 2022), https://www.insidehighered.com/news/2022/05/03/more-students-report-psychological-disabilities.

11.   *See, e.g.*, Delano R. Franklin, *Court Denies Harvard's Motion to Dismiss 2019 Wrongful Death Suit*, The Harvard Crimson (Sep. 13, 2019), https://www.thecrimson.com/article/2019/9/13/wrongful-death-suit/.

12.   *See, e.g.*, Meriwether v. Hartop (6th Cir. 2021).

13.   *See generally* Greg Harold Greubel, *In Meriwether v. Hartop, the Sixth Circuit Recognizes an Academic Exception to Restrictions on the First Amendment Rights of Public Employees*, FIRE (Mar. 29, 2021), https://www.thefire.org/in-meriwether-v-hartop-the-sixth-circuit-recognizes-an-academic-exception-to-restrictions-on-the-first-amendment-rights-of-public-employees/.

14.   *See* Steven Zhou & Nicole Barbaro, *2022 Campus Expression Survey Report*, Heterodox Academy (Mar. 22, 2023), https://heterodoxacademy.org/reports/2022-campus-expression-survey-report/; Greta Anderson, *A Perception Problem about Free Speech*, Inside Higher Ed (Sep. 28, 2020), https://www.insidehighered.com/news/2020/09/29/fire-report-students-are-censoring-their-opinions; https://www.chronicle.com/article/the-silent-treatment. *See also Scholars under Fire: 2021 Year in Review*, FIRE (July 2022), https://www.thefire.org/research/publications/miscellaneous-publications/scholars-under-fire/scholars-under-fire-full-text/ (chronicling statistics of increased "targeting" of scholars).

15.   See infra., Chapter 3.

16.   *Id.*

17.   Henry v. Brown Univ., No. 1:2022CV00125 (N.D. Ill. filed Jan. 9, 2022).

18.   Christina Fan, *Proposed Legislation Would Ban Legacy Preference at Colleges, Universities across New York*, CBS New York (Mar. 9, 2022), https://www.cbsnews.com/newyork/news/legacy-preference-new-york-colleges-universities-cornell/.

19.   Lindsay McKenzie, *EU Data-Protection Law Looms*, Inside Higher Ed (Nov. 5, 2017), https://www.insidehighered.com/news/2017/11/06/eu-data-protection-law-looms.

20.   *See* https://www.enforcementtracker.com (last accessed Sep. 15, 2023).

21.   *See, e.g.,* Joy Purcell, *Piedmont College Sues City of Demorest,* Now Habersham (Dec. 10, 2020), https://nowhabersham.com/piedmont-college-sues-city-of -demorest/.

22.   *See* 26 U.S. Code § 4968; Philip Mousavizadeh, *University Lobbies Congress for Tax Cuts,* Yale Daily News (Oct. 8, 2021), https://yaledailynews.com/blog /2021/10/08/university-lobbies-congress-for-tax-cuts/; Rick Seltzer, *How Much Are Most Colleges Paying in Endowment Tax?,* Inside Higher Ed (Feb. 17, 2020), https://www.insidehighered.com/news/2020/02/18/wealthiest-universities -are-paying-big-endowment-tax-bills-how-much-are-others-who.

23.   *See* infra. Chapter 3 and the case of Oberlin College.

24.   Josh Moody, *After DEI, Conservatives Attack ESG,* Inside Higher Ed (Apr. 5, 2023), https://www.insidehighered.com/news/2023/04/05/what-do-attacks -esg-mean-college-endowments; David Gagnon & Elizabeth Ming, *Higher Education Is Investing in ESG,* KPMG (accessed July 2, 2023), https://info.kpmg.us/news -perspectives/advancing-the-profession/higher-ed-investing-in-esg.html.

25.   *See* Chris Burt, *Strike up the Bans,* University Business (Feb. 17, 2022), https://universitybusiness.com/strike-up-the-bans-nearly-50-gag-orders-target -freedom-of-speech-in-higher-ed/.

26.   Nell Gluckman, *'This Is How Censorship Happens,'* Chronicle of Higher Education (Feb. 2, 2023), https://www.chronicle.com/article/is-this-how -censorship-happens; J. Brian Charles, *The Evolution of DEI,* Chronicle of Higher Education (June 23, 2023), https://www.chronicle.com/article/the-evolution-of-dei.

27.   Matthew Miller, *As Enrollment Falls at Most Michigan Universities, the Flagships Prosper,* Michigan Live (Oct. 13, 2022), https://www.mlive.com/news/2022/10 /as-enrollment-falls-at-most-michigan-universities-a-few-prosper.html.

28.   *See, e.g.,* the recent struggles at West Virginia University regarding program cuts and budget reductions: Liam Knox, *Shrinking Pains at West Virginia University,* Inside Higher Ed (June 23, 2023), https://www.insidehighered.com/news/governance /executive-leadership/2023/06/23/distraught-west-virginia-u-faculty-push-back.

29.   Chuck Hobbs, *The Biden Administration Marks Historic Funding for HBCUs,* Insight News (Mar. 10, 2022), https://www.insightnews.com/opinion /columnists/the-biden-administration-marks-historic-funding-for-hbcus /article_5db7bb70-9f63-11ec-b721-a7f4532b0d1d.html; Elizabeth Redden, *A Fairy Godmother for Once-Overlooked Colleges,* Inside Higher Ed (Jan. 3, 2021), https://

www.insidehighered.com/news/2021/01/04/mackenzie-scott-surprises-hbcus
-tribal-colleges-and-community-colleges-multimillion.

30.   Lian Bunny, *D'Youville Follows National Trend of Colleges Becoming Universities,*
Buffalo Business First (Feb. 23, 2022), https://www.bizjournals.com/buffalo
/news/2022/02/18/dyouville-follows-national-trend-of-universities.html.

31.   Sara Weissman, *The Name Game,* Inside Higher Ed (May 1, 2022),
https://www.insidehighered.com/news/2022/05/02/some-community-colleges
-drop-community-their-names.

32.   *See* infra. Chapter 3. *See also supra* note 3; Cummings v. Premier Rehab
Keller, P.L.L.C., No. 20-219 (Roberts, C. J.).

33.   *See* Adam Liptak, *Supreme Court Backs Georgia College Student's Free Speech Suit,*
New York Times (Mar. 8, 2021), https://www.nytimes.com/2021/03/08/us
/georgia-gwinnett-college-chike-uzuegbunam.html.

34.   Dobbs v. Jackson Women's Health Organization, 142 S. Ct. 2228, 213
L. Ed. 2d 545 (2022).

35.   Sequoia Carrillo & Pooja Salhotra, *Colleges Navigate Confusing Legal Landscapes
as New Abortion Laws Take Effect,* NPR (July 19, 2022), https://www.npr.org/2022
/07/19/1112014281/abortion-laws-college-campus.

36.   In 2016, the National Labor Relations Board (NLRB) ruled in a
Columbia University case that graduate students serving as teaching assistants were
employees. Columbia University, 364 N.L.R.B. No. 90 (2016). The NLRB had in
2004 ruled that students were not employees, *see* Brown University, 341 N.L.R.B.
No. 42 (2004), overturning a previous ruling that they indeed were, *see* New York
University, 332 N.L.R.B. No. 1205 (2000). As of 2023, Duke University is now
planning to challenge the Columbia ruling; *see* Ryan Quinn, *Duke Challenges Ph.D.
Students' Right to Unionize,* Inside Higher Ed (Mar. 13, 2023), https://www
.insidehighered.com/quicktakes/2023/03/14/duke-challenge-phd-students
%E2%80%99-right-unionize.

37.   Hamilton College formed the first such union in the fall of 2021; *see*
Duncan Freeman, *Hamilton's Admissions Workers Form a Union: How It All Happened,* The
Spectator (Oct. 21, 2021), https://spec.hamilton.edu/hamiltons-admissions
-workers-form-a-union-how-it-all-happened-f91999bb568d.

38.   Ken Campbell, *UMass Passes First Undergraduate RA Union,* Massachusetts
Daily Collegian (Mar. 6, 2002), https://dailycollegian.com/2002/03/umass
-passes-first-undergraduate-ra-union/.

39.   Liam Knox, *'We're Not Slowing Down,' Student Workers Say*, Inside Higher Ed (Apr. 26, 2023), https://www.insidehighered.com/news/faculty-issues/labor -unionization/2023/04/26/were-not-slowing-down-student-workers-say.

40.   Julian Roberts-Grmela, *'Enormous Surge' in Unions Reflects Disconnect Between Colleges and Graduate Employees*, Chronicle of Higher Education (May 18, 2023), https://www.chronicle.com/article/enormous-surge-in-unions-reflects-disconnect -between-colleges-and-graduate-employees; William A. Herbert, Jacob Apkaraian, & Joseph van der Naald, *2020 Supplementary Directory of New Bargaining Agents and Contracts in Institutions of Higher Education, 2013–2019*, National Center for the Study of Collective Bargaining in Higher Education and the Professions (November 2020), https://www.hunter.cuny.edu/ncscbhep/assets/files/Supplemental Directory-2020-FINAL.pdf.

41.   Ryan Quinn, *Temple Strike Ends after Grad Students Accept Deal*, Inside Higher Ed (Mar. 13, 2023), https://www.insidehighered.com/news/2023/03/14/temple -strike-ends-after-grad-students-accept-deal; Alcino Donadel, *Strikes and Unions: Graduate Students Marshal Their Forces Nationwide*, University Business (Feb. 10, 2023), https://universitybusiness.com/strikes-and-unions-graduate-students-marshal -their-forces-nationwide/.

42.   Mikhail Zinshteyn, *Six Takeaways for Californians after the UC Graduate Student Worker Strike*, ABC10.COM (Jan. 6, 2023), https://www.abc10.com/article/news /local/california/takeaways-for-californians-after-the-uc-graduate-student-worker -strike/103-668ef822-efc5-49e1-878d-16d088768f9f.

43.   Arrman Kyaw, *Wave of Higher Ed Union Strikes Swells Nationwide*, Diverse (May 19, 2023), https://www.diverseeducation.com/from-the-magazine/article /15447887/unrest-in-the-ranks.

44.   Philip Mousavizadeh, *University Reevaluates Global Strategy following Yale-NUS Closure*, Yale Daily News (Nov. 16, 2021), https://yaledailynews.com/blog /2021/11/16/university-reevaluates-global-strategy-following-yale-nus-closure/.

45.   *See* https://educationusa.state.gov/foreign-institutions-and-governments /educationusa-resources/partnering-us-universities (last accessed Sep. 15, 2023).

46.   Liam Knox, *A Gift or a Burden?*, Inside Higher Ed (June 2, 2022), https://www.insidehighered.com/news/2022/06/03/proposed-law-sparks -debate-over-reporting-foreign-gifts.

47.   *See* https://www.nyu.edu/faculty/global-academic-partnerships-and -affiliations.html.

48.   Ben Fuller, *College Considers Leasing New Dorms to Avoid Taking on More Debt,* The Lafayette (Apr. 26, 2019), https://lafayettestudentnews.com/71782/news /final-college-considers-leasing-deal-for-new-dorms-to-avoid-taking-on-more -debt/; Adam Sichko, *Vandy Taps Global Developer for Broadway Project,* Nashville Business Journal (May 17, 2019), https://www.bizjournals.com/nashville/news /2019/05/17/vandy-taps-global-developer-for-broadway-project.html.

49.   *See* https://www.rochester.edu/ventures/industry-partners/collaborate -with-the-university-of-rochester/ (last accessed Sep. 15, 2023).

50.   E.g., *see* https://www.stern.nyu.edu/business-partnerships (last accessed Sep. 15, 2023).

51.   Even the act of institutional "texting" cannot escape the gaze of campus counsel. *See, e.g.,* Evan Lowry, Krystal Witter, & Adam Solomon, *Reply 'HELP' or Text 'STOP?' Text Messaging Compliance for Educational Institutions,* 20 NACUANOTE 7 (Apr. 29, 2022), Nat'l Assoc. Coll & Univ. Att'ys.

52.   Alondra Nelson, *Ensuring Free, Immediate, and Equitable Access to Federally Funded Research,* Executive Office of the President, Office of Science and Technology Policy Memorandum (Aug. 25, 2022), https://www.whitehouse.gov/wp-content /uploads/2022/08/08-2022-OSTP-Public-Access-Memo.pdf.

53.   Susan D'Agostino, *Who'll Pay for Public Access to Federally Funded Research?,* Inside Higher Ed (Sep. 11, 2022), https://www.insidehighered.com/news /2022/09/12/wholl-pay-public-access-federally-funded-research.

54.   https://www.census.gov/newsroom/press-releases/2022/educational -attainment.html.

55.   See Ronald J. Daniels, with Grant Shreve & Philip Spector (2021), *What Universities Owe Democracy,* Baltimore: Johns Hopkins University Press, for a full discussion of this point.

56.   Credit is due to Josh Gewolb, Partner at Harter, Secrest & Emery, for posing a version of this question to my Cornell Law School seminar on the law of higher education.

57.   Cf, Bryan Alexander (2020), *Academia Next: The Futures of Higher Education,* Baltimore: Johns Hopkins University Press; Will Bunch (2022), *After the Ivory Tower Falls: How College Broke the American Dream and Blew Up Our Politics and How to Fix It,* William Morrow; Nathan D. Grawe (2021), *The Agile College: How Institutions Successfully Navigate Demographic Changes,* Baltimore: Johns Hopkins University Press;

Arthur Levine & Scott Van Pelt (2021), *The Great Upheaval: Higher Education's Past, Present, and Uncertain Future,* Baltimore: Johns Hopkins University Press; Ronald G. Musto (2022), *The Attack on Higher Education: The Dissolution of the American University,* Cambridge: Cambridge University Press; Gabriel Paquette, "Can Higher Ed Save Itself? Business as Usual Won't Solve the Existential Challenges We Face. Will Anything?" CHRONICLE OF HIGHER EDUCATION (Mar. 4, 2021), https://www .chronicle.com/article/can-higher-ed-save-itself?.

58.   Cf, Ronald J. Daniels, with Grant Shreve & Philip Spector (2021), *What Universities Owe Democracy,* Baltimore: Johns Hopkins Press; Richard Detweiler (2021), *The Evidence Liberal Arts Needs: Lives of Consequence, Inquiry, and Accomplishment,* Cambridge, MA: MIT Press; Wendy Fischman & Howard Gardner (2022), *The Real World of College: What Higher Education Is and What It Can Be,* Cambridge, MA: MIT Press.

Acknowledgments

All books are a team effort, and while this one is definitely a partnership between the two authors, there were also numerous other people behind the scenes who made this work possible.

First, thank you to Andrew Kinney, who saw the potential in our book proposal and helped us turn it into this finished product. Without the consummate professionalism of Andrew and the others we worked with at Harvard University Press, this book would not be in the form you see it in today. Of course, all errors of commission and omission are ours alone.

Second, thank you to those who assisted with the research on this book and who supported the concept of this book. Research assistants Caroline Block, Caitriona Carey, Joshua Gopaul, Kai Mindick, Stephen Ponticello, and Shuang Wu all patiently ran down data and references for our various hunches and made sure we were following referencing protocols. We know they will all go on, or by now have gone on, to great careers in law and education. Thank you to those current and former general counsels, lawyers, and presidents (and some in more than one of those categories) we interviewed as part of our research, all of whom were very insightful: Stephen Burbank, Brian Casey, Ona Alston Dosunmu, Mark Gearan, Robert Iuliano, Marvin Krislov, Donica Thomas Varner, and David Wippman. Thank you to our friends and colleagues Michael Baughman, Richard Grossman, Gil Skillman, Cathy Williams, Dave Winakor, the National Association of College and University Attorneys, and general counsel colleagues and friends from the "NESCAC plus" for reading and commenting on our work at various stages, or for allowing us to pitch ideas to them. And particular thanks to our assistant Amanda Blowers for checking everything along the way and keeping us on track.

Third, thank you to our spring 2022 classes, Law and Economics of Higher Education at Hobart and William Smith Colleges, and the Law of Higher Education seminar at Cornell Law School. You patiently put up with draft chapters and our clearly unfinished articulations of the themes of the book. Bouncing ideas off you in a classroom setting was invaluable, and having to write chapters in time to talk about them in class kept us on our writing path.

Finally, but most importantly, thank you to our families, who inevitably are significantly inconvenienced when we suddenly get it into our heads to spend evenings and weekends writing instead of spending time with them. Lou is forever grateful to Kirra for her steadfast support and intellectual partnership and for always pushing him to be the best version of himself. Without her, this would simply not have been possible. Lou is grateful to his cheerful toddler law clerks, Hank, John, and Emmet, for supporting his time-consuming obsession with this project; your warm smiles and love make it all worth it, and you are loved beyond measure. Joyce thanks Bill for keeping our social and family life going while she was holed up in her recliner writing. They never questioned our wanting to write this book, and without their unstinting support, we would never have gotten it done.

Index

Abbott, Dorian, 63–64
academic deference, 96–103;
    decreasing trends, 234–235; *Fisher I*
    and *Fisher II*, 99–103; *Gratz v.*
    Bollinger, 100; *Grutter v. Bollinger*, 100;
    historical application of, 74, 96–97;
    narrow tailoring and, 98–99, 101–
    102; *Powers v. St. John's University School*
    of Law, 96–97; *Pratt v. Wheaton College*,
    74; *Regents of the University of California*
    v. Bakke, 96; *Students for Fair Admissions*
    v. Harvard, 97–100, 101, 104
academic freedom, 47–53; *Garcetti v.*
    Ceballos, 51, 237; *Grutter v. Bollinger*,
    51–52, 100; individual definition
    of, 49–50; institutional definition
    of, 49–50; professional definition
    of, 48–49; *Regents of the State of*
    New York v. Keyishian, 49–50, 51;
    Regents of the University of California v.
    Bakke, 49, 50, 51–52, 96; *Sweezy v.*

New Hampshire, 49–50. *See also* free
    speech and expression
Academic Freedom Alliance, 52, 64,
    237–238
Accellion data breach, 174, 182, 192
accreditation, 128, 147, 148,
    158–161, 166, 168–169, 249
Accrediting Council for Independent
    Colleges and Schools, 161
Adams, Brian, 87
admissions, 94–109; affirmative
    action and, 50, 96, 99, 102, 146,
    239; legacy preferences, 106–107,
    142, 146, 239, 251; students'
    social media use and, 107; Varsity
    Blues investigation, 107–109
advancement, institutional, 109–114,
    239–240; cryptocurrencies and,
    110, 239; gift acceptance policies,
    109–111; naming policies and
    name changes, 111–112